Qualitative Sociology as Everyday Life

Qualitative Sociology as Everyday Life

Barry Glassner & Rosanna Hertz

Editors

SAGE Publications
International Educational and Professional Publisher
Thousand Oaks   London   New Delhi

For information:

SAGE Publications, Inc.
2455 Teller Road
Thousand Oaks, California 91320
E-mail: order@sagepub.com

SAGE Publications Ltd.
6 Bonhill Street
London EC2A 4PU
United Kingdom

SAGE Publications India Pvt. Ltd.
M-32 Market
Greater Kailash I
New Delhi 110048 India

Printed in the United States of America

Library of Congress Cataloging-in-Publication Data

Main entry under title:

Qualitative sociology as everyday life / edited by Barry Glassner
and Rosanna Hertz.
    p. cm.
Includes bibliographical references.
ISBN 0-7619-1368-8 (cloth)
ISBN 0-7619-1369-6 (pbk.)
    1. Sociology—Research. 2. Sociology—Methodology. I. Glassner,
Barry. II. Hertz, Rosanna.
HM48 .Q355 1999
301'.07'2—dc21   98-40243

99 00 01 02 03 04 7 6 5 4 3 2 1

Acquisition Editor:	C. Deborah Laughton
Editorial Assistant:	Eileen Carr
Production Editor:	Wendy Westgate
Production Assistant:	Lynn Miyata
Typesetter/Designer:	Danielle Dillahunt
Cover Designer:	Candice Harman

Contents

PART I: PUBLIC PLACES

PART II: FAMILY SPACES

PART III: INTERIOR SPACES

PART IV: WORKPLACES

Acknowledgments

This volume began as part of the twentieth anniversary issue of *Qualitative Sociology* (Volume 20[4], 1997), which Barry Glassner guest edited. We thank Peter Labella for his enthusiasm and support of this project and past endeavors and future ones. His enthusiasm for the emerging idea behind the special issue led to the decision to ask 14 additional scholars for contributions. We expanded on the idea as a joint collaboration when we asked new authors to write chapters. We also thank Human Sciences Press, particularly Frank Darmstadt, for agreeing to let us reprint the chapters. This volume then, combines original new work with chapters that appeared in *Qualitative Sociology*. Finally, we thank the contributors, who agreed to experiment with how their professional understanding of sociology is a tool in their everyday lives.

Introduction

Barry Glassner

Rosanna Hertz

How can a person draw on her or his sociological knowledge as a tool for everyday life? The intent of this book is to answer this question. Nationally recognized scholars were asked to tell us how they use sociology to understand their daily experiences. Their essays are not simply autobiographical (Berger, 1990; Goetting & Fenstermaker, 1994); instead, the authors use accounts from their lives to reflexively examine how their knowledge of sociology comes to inform their everyday experiences. The authors in this book work within the tradition of qualitative sociological research in which systematized, repetitive observations and in-depth, probing interviews form the basis for understanding why people behave the way they do and how their perspectives shape their actions. Observations over time are the key to understanding social processes and social change.

Throughout the history of sociology, there have been many outstanding studies of everyday life, beginning perhaps with Henry Mayhew's *London Labor and the London Poor* in 1861 and, in the United States, with Nels Andersen's *The Hobo: The Sociology of Homeless Men* in 1923.[1] We know of no sustained discussion in the literature about qualitative sociology as everyday activities, however.

The selection of topics that individual researchers study is no accident: The writers explain how the vicissitudes of everyday life shape their research agendas and how their interests become the "stuff" of sociological thought. This is about universal concerns that become thematic: The everyday things that happen to scholars also happen to ordinary people. Because sense-making about the world serves to counter daily chaos, everyone is in a constant search to understand their own experiences within a broader context rather than as isolated events. For the scholars in this book, moral crises and personal epiphanies are the most salient motivations to pursue one topic and askew another. Deep curiosity about how things happen to the self sustains them to continue to pursue areas of inquiry. Passion pushes them to tell the stories to audiences long after they have figured out how the pieces fit to make the puzzle.

It is folk wisdom within the profession of sociology that the job of the scholar is to take ordinary events and make them extraordinary and to demonstrate how the extraordinary is routine. In this way, sociologists transform the social world and offer new ways of seeing. Sociologists are a diverse group and, as a result, they bring different lenses to what they study and how they view what they study. Marginal individuals, as many of the scholars in this book consider themselves, challenge hegemonic views. As outsiders, they see themselves missing in the literature and their everyday lives unexplained by taken-for-granted notions. Some of the authors, however, are simultaneously insiders and outsiders—whether as parents involved in their child's school, patrons of tattoo parlors, or professors who serve as university administrators. They tell us what it looks and feels like in ways that we would otherwise not know.

For all the authors, regardless of their position within or outside of the settings they describe, ethnography is a way to find relief from painful moments using the tools of their trade to explore their lives. Partly for this reason, many of the authors chose topics that they have never written about previously. The chapters in this book discuss the major foci of the discipline of sociology: theory, methodology, small groups, family, deviant behavior, economic institutions, and complex organizations, including medical, educational, legal, and criminal justice. Throughout the discussions, gender, race, ethnicity, social class, and sexual identity are recognized as salient features and categories that both define and challenge the lives of the authors. The chapters have been divided, however, not by the major divisions within the discipline of sociology but according to the locus of the author's concern: public places, family spaces, interior spaces, and workplaces.

PART I: PUBLIC PLACES

Accepting the request to write about their own activities from their own point of view, some authors opted to examine themselves and their interactions in the larger world as they went shopping, reacted to advertisements, or found themselves feeling bored. These chapters comprise Part I and might be considered exercises in *civil attention,* the inverse of what Erving Goffman (cited in

Chapter 1) called "civil inattention" or the tendency in public places to note who is present and what is going on but without close or purposeful attention.

There are a variety of ways in which a person can be in a public place. He or she can actively participate as exemplified by Clinton Sanders's (Chapter 5) participation in the dog obedience schools and tattoo parlors. Another possibility is that a person can pay careful attention to the goings-on in the place and the meaning they have for the person as exemplified in Lillian Rubin's chapter (Chapter 2) about the nursing home and Candace West's chapter (Chapter 1) in which she describes the sequence of her passages through several public places within a single day. Yet another option is to respond to what is thrown at oneself in public places as Shulamit Reinharz (Chapter 4) does with the health warnings she comes across too frequently. Sherryl Kleinman (Chapter 3) makes public her self-identity within the context of a public workshop on racism and sexism on campus. She explores with the other participants that what one sees is not always what one gets.

Some places—a hotel room, an isolated corner of a grocery store, or a patient's room in a nursing home—look private but are really public places. The fact that there are rules and these rules are imposed make these places undeniably different kinds of spaces—public spaces. Most of us do not have a map on our homes' door instructing us where to go in case of fire even though in our homes we may perform pretend fire drills. Nursing homes try to be "family environments." In fact, however, people collectively eat at set times and are expected to participate in activities that are set by staff. It is difficult to create a truly private space within a nursing home to visit with family.

In addition to prescribed rules, sociologists are attentive to what rules proscribe and the effects that these proscriptions provoke. For instance, Christine Williams (Chapter 6) confronts a set of moral questions surrounding a sexual harassment case. She argues that sexual harassment is an example of a postmodern paradox of identity politics. Having been the recipient or victim of proscribed behavior by another serves to provide part of the victim's social identity.

PART II: FAMILY SPACES

In our everyday thought, when we think of families we think of groups of intimate people. Families are also spaces, however. They exist in physical and emotional spaces that change over time. Naomi Gerstel and Robert Zussman (Chapter 7) show how the change from a dyad to a triad takes place in an emerging family, and how this change, in turn, changes the emotional lives of the participants. The transition to parent destabilizes the physical and emotional spaces within a household. By contrast, Susan Bell (Chapter 8) and Lynn Davidman (Chapter 9) examine the interaction of quite different types of spaces.

In Bell's case, these spaces pertain to social class position and a moral dilemma of parenting—whether to advocate for one's child or for social equality for a cohort. In Davidman's case, the intersecting spaces are orthodox Judaism and the emotional space in which she comes to terms with the loss of a mother-daughter relation.

The remaining chapters in this part explore what is supposedly a hallmark of family life: the invasion of privacy. Marjorie DeVault (Chapter 10) exemplifies how the training that qualitative sociologists receive in attending systematically to what they are seeing and hearing can also aid them with such personal family matters. She foregrounds the taken-for-granted details that unconsciously enter daily life as a way of illustrating how much we censor so as not to feel constantly invaded. Peter Manning (Chapter 11) explores most directly the emotional space of family life as fragments of memories that emerge as his father's death nears. Sometimes, the unspoken thoughts of individual family members become not only spaces of privacy but also a way of sustaining family as a collective entity.

PART III: INTERIOR SPACES

To the editors of this book, the chapters in Part III have the same status as the bubbles over the heads of figures in cartoons: The authors are engaged in conversations with themselves as they go through their daily lives. Three of the chapters explicitly reveal their authors' internal dialogues and the tension between ordinary unstated thoughts and actions taken. David Silverman (Chapter 12), in pondering his experiences at cricket games, engages in a dialogue about the pacing of everyday life versus a more leisured existence. Peter Conrad (Chapter 13) also deals with a slowed down existence—the common complaint of boredom. Barry Schwartz (Chapter 14) is engaged in a dialogue with other scholars about the ages at which critical memories occur: His own recollections are epiphanies of how individual life courses are shaped by external events.

Norman Denzin (Chapter 15) and Pepper Schwartz (Chapter 16) provide vivid descriptions of how going to a new locale and engaging in new activities changes our interior space. We undergo a shift in identity. Vacations and hobbies are poignant examples of the fluidity of people's identities, but symbolically at least, many of us travel between places out in the world and interior spaces even throughout the course of a single day.

Finally, Arlene Daniels (Chapter 17) and Joshua Gamson (Chapter 18) describe the experiences of feeling as if their identities have blocked their movement in physical and social space. Joshua Gamson primarily discusses a set of sexual identities; Arlene Daniels is concerned with social class identity.

Through exploring their own identities, both authors raise questions about how the dominant cultural discourse shapes ways of being in public and private spaces.

PART IV: WORKPLACES

Sociologists are taught that similar patterns occur in places that at first blush look radically different. Several of the articles in this part illustrate the point by showing how people who were trained for one profession find that, with a shift in work locale, the same culture emerges. Derral Cheatwood (Chapter 20) uses his professional way of examining seemingly very different but remarkably similar contexts—university administrations and criminal justice systems—to explain their commonality. Barrie Thorne and Arlie Hochschild (Chapter 21) illustrate how space at work becomes similar to space at home. For Robert Dingwall (Chapter 22) and Jonathan Moreno (Chapter 23), the challenge is the movement between professional spaces and their degree of comfort in these settings—medical institutions in Moreno's case and governmental educational institutions in Dingwall's exploration.

For some of the authors, the central concern is negotiating space for one's professional identity. Allan Schnaiberg (Chapter 24) grapples with how to be a knowledgeable patient who makes use of his training as a scientific researcher to be equally conversant with the doctor. The tension between professional and patient, however, is dramatic: Despite his knowledge, he ultimately ignores medical warnings that he experiences so as not to have to return to a space that places him in the role of patient once again. Sharon Collins (Chapter 19) explains how affirmation action programs are about the creation of space in the workplace and how she as an individual fits into that space and interrogates it. She raises questions about inequality in workplaces on the basis of ascribed characteristics. Paul Hirsch (Chapter 25) explicitly puts on equal footing professional journalists and systematic sociologists. He wants to blur the distinctions that the occupants in both spaces view as sacred turf. Finally, Shirah Hecht in dialogue with Howard Becker, her mentor (Chapter 26), negotiates a space for herself as being a master-teacher and no longer an apprentice.

In this brief introduction, we selected themes that cross various chapters. Although the chapters can be read with our opening remarks in mind, they can also be used to supplement introductory sociology courses. In the spirit of Park and Burgess, the chapters provide glimpses of scholars who are vividly living the tenets of qualitative sociology as they actively seek to understand the social world through their own encounters. The tools of qualitative sociology enrich and deepen the imaginative insights presented in this volume.

NOTE

1. The famous major work *Introduction to the Science of Sociology,* by Robert E. Park and Ernest W. Burgess (1921), is a timeless classic that covers the entire discipline. Robert E. Park urged students and colleagues to study everyday life. The early *University of Chicago Sociological Series,* published by the University of Chicago Press, reflects the call for empirical studies. On the editorial committee of the series was Ellsworth Faris, Robert E. Park, and Ernest W. Burgess. Studies include Robert E. Park and Ernest W. Burgess, *The City: Human Behavior in the Urban Environment* (1925); Ernest R. Mowrer, *Family Disorganization: An Introduction to a Sociology Analysis* (1927); Louis Wirth, *The Ghetto* (1928); Ruth Shonle Cavan, *Suicide* (1928); Ernest Theodore Hiller, *The Strike: A Study in Collective Action* (1928); Frances R. Donovan, *The Saleslady* (1929); Harvey W. Zorbough, *The Goldcoast and the Slum: A Sociological Study of Chicago's Near North Side* (1929); Clifford Shaw, *The Jack Roller* (1930); and Paul G. Cressey, *The Taxi Dance Hall: A Sociology Study in Commercialized Recreation and City Life* (1932). There are also theoretical works that deal with the concept of everyday life as fundamental to sociological study, including the works of Erving Goffman, Harold Garfinkel, and Alfred Schutz.

REFERENCES

Berger, B. M. (Ed.). (1990). *Authors of their own lives: Intellectual autobiographies by twenty American sociologists.* Berkeley: University of California Press.

Goetting, A., & Fenstermaker, S. (Eds.). (1994). *Individual voices, collective visions: Fifty years of women in society.* Philadelphia: Temple University Press.

PART I

Public Places

Not Even a Day in the Life[1]

CANDACE WEST

If I squint, I can make out the red glow on my alarm clock: 7:20 a.m. Mentally subtracting the extra 20 minutes this clock runs fast, I realize it's actually only 7:00. For a moment, I wonder how many other people are compulsive enough to set their clocks 20 minutes ahead (and their bathroom scales 5 pounds heavy) lest they find themselves running late (or over). Then, I confront the inevitable question: Is this a school day or not? If it's a school day, there's not a minute to spare: I'll need to grab some coffee, throw on some shorts, and jump on my stationary bicycle. Cycling for 15 miles while watching CNN news and bolting coffee, I'll have just enough time to wake up before running the dogs and getting things together for school. But if it's not a school day, life can proceed at a more leisurely pace: I can dispense with the bike until Monday, I can drink coffee rather than bolt it, and I can read the news instead of watching it.

Of course, school days and non-school days don't mean the same thing as they did when I was a student. Whether I have to teach today or not, there are still 35 letters of recommendation to be written, 7 manuscripts to be reviewed, and an article with a rapidly approaching deadline. Whether it's Tuesday or Sunday, I can't forget the tasks that remain once class is over and committee meetings are done with. As Eviatar Zerubavel (1979) has argued, professional commitments don't disappear at specified hours on the clock or on designated

AUTHOR'S NOTE: For their helpful comments on an earlier draft, I am grateful to Sarah Fenstermaker, Carol Brooks Gardner, Valerie Simmons, Frank Talamantes, and, especially, Celine Pascale.

days of the week. The hallmark of some professions (e.g., physicians) in comparison to others (e.g., nurses) is that their practitioners are, at least in theory, "on call" around the clock. Zerubavel studied a hospital to reach this conclusion, but he clearly knew a thing or two about the structure of academic life.

On reaching the happy realization that it's Saturday, I (temporarily) banish Zerubavel from my mind, fill a travel mug with coffee, put the two dogs on leashes, and head for the park. The dogs are obviously delighted, suffering from no confusion about school days, professional commitments, or days of the week. We stroll rather than run, allowing them plenty of time to sniff things and me plenty of time to enjoy my coffee. When we get to the park, I note further signs of middle-class "Saturdayness": 40- and 50-year-old basketball players, weekend fathers with toddlers, and over a dozen dogs with owners, rather than the usual weekday group of four or five. Here are Bella (a Labrador), Boris and Brandy (two Samoyeds), China and Max (two standard poodles), Lily (a Dalmatian), Paco (a Brittany spaniel), both Sadies (an English bulldog and a Heinz 57 variety), Shadow (a Border Collie), Sammy (a Rottweiler), Shiloh (a German shepherd), and, of course, Míja and Feliz (my Afghan hound and collie).

As I reach the dog area (so designated by signs admonishing owners to pick up after their pets), I unleash my two and see a man standing apart from the others with what looks like a Labrador-shepherd mix. "Would she like to play?" I ask, noticing that the man is intently watching the other dogs run. "She's too old" he replies (as if dogs' sociability had an expiration date). "Are you sure?" I ask, then adding: "My Afghan-who-died lived to be 14 years old and he loved playing with the other dogs right up until the end." "Not this one," he answers, making no move to unleash his not-so-old-looking dog. "Well, if you change your mind, the others are very friendly," I say, turning to join the rest of the owners up by the path.

"He's a strange one" says Anne, reaching into her pocket for the dog biscuits that Míja and Feliz are already nosing around for. "Look at that—he's wearing a velour running suit and gold chains to walk that dog!" (The rest of us are dressed in our rattiest jeans or sweats to protect our Real Clothes from paws, claws, and mud). I nod, saying, "That's not all. He claims his dog is 'too old' to play." Several of the owners shake their heads at the same time, thinking, perhaps, of the geriatric canines we have known—dogs whose sole reason for going on seemed to be their daily romp with other dogs.

After 20 minutes or so of watching our dogs at play, the strange man approaches, his Labrador-shepherd still on a leash. The other dogs are busy chasing one another across the grass, so they don't notice this new arrival. As the man comes abreast of us, he asks, "You folks live around here?" This makes me a little nervous: None of us has ever asked another owner for such personal information on first making their acquaintance. In fact, we who are "regulars" got to know all our dogs' names very quickly, but we didn't learn one another's names until we'd been coming to the park for several months (and then, the reason we came to exchange names was a petition to have the city council formally approve a dog area in this park). Despite the man's intrusive question, several owners reply "Yes" and nod politely, some pointing vaguely to streets beyond the park. "And do you come here often?" the man continues, setting off alarm bells in my head. Again, several people respond affirmatively, pointing out how well the dogs get along. "My name's Paul" says the man—eliciting "I'm Pete" and "Jason" from two of the men but nothing from any of the women, including me. "And I'm an animal control officer" Paul adds, pulling an official-looking badge and identification card out of his pocket.

Furious at my Saturday slowness, I think immediately of "Dogs and Their People" (Robins, Sanders, & Cahill, 1991). My students love this article, not only for its focus on an everyday feature of their own lives (pet-facilitated interaction in a public place) but also for its illumination of Erving Goffman's (1963, pp. 83-84) concept of *civil inattention*: that is, sufficient attention "to demonstrate that one appreciates that the other[s are] present" but not enough to suggest that they "constitute [targets] of special curiosity or design." Robins et al. (1991) found that, in the park they studied, dogs served as warrants for breaching civil inattention among owners, but only for very limited conversations: On encountering strangers with dogs, it was appropriate to ask them for "personal" information about their dogs (e.g., their dog's name, age, breed, or habits); it was not appropriate to ask them comparable information about themselves. The exchange of people-personal information had to wait until newcomers became regulars—in other words, not strangers any longer. This, of course, was the basis for my nervousness about Paul the animal control officer: He had been pressing us for information he had no business asking, accompanied by a dog or not. Then I remember Carol Brooks Gardner (1995, p. 93), who characterizes persons accompanied by dogs as "open people" (i.e., people who may be "approached at will with no pretense of stranger etiquette"). Gardner is the one who developed the idea of "access information"; that is, information "that would lead to the discovery of an individual's immediate or ultimate destination or a place where the individual can later reliably be found" (p. 122). Consistent with Gardner's view—that breaches of the rule concerning civil inattention can lead to leaks of access information—Paul is now checking each of our dog's collars for current tags and taking addresses for those of us (including me) who have failed to register our dogs.

I listen to him announce that I'm in for $36.00 in dog registration fees and an additional $10.00 penalty for failing to register before now. The Afghan will cost twice as much to register, he says, because she hasn't been spayed. What's more, I'll need a certificate from a vet confirming that I am sequestering her properly when she comes into heat and that I am not involved in any unlicensed breeding. With the clarity of vision that comes from hindsight, I see that I am only making sense of this situation and invoking the rule about civil inattention now that it has been violated (to which Harold Garfinkel [1967] would doubtless reply, "But of course." If norms really regulated behavior, I should have been out of there as soon as this stranger asked us our names).

Returning home, I see that the dogs are in no way chastened by their newly declared status as outlaws. They line up in perfect "sit" position for treats and look expectantly at the kibble container, figuring that breakfast comes next. I respond by filling both bowls with kibble, thinking all the while that living with dogs is much like living with Dustin Hoffman's character in *Rain Man* (this character was autistic and perfectly amiable—so long as his days proceeded in orderly fashion. Lunch on Friday had to consist of exactly eight fish sticks at precisely 12:30).

The phone rings, disrupting my train of thought. My first reaction is to ignore it—it's Saturday, after all. After obediently answering ringing phones all week, I'm ready for a break. As it rings again, I remember that weekend calls are often from friends and family, and I pick up the receiver. "Hello?" I say, cradling it on my shoulder while pouring more coffee into my travel mug. "Mrs. West?" says the voice at the other end of the line. Instantly, I am on guard. Although this two-turn exchange has so far displayed all the prototypical features of a phone call's conversational opening—for example, the answerer spoke first, the caller tried to display recognition of the answerer's voice (Schegloff, 1968, 1979)—I know that something is very wrong. For all that the caller dispensed with "Hello" and moved to an attempted identification of my voice, "Mrs. West" is not my name (and wouldn't be, even if I were married). Remembering a sociolinguist's advice from years ago (Sharon Veach, personal communication), I reply "I'm sorry, she's not here right now. Can I take a message?" "No," says the caller, "Just tell her MCI called and we'll call back later." Hanging up the phone, I note, "That kind of 'nonmessage' is like the cases Manny Schegloff [1980] talks about in 'Preliminaries to Preliminaries' " (e.g., Questioner: "Can I ask you a question?" Answerer: "You already have.")

Elated to have outsmarted an MCI salesperson (especially after having been duped by an animal control officer), I grab my car keys and set out to do a few Saturday morning errands. The first one takes me downtown, which is already looking awake and alive. As I drive down the main street, I see several shabbily dressed people with backpacks and bedrolls, some gesturing and reaching out to the pedestrians who walk by. Stopping at a stop sign, I see holiday shoppers averting their eyes and/or crossing the street to avoid contact with these folks. I think of my work with Celine Pascale (Pascale & West, in press) showing how civic leaders in Santa Cruz justify ordinances and policies that exclude people who are homeless from public places and hence from public purview. I know that the people I see on this street represent but a few of the estimated 2,000 to

3,000 people who are homeless in this community. As the holiday shopping season builds to a fevered pitch, they are becoming less and less visible to the public eye.

After parking the car, I walk toward the bookstore, window shopping as I move along. I notice a number of display windows that say "Feliz Navidad" as well as "Merry Christmas" (though none says "Feliz Hanukkah"). Some display what look like African American angels along with white ones, although both have decidedly European features. One window stops me dead in my tracks: a carefully arranged potpourri of artistic objects from very different parts of the world. Masks from Bali form the backdrop for man-with-burro figurines from Mexico, with Chinese slippers on one side and African spear-holding statues on the other. The whole display is framed in shiny gold tinsel, with red and green glass balls hanging from ribbons up above. I shake my head despairingly, recalling my attempts to explain to students that there is no such thing as Ethnic with a big *E*: If they mean Thai food, they should write "Thai food"; if they mean Chinese food, that's what they should write (I also point out that they don't use "Ethnic" when they mean French food, and this finally gets through to the slower ones). This window, by contrast, lumps Balinese, Mexican, Chinese, and African objects all together—as if they came from a single culture or were somehow indistinguishable from one another. It brings to mind Marianna Torgovnick's (1990, pp. 75-76) description of turn-of-the century Western museum exhibits, which displayed "primitive" objects—especially African ones—all in a mixed-up heap (as if to suggest "that African life was messy, chaotic [and] in need of Western order" (p. 76).

Remembering that I haven't got all day to spend window shopping, I leave the window display and move on to the bookstore. I join the queue of people at the bookstore's counter, waiting to pick up my special order. When my turn comes, I look down at my planner to verify the title of the book I ordered, so I'm not looking when the clerk says "Hey, Dr. West!" Glancing up, I recognize a former student who took my methods class last year. "I was in Soc 103" says he, none too sure that I will know him. "And did you pass?" I ask teasingly, knowing full well that he did. It occurs to me that, for a professor, running into students everywhere you go is one of the advantages of living in a small town: For example, you never have trouble getting your checks cashed. Then I recall that, for a professor, running into students is also one of the disadvantages of living in a small town: For example, you're never assured of anonymity. There was that time I took a prospective colleague and his wife out to dinner, in an attempt to show them the joys of living in Santa Cruz. Since they were from Australia, I wanted to pick a restaurant that showed some cosmopolitan sophistication; however, since they weren't keen on spicy food, our best restaurants (Indian, Mexican, and Szechwan) wouldn't do. I settled on an Italian restaurant, which, although no competition for Italian restaurants in New York, served reasonably decent food. The problem was, the night we were there, it was staffed exclusively by university students. The wine steward sought my advice on his senior thesis while simultaneously crumbling the cork in our wine bottle to pieces and confessing that he had never used a "professional wine opener" before. The waitress polled each of us at the table on the question of whether she should change her major from psychology to sociology. To top things off, when the check and my credit card disappeared to the cash register in the back of the restaurant, we heard a delighted cry: "Candace West? That's my teacher!" The cook (my student) came out to greet us, quite unaware of my embarrassment at how provincial Santa Cruz must have seemed to Australian sensibilities. In the bookstore, though, I am pleased by the provincialism, which gets me in and out in record time.

My next stop is a bagel shop, which is doing a very brisk business. Serving "New York-style" bagels like its parent shop in Berkeley, this establishment stimulated a lot of controversy when it first opened here. Many people feared that the advent of "bagel chains" would, like the advent of other chain stores, lead to the demise of the independent small businesses in Santa Cruz. Hence, many (like me) are scrupulous in alternating our patronage between chain shops and independent shops—our palates conditioned as much by guilt as by taste. Standing in line, I notice a supreme test of civil inattention just outside the window of the shop: A man is walking down the street with black grease paint on his face, a hat with Viking horns on his head, and a huge spear, which he is carrying upright in his fist. His appearance is otherwise unremarkable: jeans, running shoes, a sweat shirt, and a flack jacket look pretty much like what everyone else is wearing this Saturday morning. As he moves toward other pedestrians, they do their best to seem urbane: catching sight of him from about 8 feet away and averting their eyes as they near him—but whipping their heads around to stare at him, just after he passes by. I laugh, recalling the vampire I met on the street one Halloween morning, just after I moved to Santa Cruz.

My final destination today is the cigarette shop—now, the only store in town that allows smoking on its premises. Arriving at the doorway of this shop, I am aware of other pedestrians who studiously avert their eyes from me as I enter. Buying cigarettes these days feels like buying tampons did when I was 13—making an acutely stigmatizing purchase that you hope nobody notices. Moreover, things have gotten even worse than they were when Joseph Schneider (1984) documented them: Not only do nonsmokers look away from smokers as the latter enter this shop but also smokers themselves avoid looking at one another as they pull their cartons from the shelves. Skulking out with my plain unmarked bag, I console myself with thoughts of Charles Edgley and Dennis Brissett's "Health Nazis and the Cult of the Perfect Body" (1990).

I drive home with my mental calculator running, itemizing Things I've Got To Do Today. My first priority has got to be e-mail, I realize, since I haven't touched it in 48 hours. Although I appreciate its advantages, I hate e-mail for making me ever-accessible. The article comes next, I figure: I can work on that while my brain is still fresh and switch to the letters of recommendation when I start getting tired. There aren't that many letters with deadlines this week— once I finish them, I can review at least one of those journal manuscripts. Realizing that this set of priorities will leave some hapless author with a very frazzled referee, I promise myself that I'll double-check any review I write before sending it off on Monday morning.

The screen of my computer brightens as icons begin to appear. I look longingly at the file with my emergent article in it, then dutifully click on my e-mail program. I have 44 messages, I learn with dismay (knowing that this will kill the better part of 2 hours). I list all 44, resolving to be brief, to answer only those that must be answered by Monday morning and to save the others for the week to come. The first one to appear, however, is a message from an irate student. Although he is enjoying my methods class very much, he says, he is upset at my remark last Thursday that "even Hitler was kind to his dog." He is Jewish, he tells me, and several of his relatives died in the Holocaust. He says he believes Hitler was a monster; therefore, he finds my comment very distressing. I think back to the context in which I made this remark: well after our discussion of ethics and politics in social research (including Jack Galliher's "Social Scientists' Ethical Responsibilities to Subordinates" [1980] and Barrie Thorne's " 'You Still Takin' Notes?'" [1980]) and well into our discussion of field research itself. What I had been trying to convey in class was the necessity of capturing the whole of an informant's worldview—however complicated it might be—in one's field notes and analysis; but what he'd gotten out of my remarks was my apparent appreciation of Adolph Hitler. I sit for several minutes, thinking of how to best explain myself "Dear Keith," I finally write,[2]

> I'm very sorry to have caused you such distress—I certainly didn't mean to. In fact, I chose Hitler for my example precisely because of his infamy, and the nearly universal loathing people feel for him.
>
> But the job of researchers who conduct unstructured interviews is to capture the point of view of those they are studying. This means including what makes sense to the people they are studying—and why it makes sense to them—regardless of how repugnant it might seem to the rest of us. Your reaction to my comment reminds me of my own reaction a few years ago, when I was asked to review a manuscript about pedophilia by an author who was obviously a pedophile. I actually cringed as I read the first page of this manuscript, thinking, "What is sociology coming to?" I realized, however, that if we really want to eliminate pedophilia, we're not going to accomplish it by dismissing those who practice it as "monsters" or somehow inhuman (remember Bosmajian [1974]?). Rather, we're going to accomplish it by understanding what things look like from their point of view.
>
> Candace.

As I sign off, I make a mental note to look for Keith in class on Tuesday and make sure that I've resolved this misunderstanding. He's a good student, and this is the second course he's taken with me; if there weren't 230 other students in the room, I suspect he'd have posed his question in class on Thursday.

The next message on my screen is more disconcerting still. It's from a senior administrator in my department, concerned about the problem of "gender balance" on our Departmental Policy Committee.[3] He notes that two of the five women faculty members in our department have taken unexpected leaves this term; as a consequence, there is no "gender representation" of women on the committee that makes executive decisions for our department. So, he is asking me and the other senior woman on duty this term "if [either of us] would like to serve on this committee"—in addition to our already full loads of existing committee responsibilities.

In irritation, I think of Rosabeth Moss Kanter's (1977) contention that it's women's status as tokens—not gender—that determines their experiences in the workplace. If there were more women faculty members in our department than the existing 5 (out of 16), we wouldn't have to do more service than men faculty (to ensure that "the woman's point of view" is represented on every committee). But then I remember my own work with Sarah Fenstermaker and Don Zimmerman (Fenstermaker, West, & Zimmerman, 1991; West & Fenstermaker, 1993, 1995; West & Zimmerman, 1987). And I remember the tacit assumptions of work like Kanter's: that one's gender might be interactionally "overcome," that it might someday be no longer worthy of note; that it might eventually no longer require accommodation (Fenstermaker et al., 1991, p. 292; Zimmer, 1988). I realize that this view (like the view of the senior administrator who has sent me this message) still retains the notion of gender as an individual characteristic rather than "an achieved property of situated conduct" (West & Zimmerman, 1987, p. 126). In holding my colleague and me accountable as women for the "gender imbalance" of the Departmental Policy Committee, this administrator is engaged in not only the ongoing accomplishment of gender but also the ongoing production of women's greater workloads.

"Enough already," I tell myself in exasperation. I'll call my colleague later and see how she thinks we should handle this. Meanwhile, I'll let the e-mail just sit there and get to work on my article. I open the file full of drafty, unpolished prose, speculating that one reason this article is taking me longer to write than I'd like it to is its lack of a proper title. Thinking of it vaguely as a piece on "Qualitative Sociology as Everyday Life" isn't getting me anywhere; what I need is to put my own stamp on it as the author. Let's see . . . "Everyday Life" . . . no, "A Day in the Life" . . . no, "Almost a Day in the Life" . . . maybe that's it. . . .

POSTSCRIPT

I have exercised some literary license here: The events I describe did not all happen on the same day, although they did all happen (and some, very recently). Condensing them the way I have seemed the most economical means of fitting them into the space allotted.

NOTES

1. Reprinted with permission of Human Sciences Press, Inc. (1997).
2. "Keith" is a pseudonym.
3. "Departmental Policy Committee" is a pseudonym.

REFERENCES

Bosmajian, H. (1974). *The language of oppression.* Washington, DC: Public Affairs Press.

Edgley, C., & Brissett, D. (1990). Health nazis and the cult of the perfect body: Some polemical observations. *Symbolic Interaction, 13,* 257-279.

Fenstermaker, S., West, C., & Zimmerman, D. H. (1991). Gender inequality: New conceptual terrain. In R. L. Blumberg (Ed.), *Gender, family, and economy: The triple overlap* (pp. 289-307). Newbury Park, CA: Sage.

Galliher, J. (1980). Social scientists' ethical responsibilities to subordinates: Looking up meekly. *Social Problems, 27,* 298-308.

Gardner, C. (1995). *Passing by: Gender and public harassment.* Berkeley: University of California Press.

Garfinkel, H. (1967). *Studies in ethnomethodology.* Englewood Cliffs, NJ: Prentice Hall.

Goffman, E. (1963). *Behavior in public places.* Glencoe, IL: Free Press.

Kanter, R. M. (1977). *Men and women of the corporation.* New York: Basic Books.

Pascale, C. M., & West, C. (in press). Social illusions: Responses to homelessness in Santa Cruz, California 1989-1994. *Perspectives on Social Problems.*

Robins, D. M., Sanders, C. R., & Cahill, S. (1991). Dogs and their people: Pet-facilitated interaction in a public setting. *Journal of Contemporary Ethnography, 20,* 3-25.

Schegloff, E. A. (1968). Sequencing in conversational openings. *American Anthropologist, 70,* 1075-1095.

Schegloff, E. A. (1979). Identification and recognition in telephone conversation openings. In G. Psathas (Ed.), *Everyday language: Studies in ethnomethodolog* (pp. 23-78). New York: Irvington.

Schegloff, E. A. (1980). Preliminaries to preliminaries: "Can I ask you a question?" *Sociological Inquiry, 50,* 104-152.

Schneider, J. W. (1984). Morality, social problems, and everyday life. In J. Schneider & J. Mtsuse (Eds.), *Studies in the sociology of social problems* (pp. 180-205). Norwood, NJ: Ablex.

Thorne, B. (1980). "You still takin' notes?" Problems of informed consent in field research. *Social Problems, 27,* 284-297.

Torgovnick, M. (1990). *Gone primitive.* Chicago: University of Chicago Press.

West, C., & Fenstermaker, S. (1993). Power, inequality and the accomplishment of gender: An ethnomethodological view. In P. England (Ed.), *Theory on gender/feminism on theory* (pp. 151-174). New York: Aldine.

West, C., & Fenstermaker, S. (1995). Doing difference. *Gender & Society, 9,* 8-37.

West, C., & Zimmerman, D. H. (1987). Doing gender. *Gender & Society, 1,* 125-151.

Zerubavel, E. (1979). Private time and public time: The temporal structure of social accessibility and professional commitments. *Social Forces, 58,* 38-58.

Zimmer, L. (1988). Tokenism and women in the workplace: The limits of gender-neutral theory. *Social Problems, 35,* 64-77.

CHAPTER 2

The Nursing Home

LILLIAN B. RUBIN

"Damn, when do I get to be old," I think resentfully, as I drag myself out of bed just after dawn. It's one of those beautiful San Francisco mornings when a billowy fog bank hangs over the ocean, its lacy tendrils creating magical forms as they spill over the Golden Gate Bridge. But I have no time to linger.

Forty-five minutes later, I'm hurtling down the freeway in a taxi, heading for the airport to catch the 8:00 a.m. flight to Miami where my 94-year-old mother lives. I look out at the Bay, the water cool and green in the morning light, and brood: "Twenty years ago, it was 50-year-old 'children' taking care of their 70-year-old parents. Now it's 70-year-olds looking after the 90-plus old folks. I'm too old for this," I tell myself, "too tired. These trips take too much out of my 70-year-old body."

At the gate, I hand over my ticket in return for a boarding pass and prepare to wait. This is the third trip this year, and the year isn't yet half gone. My husband and daughter keep asking why I go. "She doesn't recognize you," they argue, "and even if she did, it wouldn't make any difference to her. All she wants is your brother, and he's dead."

They're right; my relationship with my mother has been troubled since I was a very small child, and my being there makes no apparent dent on her consciousness. Yet I go, not so much for her but for me: for the child inside who still hopes for something, not approval exactly, but some way to define the relationship more positively, and for the adult who knows she has to do it "right" now to avoid guilt later.

The plane is due into Miami at 5:30 in the afternoon—too late, I tell myself, to go to the nursing home where my mother has resided for the past 6 months. It's not too late, of course, but it's the excuse I need to have dinner with a friend. He's my gift to myself whenever I make this journey—a long, leisurely, lovely dinner among the young and the beautiful who inhabit Miami's South Beach: my antidote to the absurdity of life and death in a nursing home.

The next morning, I dawdle over breakfast, putting off my visit as long as conscience allows. It isn't just seeing my mother that's so difficult; it's the whole atmosphere—the sights, the sounds, and the smells. Worst of all, it is the confrontation with my future. At 70, it's impossible to be here without asking, "Is this what's in store for me?" I tell myself that I'll never let it happen, that I'll take my life before I live this indignity. Brave words. But can we ever know what we'll do when the moment is upon us?

Finally, I enter the building, check in at the front desk, and take the elevator to my mother's third-floor room. As I step into the corridor, I'm greeted by five wheelchairs facing the elevators expectantly. For a moment, my mind trips out in an image of the chairs gliding off by themselves into some adventure. In reality, the chairs are occupied by three women and two men, all clearly living in some other universe in their minds. Their bodies, slumped in the chairs, are so limp that they seem to have no bones. One woman mumbles incoherently, a rhythmic set of nonstop sounds that no one understands; a man's palsied hands shake uncontrollably; the others sit quietly, with their eyes closed and their heads lying lopsided on their shoulders as if the muscles and tendons that used to hold them in place have worn out.

"What are they doing here?" I ask an attendant at the nursing station nearby. "Oh," she replies cheerily, "it recreation time; they're waiting to go down to the rec room." Recreation time? Am I crazy, or are they?

The scene at the elevator and the explanation follow me as I make my way down the hall to my mother's room. I remember that when I came to make the arrangements to move my mother into this place, I was impressed when the director showed me around and outlined all the activities available for residents. Now, I wonder fretfully whether I blinded myself to the reality that these "activities" are little more than a bureaucratic response to state licensing requirements. But perhaps I'm being uncharitable. It's possible, too, that this pretense that some semblance of normal life exists here is the only way the staff can cope with the incongruity of dealing with the living dead.

I enter my mother's room preoccupied with the realization that if I had allowed myself to "see" then what is so obvious now, I might have been forced to look for another solution. But what would it have been? My mother couldn't live alone, nor was the euphemistically named "family residential center" in which she had resided for 2 years able to continue to care for her. It was a nursing home or my home, and that I couldn't do. I flinch when I see those words staring back at me, fearful that the world out there will know me for the selfish daughter my mother always said I was.

My attention is diverted by my mother's new roommate. She's younger than most of the people here and seems fully competent as she sits up in her chair, a tray table in front of her. "I'm Pat," she says, her right hand patting her chest as she speaks. "I can't walk." I smile, say a few of words of greeting, and turn to my mother who lies still and frail in her bed. "Hi, mom," I say. Her eyes flicker open and look at me vacantly. "Mom, it's me, Lillian, your daughter." She turns away, mumbling, "I have no daughter; she died." "No," I insist, even as I understand the folly of my attempt to penetrate her fog, "I'm here, right here."

In the background, I hear Pat patting her chest noisily and repeating, "I'm Pat; I can't walk"—a mantra meant perhaps to remind herself that she's still a person. "Maybe if I talk to her, she'll settle down," I think. But there is no conversation; she has no other words, at least none she's willing or able to share with me.

I sit at my mother's bedside, Pat's words like a soft drumbeat in the background, and feel the anger rising inside me. My mother is dying, yet she won't give an inch. If I were my own patient, I'd ask: "So why would you think it would be different now?" I don't "think" so, but I can't help wishing it were so.

It's hard seeing this woman, once so all-powerful in my life—the person I feared, hated, loved—now lying helpless before me. It isn't that I want her to live; rather, it's nearly intolerable to see her so diminished, so demeaned. She was so tough, so fiercely independent, so unyielding. Now here she is, broken, her mind wandering in and out of a reality that's intolerable, kicking, clawing, biting, cursing at her attendants who come to clean her up—to change her diapers. The image is blinding, incomprehensible. My indomitable mother, a woman for whom control seemed to equal survival, now suffers the ultimate loss of control. Who wouldn't want to kick and scream, to curse the helper instead of the God who abandoned her to this living death?

I, too, want to scream my protest: "This isn't a fitting end to her life." Or to mine. It's impossible to sit here without conjuring with my own demons about aging, without confronting my own pained understanding that I'm not far behind.

Anita, my mother's attendant for the day, interrupts my thoughts. "You're her daughter, huh?" she asks, as she comes into the room. "She's tough, your mama; she don't do nothing she don't want to do." On the inside I think angrily, "Boy, don't I know that!"; outside I shrug my assent wordlessly. At that, Anita turns toward the bed and shouts, "It's time to get dressed, Rae." No answer. Impatient, she shouts louder, "Rae, did you hear me, Rae. It's time to get dressed."

"Why doesn't anyone here talk to these patients in a normal tone of voice?" I think irritably. Aloud, I say, "She's not deaf; you don't have to shout so loudly." "Well," she says, vexed at the perceived criticism, "you can't always tell."

But it isn't only an inability to "tell" that makes people shout at the old. It has to do also with our cultural assumptions about the aged, with the deeply held, if unarticulated belief, that the aged are also infirm, not just physically but mentally. So we shout because we feel helpless in the face of infirmity, because somehow shouting seems to give more force to our words, to offer more hope that we'll be heard and understood. Moreover, the old are a mirror on our future, a terrifying image that threatens our denial of our own mortality, one from which we turn in angry disgust as we try to shout it down.

After a brief struggle, Anita gets my mother dressed and into a wheelchair, while I prepare to take her out for a walk by the beach. We walk in the warm sunshine until it's time for lunch, which, I remember from previous visits, is served in what they call the recreation room. When we arrive there, I see a semicircle of wheelchairs, all occupied by people like those who greeted me at the elevator. Inside the circle, an attendant sits beside a portable stereo that's playing music so loud that those in the room who are still competent are covering their ears.

I settle my mother in a corner as far from the music as I can get, but neither thought nor conversation are possible in the din. Unable to stand the noise for very long, I go up to the aide, tap her on the shoulder to get her attention, and shout, "The music is much too loud, can you turn it down, please." She looks at me offended, draws herself up to her full height, and says, her sweeping gesture taking in the near comatose people around her, "I can't turn it down; this is their music lesson." Then, as I stand there wide-eyed, wondering if I've entered a loony bin instead of an old-age home, she says, as if it explains this bizarre scene, "We do it every day at this time."

I cross the room to where my mother sits, thinking, "Maybe it does explain it." Not the music lesson, but the attendant's prideful response. We all do it in one way or another. We make sense out of senseless events by imbuing them with meaning. It's God's will; it's nature's way; it's fate, kismet—anything that allows us to avoid confronting the inexplicable, the randomness of so many of life's events.

For this woman, as for others who work in nursing homes, life on the job is filled with the senseless because the senselessness of both life and death is particularly acute in this setting. It's easier to come to work every day if she can make herself believe that she's doing something useful, that her activities here have some meaning. So when she gathers her charges together, she's not just surrounded with people who long ago lost consciousness, she's bringing them pleasure with her music lesson.

"Who's to say she isn't?" I muse as I walk back across the room. "How do you know what's going on in their heads and hearts?" I shake my head, impatient with my thoughts. Am I, too, determined to make sense out of the senseless?

My mother refuses to eat any lunch, so I take her back upstairs. I sit at her bedside, Pat's unending mantra providing the background music to my thoughts, when a woman wanders into the room, plops down on my lap, and puts a finger in her mouth. She's a small person, dressed in a kind of clown's outfit—brilliant green shirt, hot pink skirt, harlequin stockings, and no shoes. My astonishment strikes me dumb for a moment, then I gently stand both of us up and say, "Hello; what's your name?" She beams—a brilliant smile that lights up her face—and replies with an incomprehensible stream of sounds. She's young looking, middle fifties, I imagine—too young to fit my classic image of the Alzheimer's patient.

I don't know if I've made contact with her, but she seems perfectly happy to be babbling at me. Not knowing what else to do, I sit down again and so does she, taking her place once more on my lap. Soon an attendant comes looking for her: "You can't stay here Lita; you know that," she scolds. Then, as she takes her by the hand to lead her down the hall to her own room, the attendant turns to me: "She wanders," she says apologetically.

Wandering Lita won't stay put, however. So we replay the same scene repeatedly through the afternoon as she comes for the comfort of my lap and the attendant comes to take her away. "Let her stay," I finally say, "she's not doing any harm." "I can't," the attendant replies, "it's against the rules." "What rule says a patient can't find comfort somewhere; I don't mind if she's here." But the rules say no and there's no give.

I sit there angrily, thinking of the time when my mother fell out of bed and broke her hip 2 days after she'd been admitted here. "Why weren't the rails up on her bed during the night," I demanded to know. "The state of Florida has a rule against any restraints," explained the director. "Even when it jeopardizes the health and safety of the patients?" I asked incredulous. "Yes," he said, "If an inspector came and saw the rails up on the beds, we'd loose our triple A rating."

It's easy to understand the thinking behind the rules. For so long nursing homes abused their patients with unnecessary restraints—physical, chemical, or both. But as with so many rules that are designed to correct such problems, their bureaucratic application often creates new difficulties, sometimes as bad as the ones they sought to cure.

Now that Lita is gone, my attention is caught once again by a man, probably in his late seventies, who, with one foot, has been propelling himself up and down the hall in his wheel chair. Up and back he goes, each rhythmic energetic push scooting him along at an impressive pace. What does this journey to nowhere mean to him?

I move toward the hall and watch from the doorway. After a few trips, he stops before me and says, his voice edged with hostility, "What're you looking at?" "You," I reply, "I can't help wondering why you do that all day." "What would you do if you were in this crazy place?" "I don't know; maybe I'd read a book," I say. "I can't do that; it's too hard to concentrate on anything," he answers. "You look and sound pretty good to me. What are you doing here anyway?" I ask. "What am I doing here?" he snorts, a bitter anger suffusing his features:

> What am I doing here? Ask my damn kids. They'll tell you. I had this stroke, and as soon as I couldn't take care of myself like they thought I should, they shoved me in here, threw me away like a piece of garbage.

I shudder, thinking, "That's what my mother said when I brought her here." "But she needed to be here; she couldn't take care of herself anymore," I tell myself. Words that don't still my guilt which asks, "Is that what we 'children' always tell ourselves? Is that what we need to believe so we can live with the choices we make?"

I turn back to my mother and leave the man outside to his frantic pacing. The day is almost gone; I'll leave soon to catch my 6 p.m. flight back to San Francisco. I lean over and kiss my mother's dry, weathered cheek. "I'm going to have to leave," I say into her ear. She turns away, and so do I. It's the same in death as it has been in life. We have always turned away from each other, my mother and I, always since I was a small child.

I collect my things, stroke her hair one last time, and say good-bye to the staff. Outside I hail a cab, sit back, and expect to be flooded with relief at the prospect of being home in a few hours. Instead, I begin to weep, quietly at first, then in big gulping sobs. "Anything I can do for you lady?" the cab driver asks, looking anxiously in the mirror. But there's nothing anyone can do. I know I've said my last goodbye to my mother—a farewell that was as painful and unsatisfying as our lifetime of hellos have been.

Two weeks later, at 7 o'clock on Saturday morning, the phone rings. I know before I pick it up what I will hear. "Your mother's running a fever, and the doctor wants to know if you want her treated?" I had left explicit orders saying "no treatment," but now, faced with the question, I gulp nervously. I turn to my husband and tell him the news. He shakes his head wordlessly. Finally, I eke out the one word, "No."

It's Sunday now. A chill passes through my body as I pick up the phone to hear that my mother is dead. *My mother is dead!* My mind stands still for a moment, then thought and feeling collide. For her it's over. For me, it's both an ending and a beginning—or perhaps the beginning of the end—as I move to the head of the generational line.

CHAPTER 3

Essaying the Personal[1]
Making Sociological Stories Stick

SHERRYL KLEINMAN

I like to think I was always a sociologist. As a child, I asked my mother why I had to hide my pale skin under a deep tan in the summer while white people hated black people's dark skin. In my early teens, I didn't understand why sex was good for boys and bad for girls, why my 19-year-old sister felt embarrassed about not having a fiancé, or why my brother never did the dishes while my sister and I were supposed to help my mother clean the whole house.

Maybe Simmel (1993) was right—people on the margins have the distance required to stand back and analyze the mainstream world. Although I lived a conventional life as a girl in a lower-middle-class "intact" family, got good grades, and never ran away from home, I was also a Jew living in English (Protestant) and French (Catholic) Quebec.

I had good questions and observations back then but no analysis. I hadn't yet learned, as C. Wright Mills (1959) put it, to turn private troubles into public issues. That came later.

When I started college in 1970, I thought I'd become a psychologist. I was, after all, interested in how people thought and felt about things. In the first part of the two-semester Introduction to Psychology, we never got to humans. I

AUTHOR'S NOTE: Thanks to Prue Rains for early conversations about this piece. I am also grateful to Michael Schwalbe, Barbara Stenross, Martha Copp, Martha Roth, and members of my writing group—Jane Brown, Marcy Lansman, Wendy Luttrell, Sarah Shields, and Fabienne Worth—for commenting on several drafts of this chapter.

vaguely remember reading about the stickleback (though I no longer know why). And I can still see Harlow's tortured monkeys, clinging to terry cloth surrogates of their mothers. The second semester didn't get much better, as my behaviorist professors tried to convince me that I could understand people through operant conditioning.

I took a sociology course the next fall and discovered Blumer (1969), Goffman (1959), Mead (1934), and then Berger and Luckmann (1966).

I learned that people created worlds, which meant, to me, that those worlds could change. All the things I didn't like—like having to get married and have kids or being sure to fall in love only with Jews—were social conventions that benefited some more than others. I learned that talking to people about things that interested me was called "research" and I could get course credit for doing it. For instance, I thought I was the only woman missing out on the sexual revolution, so I did interviews with female undergraduates on "premarital sex." I found my own doctors unsympathetic about menstrual pain, so I interviewed gynecologists about their understandings of "dysmenorrhea" and the women who came to them for help.

At the time, a teaching assistant in sociology told me that I had a knack for this kind of work and if I worked hard and got a PhD I could eventually get paid for doing it. I was relieved to know I wouldn't have to go to law school, the fallback for students of my generation who didn't like their major.

Sex and menstrual pain interest a lot of people, but I wrote those stories only for sociologists. This has been true for most of my work; I've published articles and books in places that few nonacademics know about. We can sociologize this pretty easily—I'm part of an academic community where rewards (like tenure and promotions) are tied to winning approval from that community. Other communities, other audiences, haven't mattered as much.

So it is probably the privilege of job security that now makes it possible for me to think of bringing sociological messages to a wider audience. Why do this? As Barry Glassner (personal communication) put it, qualitative sociology is a "way of seeing." For me, it's potentially a life-changing and world-changing way of seeing. As a sociologist of everyday life, I notice and try to understand what I—and those around me—think, feel, say, and do. What a symbolic interactionist-based qualitative sociology offers, I think, is a double vision: We are all individuals who act—and action can mean anything from resignation to making trouble. At the same time, we are all stand-ins for groups, classes, and social categories. So, we are products of social-historical circumstances and we act with or upon them. If we understand how conditions and culture constrain us, and how our actions affect others and ourselves, then we have the potential to make changes in ourselves and in the world. If, as a sociologist, I bring these analyses to people outside our borders, then they too can understand their own experiences socio-logically and perhaps think about how they might do things differently.

We can, of course, opt to keep our analyses to ourselves. My job provides little incentive to communicate sociology to people outside the academy. But as someone who sees the liberatory potential of sociology, I now feel obligated to bring a sociological sensibility to others. Am I abandoning sociology? Quite the contrary. I want to reach those who either don't know what sociology is or who took that one intro course years ago and found it useless or boring.

What's the best way to communicate sociological analyses to those outside our circle? Storytelling, whether in fiction or nonfiction, is a time-tested way to get readers to care. As I've learned in teaching courses in race, class, and gender, writings that "show" more than "tell" a story of interaction, inequality, and power get students to listen and then to understand that life is more than a drama of personalities. For example, students read about a black undergraduate's experiences at a predominantly white university and learn about subtle-to-blatant racism among white students who see themselves as liberal (Simmons, 1995); or they read one reporter's (Griscom, 1995) account of a lesbian's long struggle with doctors, lawyers, and families to gain legal guardianship of her recently disabled partner and learn to see connections among heterosexism, sexism, and ableism.

Ethnographic analyses written for sociologists are also stories, but we often write them in ways that keep only specialists turning the page. When I write what I clumsily call "sociologically informed personal essays," I don't have the luxury of assuming the reader's attention. I'll have to earn it with every sentence. Readers (like students) will stay interested in the sociology only if the story sticks.

I offer one of my essays-in-progress as an example of how we can use our qualitative perspective in writing personal essays (or "creative nonfiction") for the educated public. After the essay, I discuss similarities and differences between this kind of writing and conventional ethnographic tales.

THE NOSE JOB

In the first weeks of my courses on race, class, and gender, some of the white students say they keep quiet because they worry that their words will "offend someone." When I probe, the students admit what they're really afraid of: looking like bigots in front of their peers. Today, I'm getting a taste of their fear.

It's the start of a 2-day workshop on "Racism and Sexism on Campus." Those of us who are getting money to devise or revise undergraduate courses that fulfill the cultural diversity requirement have to attend the workshop. I've heard it's run by psychologists, so I'm sure we'll explore our own racism. I'm the white feminist who's taught race, class, and gender for 7 years, so I'm supposed to know something. All I know today is that I've got a big case of performance anxiety. The faculty are my peers and I don't want to lose face. Like the students in my classes, I wonder, "Will I get caught?"

I'm still analyzing my anxiety as I enter the cold conference room. Chairs line three of the walls. If this were my class I'd move the chairs into a circle. But I'm not in charge here.

I recognize 3 of the 11 faculty from brief contact in the past. I do a quick race and sex count: two men of color, two women of color, five white women (including me), and two white men. I'm relieved to see students in the room; they'll be more forgiving. I scan their faces, hoping to find someone who has taken a course with me. Not one.

The workshop leaders, a white man and a black woman, both middle-aged and smiling, introduce themselves. As we go around the room, 13 of the undergraduates say they are African American. One says he's biracial but doesn't give the details. Another says Native American. Only 3 are men.

After the rest of us say something about ourselves, we break into small groups and talk about our goals for the workshop. Then we resume our seats along the walls. Phil tells us to count off—1,2,1,2,1,2. . . . Then: "All the 1's should stay in this room, all the 2's should go into the next room." Whispers, then pockets of laughter, as it becomes clear that many of us have already forgotten our numbers.

I follow Phil into the next room and we move our chairs into a circle. We sit and he asks us to relax. "Close your eyes, if it feels comfortable." Oh, he's going to lead us in a guided meditation. I've done these before, so I can put aside my performance anxiety and relax into the assignment. He tells us to think back to when we first met a person of a different race, ethnic group, or religion. Any difference we can remember.

I know what's going on: We're supposed to search for an experience that left a big impression on us, so we can explore how we interpreted the encounter at the time and discover how we've generalized about the group from that first experience.

Try, Sherryl. You grew up in the province of Quebec, a place filled with difference. Think of the first French-Canadian you met. The French were the "white niggers" of Canada, as Pierre Vallières put it in a book that I read for a French-Canadian lit class while an undergraduate at English-speaking McGill.

It's not working.

Think about growing up Jewish. How young was I when I learned to fear the French, the troublemakers who wanted to separate Quebec from Canada? Somehow I learned to equate Quebec separation with trouble for the Jews. The WASPS—the real English—have the power, but we'll be the English speakers to blame. Scapegoated, once again. Yet I can't remember my first encounter with a Québecois. Was it with a clerk at Morgan's, a department store in downtown Montreal? Or with a bus driver taking me to Morgan's?

An image of my family appears. What are they doing here? I'm supposed to be thinking about some other group. I close my eyes tighter, trying to squeeze them out. But they won't go. I see my mother, my father, and my brother. My sister lurks in the background.

They're looking at my nose.

I can hear what they're thinking: Sherryl is ugly and it's all because of her big nose. The nose is the focal point; the rest of the body is understood, judged, in relation to the nose.

Another image: I'm in a dressing room with my mother, trying on what she calls "an outfit." Not a skirt from this rack and a blouse from that rack, but a two-piece set. She enunciates "outfit" with military precision, but with a glint in her eye. It's a sexy uniform.

The pieces match, but I'm no match for the outfit. "You're so skinny. Clothes hang on you." I am 7, 10, 13. "Why don't you have a nice figure like your sister?" My sister is 5 years older. She also has a nice nose, like my mother. But this boy mannequin on which girl clothes hang like heavy drapes is only part of the point: The nose stands out because it's glued to a long, skinny face.

When did my nose become a family joke? My father has a big nose, but that's not so bad. "You have a nose like daddy," my older brother announces. That's the joke. A girl with a man's nose.

It's 1965. I'm 13, sitting on my bed in the room I share with my sister, admiring the coeds in *Seventeen*. My mother hesitates at the door, then walks in, slowly, as if the weight of her thoughts had sunk to her legs. God, she's going to tell me someone died. "I've talked with your father," she says, "You know we don't have a lot of money, but we're going to pay the thousand dollars to give you a nose job." A thousand dollars? I'm dizzy. I see bubbles of zeros floating around my mother's head. Now I know the truth: My parents are willing to go broke to make me look better. This nose is worse than I thought.

"It's that bad?" My eyes are stinging and I'm sure my nose is turning red and puffy, growing as wide as it is long, right before my mother's eyes. "No, no, it's not *terrible*. Let me show you." *Show* me? Does she have before-and-after pictures?

"Just two things to fix. And each one only needs a little fixing." Like a finger painter, she lightly sweeps my bump with her index finger. "We take just a little off that, see?" Then she moves her finger to the tip of my nose and pushes it up, gently. "And just a little lift here, not much at all. A small job."

While she steps back and eyes the new me, I remember something else she once said: "Never let someone take a picture of your profile. Lift your head when someone takes a picture of you from the front; your nose will look smaller."

My mother means well. To help me get a good Jewish husband—"a professional man"—I should look less Jewish.

I try to remember where I've read about nose jobs, maybe in the *Montreal Star.* They break your nose in order to fix it, that much I know. I run from the room crying. I will not do this. Am I afraid? Yes. Do I think it's wrong to change my face? Yes. But for years I wonder, Did I chicken out or did I have principles?

My mother doesn't mention surgery again, though I know her offer is open-ended.

After I save my nose from the knife, I figure out how to save myself. I get funny. I make better jokes about my nose than anyone else, even my grown-up brother. Necessity must have been the mother of self-deprecating Jewish humor.

Phil's voice pulls me back to the circle. "Open your eyes, slowly." He pauses. "Would anyone like to share what they saw?"

I'm not going to tell my story. It doesn't fit the assignment. Well, that's not the only reason. Look who's in the room: Barry, a Jewish leftist. He'll think I'm giving away tribal secrets or wasting time on trivia while capitalist greed ravages the planet. Even if Barry weren't here, I'd worry about reinforcing anti-Semitism or creating new anti-Semites in the room. "Gee, I thought Jews were at least good to each other. But doing that to a 13-year-old child? Shame on them!"

I convince myself that I'll learn more by listening. Tracy, an African American student, tells us about touching her white teacher's hair and how nice it felt, unlike her own hair. Monica, another African American student, remembers the crush she had on a white boy when she was 6 and how she chased him "round and round" until he turned to her and said, "Why do you have such fat lips?" Then she shows us how she bit her lips—for hours a day—to make them smaller.

Phil says, "Did you talk to your mother about it?" "No." Sybil, a white professor, says, "And if you had, you know what a mother would have said, 'You're beautiful as you are. You don't need to do that.' "

Astonished, I look at Sybil: "I would *never* have heard that in my family. It's in my family where I felt ugly." So this truth has tumbled out of the mouth I willed silent. Twelve faces beam question marks at me. I can't stop now, I can only hope to make things better by adding words.

I turn to Phil. "I couldn't think of an encounter with another group, only with my 'own' group." Cold sweat drops from my armpits to my waist. Barry looks at me with a look I can't decipher, and I feel heat spread up my neck and across my face.

I tell the story of my nose.

When I'm done, I'm convinced my mother has overheard and a telegram will arrive any minute: Why did you have to *tell?* STOP. Your hurt mother. STOP.

I jump to analysis, hoping my sociology wards off the anti-Semitism I'm sure will follow. "As I see it, this story is about internalized oppression—gender oppression as well as internalized anti-Semitism," I say, "It was bad to have a Jewish nose, even if you were a man. After all, it was a *Jewish* nose, not just a big nose, that was the problem. It was clear that my brother was relieved *not* to have my father's nose. But the real tragedy was when a *girl* had that nose."

A few heads nod.

Phil says, "I'm glad you told that story. We don't learn about our differences only when we meet people outside our group. We also take in messages about ourselves *inside* our groups. The target group—the group that has less power—can take on the messages of the nontargets, the powerful group, and pass those on to insiders."

Barry says, "I think Sherryl's story is powerful because it shows us the narrow range of acceptable images out there." "Yes, there's a narrow range—whether it's lips, hair, or noses," I say. Sybil adds, "All the stories are about girls learning what's acceptable for their appearance. It's sad that the images are so limited and limiting."

I'm worried about having put my story in the same league as Tracy's and Monica's. "In my classes I like to point out that not all instances of oppression are the same," I say, "The three of us suffered because of gendered images of beauty we couldn't live up to. But being Jewish, I can pass as non-Jewish and I can have most of the privileges of white people. When I walk down the street most people won't think 'there's a Jew' and they won't even notice my nose."

Phil says we have only a few minutes before we must join the other group. When he asks for final comments, Susan, an African American professor, says in an even tone, "I'd like to hear from the brothers. Why do you put this trip on us?"

Silence.

Finally, one of the African American students talks about what women looked like in the magazines he read and the movies he saw while he was growing up. Before we can hear more from the men, time's up.

As I gather my stuff to move back to the larger room, I think about what I didn't tell the group: Knowing I have white privilege doesn't dissipate my anger as I think back to my near surgery 30 years ago. "Ancient history," my mother would say, as she always does when I bring up family done-me-wrongs from the past.

I thought I'd made peace with my nose. Nine years ago when I visited Montreal and was rail-thin from a strict diet to get my cholesterol down, my brother greeted me at the door in sing-song: "As the face gets thinner, the nose gets bigger." He might have added, "Short hair accentuates the nose." I vowed that day to stick with my 1-inch haircut for life.

I kept my nose and rarely dated Jewish men; I figured I'd spent enough years warding off nose jokes from my brother and father. A friend convinced me I'd like a Jewish philosopher she knew. Things went well until he told me, "You look like SpiNOZa."

It's anti-Semitism that has led Jews to hate "Jewish noses," but not every Gentile is anti-Semitic. Ironically, I learned I could be beautiful only outside the Jewish community. I linked up with Gentiles who didn't know what a Jew was. And for whom my nose was just a nose.

In his introduction to *The Art of the Personal Essay* Phillip Lopate (1995, p. xxxviii) tells us: "All good essayists make use at times of storytelling devices: descriptions of character and place, incident, dialogue, conflict." I kept those devices in mind as I wrote the essay-in-progress you just read. Some sociologists recommend that we use these techniques in our ethnographic writing. To make sociology come alive on the page, Richard Mitchell and Kathy Charmaz (1996, pp. 144-145; see also Charmaz & Mitchell, 1996) tell us to "(a) pull the reader into the story, (b) re-create experiential mood within the writing, (c) add elements of surprise, (d) reconstruct the experience through written images, and (e) create closure on the story while recognizing it as part of an ongoing process." Who would argue with their suggestions? If our ethnographies promised a good read, we'd probably read more of them, and so would people outside our borders. But does this mean that sociologically informed personal essays and ethnography are the same? I don't think so. As I wrote "The Nose Job," differences between these two genres became clear to me.

When I read (or write) field studies, I bring particular expectations with me: I expect the author to be as accurate as possible; I expect the work to be about a piece of social life rather than mostly about the author (even if she belongs to the group she studied); and I expect an integrated analysis that covers a lot of the data.

When I read personal essays, I expect the author to care as much about what "works" in a scene as about what she remembers; I expect the author to give me her take on things, even if she speaks of others; and I expect her to show, more than tell, the story.

Every fieldworker knows she can't give a complete picture of the piece of the world she has come to know. We pick and choose, even if our mentors told us to "Write everything down." But in the personal essay, I took more leeway with reporting the facts than I would have taken in a qualitative study. I know it's rather old-fashioned to speak of facts, but there are things that either did or did not happen, and I can easily point them out to you.

For instance, I mentioned in my essay that I was reading *Seventeen* when my mother told me that she and my father had decided that I should have a nose job. Well, I don't remember if I was reading *Seventeen,* or any other magazine, when she came into the room. Does this make my story fictional? No. This is what I think of as a plausible detail. I did read *Seventeen* at that age. I did admire the coeds in it and wanted to look like them—clothes and nose. I fantasized about turning into these swans after my gawky teens. Yet, as it turned out, I wasn't willing to have my nose broken to make me into them.

I worried about putting this detail into the essay: Did this make my story untrue? That worry, I think, reflects my being an old hand at doing qualitative research and a novice at writing personal essays. Playing with the facts in the ways I've done in my personal essay is allowable, even expected, in what's called creative nonfiction (Broughton, 1995; Franklin, 1986; Gutkind, 1995; Lopate, 1995).

Let me compare this detail from my personal essay with a scene from "Renewal," a holistic health center I studied and wrote about (Kleinman, 1996). On the day I stepped into Renewal, a woman, a novice practitioner it turned out, came out of the bathroom towel-drying her hair. This scene captured the informality of Renewal in a vivid way, so I included it in the book.

What if I hadn't witnessed Karen emerging from the bathroom? Suppose another participant had said to me, "Karen once came out of the downstairs bathroom with wet hair, having just showered." I might have included it as something someone else told me. If someone had told me that, I might have thought, "Writing it in the first person as if I'd witnessed it would make the scene live in a way that reporting it from an interview would not." No dilemma there. I simply wouldn't have done it. When I read qualitative studies, I want to know if the sociologist saw or heard what she says she did. If a secondhand account is conjured into a scene, as if the researcher had witnessed it, I'd call it lying. My guess is that most field-workers would call it that too.

When I read personal essays, I have different expectations about accuracy. If, in an essay, the writer uses dialogue from her childhood, I know she's telling me this is how she remembers it, but she could be wrong. Field notes aren't perfect either, and we don't always get to tape-record what people say, but we have better records than when we write only from headnotes (Ottenberg, 1990). In my qualitative work, I try to capture things as I remember them; in a personal essay, I care as much about "what works."

In my experience, fieldwork is done best when we know who we are and what we feel throughout the research. (I've written about this with a colleague elsewhere [Kleinman & Copp, 1993], so I won't belabor the point). Yet I expect the qualitative story to tell me about others, not about the author. Yes, we all write about ourselves in whatever we do, but when I read the study I want to learn about a piece of social organization or members of a social category. I want a tale of *the field*. If the author is a member of the group, I want her to use herself as data. For example, in *Opposing Ambitions,* the study I mentioned earlier, I wrote about similarities between myself and members of Renewal: I showed how recognizing those similarities helped me explain their contradictory goal—establishing a legitimate alternative organization. Readers of the book learn some things about me, but they learn a lot more about members of Renewal. When I speak about myself, I'm a vehicle for understanding *them.*

I hope my personal essay isn't only about me; I'm a stand-in for women in a culture that equates their appearance with moral worth, Jewish women living in a Gentile culture, daughters of mothers who want to help them fit into the culture, and so on. But I also know I've put myself center stage; the piece is my take on things, and I make no claims to having done a long-term, systematic study of Jewish-women-whose-parents-have-tried-to make-them-look-Gentile. "The Nose Job" is a personal essay; it begins and ends with me.

I expect a field study to give me an argument—even if it's complex and I can't put it into one sentence. I expect the author to give me the analysis, using details—yes, vivid ones—to support that analysis. I want to know what the argument is, what the pieces are, and I want the author to tie them together for me. In my book on Renewal, I hope I pulled the reader in and gave compelling details, but I also hope that I told the analysis well enough for readers to say, "Sherryl Kleinman found that. . . . " In contrast, "The Nose Job" has no introduction or conclusion. I invite the reader in as a collaborator, hoping she'll compare her experiences to mine and accept or resist the images I offer. I want the reader to complete the story.

Those of us who want to write lively ethnographies should proceed with caution. We need to ask ourselves, page by page, whether we're futzing with the facts to make a scene work, showing the story because telling would require more analysis than we're willing to do, or talking about ourselves without linking that material to those we studied. The romance of fieldwork may seduce us into writing an adventure story, one that risks omitting the mundane details that make up much of social life. As John Van Maanen (1988, p. 135) wrote, "The need for action, drama, high jinx, colorful characters, and purple prose may drive out the calmer, more subtle and sublime features of the studied scene." If we adopt literary tales as our models, the textual form may drive the content rather than the other way around (Agar, 1990, p. 87).

Those of us who want to write sociologically informed personal essays should read essays by those who know how to write them and learn how to use their techniques. And when we write ethnography, we can use those techniques to enliven our work, provided that accuracy and analysis remain our primary goals.

NOTE

1. Reprinted with permission of Human Sciences Press, Inc. (1997).

REFERENCES

Agar, M. (1990). Text and fieldwork: Exploring the excluded middle. *Journal of Contemporary Ethnography, 19,* 73-88.

Berger, P., & Luckmann, T. (1966). *The social construction of reality.* New York: Doubleday Anchor.

Blumer, H. (1969). *Symbolic interactionism: Perspective and method.* Englewood Cliffs, NJ: Prentice Hall.

Broughton, T. A. (1995). Some notes on the art of lying. In J. Heffron (Ed.), *The best writing on writing* (pp. 3-14). Cincinnati, OH: Story Press.

Charmaz, K., & Mitchell, R. (1996). The myth of silent authorship: Self, substance, and style in ethnographic writing. *Symbolic Interaction, 19,* 285-302.

Franklin, J. (1986). *Writing for story.* New York: Penguin.

Goffman, E. (1959). *The presentation of self in everyday life.* New York: Doubleday Anchor.

Griscom, J. L. (1995). The case of Sharon Kowalski and Karen Thompson: Ableism, heterosexism, and sexism. In P. Rothenberg (Ed.), *Race, class, and gender in the United States* (pp. 253-263). New York: St. Martin's.

Gutkind, L. (1995). From the editor: Permission to lie? *Creative Nonfiction, 5,* 1-3.

Kleinman, S. (1996). *Opposing ambitions: Gender and identity in an alternative organization.* Chicago: University of Chicago Press.

Kleinman, S., & Copp, M. (1993). *Emotions and fieldwork.* Newbury Park, CA: Sage.

Lopate, P. (1995). Introduction. In P. Lopate (Ed.), *The art of the personal essay: An anthology from the classic era to the present* (pp. xxiii-liv). New York: Doubleday.

Mead, G. H. (1934). *Mind, self, and society.* Chicago: University of Chicago Press.

Mills, C. W. (1959). *The sociological imagination.* New York: Oxford University Press.

Mitchell, R., & Charmaz, K. (1996). Telling tales, writing stories: Postmodernist visions and realist images in ethnographic writing. *Journal of Contemporary Ethnography, 25,* 144-166.

Ottenberg, S. (1990). Thirty years of fieldnotes: Changing relationships to the text. In R. Sanjek (Ed.), *Fieldnotes: The makings of anthropology* (pp. 139-160). Ithaca, NY: Cornell University Press.

Simmel, G. (1993). The stranger. In C. Lemert (Ed.), *Social theory: The multicultural and classic readings* (pp. 200-204). Boulder, CO: Westview.

Simmons, C. R. (1995). Silent scream. In P. Rothenberg (Ed.), *Race, class, and gender in the United States* (pp. 263-265). New York: St. Martin's.

Van Maanen, J. (1988). *Tales of the field.* Chicago: University of Chicago Press.

CHAPTER 4

Enough Already![1]
The Pervasiveness of Warnings in Everyday Life

SHULAMIT REINHARZ

I would like to get through a day without being assaulted by warnings. I find this barrage of dire information intrusive, pervasive, and depressing. All day long, cashiers, gas station attendants, waitresses, dry cleaning clerks, bureaucrats, and strangers tell me to "have a nice day." And yet, the signs, newspaper articles, radio reports, and labels tell me to "watch out." They let me know that life is dangerous. It's almost foolhardy to be in the sun, to be in a car, or to take food (poison?) from a supermarket shelf. Do I buy margarine or butter, knowing, as I have learned, that both are bad? Is it better to be overweight or risk the "serious health consequences of dieting and yo-yoing weight" (Klein, 1996, p. 13).

As a qualitative sociologist trained in participant observation, I suffer from the occupational hazard of being extremely attentive to the social and built environment. Ethnographic sensitivity allows sociologists to notice patterns in the mundane experiences of everyday life. Paying attention to different kinds of messages—speech, signs, media material, and laws—and how they reinforce each other is a way of doing unintrusive sociology, that is, sociological research that does not rely on interviewing or questionnaires. Feminist consciousness adds to my sociological awareness by introducing questions of gender differences and power relations in all of my observations (Reinharz, 1992). Everyday life thus becomes a source of rich data for developing hypotheses about social problems, social structure, and social change.

Attention to these messages makes it clear that warning signs have become extraordinarily repetitive. Can't we assume that everyone already knows that "smoking is dangerous to one's health"? Can't we assume that I know "the 10 danger signs," without having to open a cookbook sponsored by the American Cancer Association and find warnings related to many body parts. You can lose your appetite! You can lose pleasure. You can lose a sense of being comfortably in your body. Instead, your body becomes an enemy of your health (Bordo, 1993).

In fact, I don't like walking outdoors past buildings because that is where I am forced to experience "secondary smoke." Do I have to automatically dislike and feel endangered by all these people just because they smoke? Do I have to be reminded of danger constantly? Do I have to know that it is not only "my" smoking that's bad for me, but also inhaling other people's smoke, leaving the choice quite silly as to whether I'm in the "smoking" or "nonsmoking" section of a restaurant. How about seat belts? Do I have to disparage everyone who doesn't wear them? And how can I feel good about someone who is obese when I know they are endangering themselves?

I don't believe I am the only person who feels invaded in this way. I remember casually asking a colleague in his late 50's how he was doing, and he said, "Well, I'm usually obsessed with a cancer-of-the-week, but other than that, I'm fine." Or once I heard a woman say that she is so terrified of getting breast cancer that she has had to train herself to reduce her breast self-examinations. She now has them down to one per day!

Should I eat salt or not; eggs or not? Should I read medical literature continuously to keep up with the latest information about which is the least dangerous way to eat/live? Yes, I did have my annual mammogram, pap smear, eye checkup, dental exam, and on and on. Now the newspapers are recommending an annual lung X ray too. Yes, I know what the dangers are when I pass the age of 50, as I just have. But do I have to check my calendar for what's next to examine?

Lung cancer information is forced not only on those who buy cigarette packs, but on the rest of us, too, by warnings "writ large" on billboards. Colon cancer information is forced on me when I sit down for breakfast cereal because of the national media campaign to promote bran cereal consumption. This campaign consisted of "television commercials, public relations materials, and special cereal packaging" (Flora & Cassady, 1990, p. 146). Does anyone care, however, if people are distressed by the messages? If people would prefer a less gloomy breakfast?

Today, I take my office mail out of my briefcase and there is a one-page issue of the monthly Health Newsletter put out by the Health Services in my university. It starts, "What you can do to prevent cancer." Answer: Eat right. Then it tells me how many portions of what to eat every day. Am I doing the right thing?

Never having been heavy, I don't count calories, so I don't pay much attention to exactly what I am eating. Is this living dangerously? I attend a meeting of a women's volunteer group that I belong to, concerned with a particular political issue, and I learn that they have now taken on issues of special concern to women—domestic violence and breast cancer—neither of which was in their original mission.

I innocently walk into the bathroom of a large synagogue after a bar mitzvah celebration and find myself in a stall facing a poster that tells me what to do about rape, suicide, mental illness, AIDS, and more. I am in another city, using the bathroom of a restaurant, and a plastic sign hangs from the coat hook suggesting that I do monthly breast examinations, with detailed instructions about how to carry them out. I visit another university, and its bathroom walls have flyers offering help in many languages for domestic violence problems I might be having. I go to a manicurist and when she cuts my cuticle, there is a tiny bit of blood. Will I get AIDS?

The muzak is in the elevators, soothing us with musical syrup. What is on the outside? Continuous alarm. Pajamas might catch on fire; your stroller can get entangled in an escalator. And what's the first thing we see when we enter our hotel room? The way to deal with fire in the hotel is to memorize your exit, double-bolt your door, remember not to use the elevator, follow the instructions, put a wet towel on your face, and crawl along the floor, testing first to see if the door is hot.

Is there too much weight in the elevator? How recently was it inspected? And now that I think about it, how recently was my mammogram machine inspected? Can the bridge carry the tonage of the trucks going over it? I know that the images in my side-view mirror are closer than they appear. I've read that message countless times and tried to figure out what it means.

If I stop on the way home from work and buy a pizza, I know that I will see smiling faces of children with leukemia urging me to put quarters in the special slots of a paper display. I have to make sure that I have gotten enough exercise—is running good or bad for me? How about aerobics? Swimming and walking are good, right? At least that's what this month's medical news is reporting. I remember the joke about Ralph Nader, told when people were criticizing him for overdoing warnings. It was said that soon he would declare the human foot unsafe to walk on. Well, I wouldn't be surprised—except now it could come from anyone, not just Ralph Nader.

I pick up a package with photos of children who have been abducted and what their kidnapper might look like or the way the child might look after the passage of the intervening years. In the window of the store is a poster about a walk that will take place to support the fight against AIDS. My neighbor calls to say she is raising funds for the Crohn's and Colitis Society, and another person calls to tell me that she is running the Dana Farber annual gala ball this year. One of my friends in another town told me that every neighbor on her street has a different organ for which they advocate.

I come home from work, empty my mailbox, and find catalogs advertising books concerning women who have lost a breast, who are coping with chemotherapy, or who are suffering in some graphic, disturbing way. An ad for a fitness center has the photograph of a missing child on the reverse side. I reach into the refrigerator and take out a carton of orange juice. There on the side of the package is a sketch of a woman running—the text discusses the race for the cure against breast cancer. I put some leftover food in a plastic bag and am warned that the bag may suffocate a baby. But, if I pay attention to all of these warnings, I actual feel suffocated! What if it turns out that warnings are stressful and bad for one's mental health?

I open the newspaper and it tells me that women who are depressed are more likely to have heart attacks than are women who are not depressed. I do a quick mental checkup: Am I depressed? Am I a likely candidate for a heart attack? I turn on the radio, and I learn that one pharmaceutical company has produced a flu vaccine that is not quite as powerful as expected. Listeners who did have a flu shot this year are advised to ask their doctor if they need to be revaccinated. Then the radio news moves on to inform us that air bags are killing children.

This is the holiday season. I am getting appeals from many different organizations to make donations. Paralyzed veterans, homeless women, starving children, Chernobyl victims, abortion rights, Jewish women's breast cancer coalitions, and more. The more graphic the descriptions, I presume, the greater the effectiveness of the promotional materials. So, the assault on my senses is perhaps particularly strong now.

Maybe I should take a trip. I expect to be lucky and not have fuel tanks blow up midflight. Nor will I investigate what type of plane is used for which flights, as do others who know the accident record of different types of planes and choose their flights accordingly. Of course there will be security checks with their signs about bombs on airplanes, terrorists smuggling in weapons, and other delightful thoughts. "No, I did not take any packages from strangers onto this flight and yes, I did pack my own bags." On every flight, I am told how to evacuate the plane if we land over water or if there is some other emergency. Have a nice flight!

Taped messages I am forced to listen to while "on hold" waiting to make an appointment in my health maintenance organization tell me that if I plan to travel to an exotic place, I should inform my physician at least 6 months in advance so that I can be vaccinated against various horrible diseases (my words) such as malaria. Traveling to Europe? Leave all valuables behind. Do not leave anything in your car, we are not responsible for thefts. Do not leave anything in this coatroom (?), we are not responsible for thefts. If the diseases don't get you, the criminals will.

After I finish my work at the end of the evening, I get ready for bed and turn on the television. Big mistake. Nightly entertainment consists of people being shot, tortured, arrested, punched, or perhaps simply becoming ill from some horrible illness or another. I switch to a comedy station. Rosanne Barr's children are talking about premenstrual syndrome and using it to explain their mother. I switch to the news. The newscaster offers us some additional gruesome medical news and, having had a "nice day," I drift off to sleep. Only to awaken the next day with new information.

Every woman is subject to rape, I learned (and believe). So, always be fearful if you walk alone (an attitude I resist as a feminist). But, when my teenage daughters begin to date, what do I tell them, now that I have learned all about date rape?

In the spring, signs inform me that lawns are dangerous to walk on because of pesticides. I could go for a walk in a field instead, but then, there's Lyme disease. Try as we might to make things attractive and enjoyable and safe, they end up killing us or making us sick. Even when we are doing nothing at all, we may be in danger. Information about danger may be spoiling our interpersonal relations.

THE DANGERS OF PREVENTION

As a modern human being, I am, of course, a believer in education, information, and prevention. So, one would think I would be pleased that there is so much relevant information out there. In fact, between 1972 and 1982, I was a faculty member in the Community Psychology division in the University of Michigan's Department of Psychology, where we focused entirely on prevention (Heller, Price, Reinharz, Riger, & Wandersman, 1984). We sought measurable, documentable strategies for improving mental health and physical health by preventing problems in the first place.

Clearly, we were in favor of letting people know about the dangers of smoking by mandating printed information about carcinogens on the outside of cigarette packages. We were in favor of teaching people good eating and behavioral habits so that they can lead long, healthy lives. We were in favor of warning people before Halloween that their neighbors might be putting razor blades in apples for unsuspecting children. We were in favor of "Neighborhood Watch" programs with signs posted in deceptively harmless neighborhoods. We were in favor of antitamper labels on seemingly helpful over-the-counter medications to prevent poisoners from injecting harmful substances. We were in favor of inserting pamphlets in tampon boxes warning users of their risk of toxic shock syndrome from this seemingly medically irrelevant product. We were in favor of requiring patients to sign "informed consent forms" so that they could know all the possible ill consequences of their decision to undergo procedures.

Never did we think, however, that prevention itself intrudes on the quality of life, foregrounds danger, and makes it harder to enjoy everyday experiences. Never did we consider the implications of having warnings and descriptions of catastrophic illnesses continuously thrust into consciousness.

My sociological question is, can prevention become so overdone that it becomes deleterious in and of itself? We strive to find balance in our lives, between work and play, between work and family, between earning and spending, between being alone and being with others, between pride and self-criticism. Is there a balance we need to achieve about warnings so that the warnings themselves don't become the problem? Do we need to prevent some of this ubiquitous prevention?

SELF-DOUBT

I wonder if I am oversensitive. Do other people notice this deluge of information about the most unpleasant experiences imaginable? Or am I appropriately sensitive, paying the correct amount of attention to the warnings and messages out there? Is anyone becoming confused by contradictory messages? Watch out for danger signs! Have a nice day! Is anyone being desensitized because of an overload of messages? Have prevention of disease and advocacy for research dollars to combat disease gotten so out of hand that they themselves have polluted our environment?

Can our environments create a sense both of safety and of peace; of enjoyment and pleasure; of security and anticipation of good things? Would that be a pollyannaish, put-your-head-in-the-sand, silly world? Is mentioning danger a way of being adult, responsible, serious, and good? Is all this danger-signage a by-product of our litigious society, always telling us that if something bad happens to us, it's our fault, and we have no one to blame but ourselves?

I am concerned that because there is so much information of this sort, people are beginning to think that catastrophes are almost inevitable. When we learn that someone has become ill, do we almost automatically wonder, "what did they do wrong?" Not eat right? Not go to the doctor early enough? Smoke? We assume they were personally irresponsible because we are told that we must be responsible for our health. There is, in the U.S. today, a health movement ideology that "emphasizes the necessity of doing whatever is required to prevent illness" (Goldstein, 1992, p. 34). But ironically,

> what is required is the ability to restrain oneself from participating in behavior that is considered normal, if not desirable. . . . Limiting sweets, staying out of the sun, not smoking or using alcohol, keeping one's weight down, and participating in

vigorous exercise are all behaviors that must be attended to regularly, if not religiously. . . . Furthermore, the restraint and denial required to achieve wellness are not one-time things. The possibility of being seduced into unhealthy behavior is omnipresent. One's vigilance must be lifelong. (p. 34)

How did people live in the past? How do they live elsewhere? Did everyone die young because there were no danger signs out there? What did people do before they learned to check all over their bodies for moles and changes in warts?

THE ROOTS OF WARNINGS

Obviously, some of the information I am receiving is related to selling me something or trying to persuade me to contribute to something or another. But, I think that only very little of it actually has that intention. Surely, when the label tells me that cigarettes have carcinogens, that information does not encourage me to buy cigarettes.

Rather, I think the pervasiveness of warnings might have four roots: (a) the increased emphasis on litigation in our society, (b) the medicalization of everyday life, (c) the emergence of political advocacy around illnesses and social problems, and (d) the respect for science. Moreover, these four factors intersect with and reinforce one another.

To explain the first (litigation): The warnings related to products protect the producers against claims of injured parties. The warnings related to eating, exercise, and early signs of illness reflect the strength of the public health mentality, which is also related to litigation. But more than that, the acceptance of the concept of public health enables society to medicalize everything, from purifying drinking water to dealing with domestic violence.

Political advocacy around illness is related to the respect for science in the sense that people try to raise dollars or convince the government to spend dollars on research to eradicate the problem at hand.

Given that these four factors can be expected to remain strong in society—litigation, medicalization, political advocacy, and respect for science—it is unlikely that I will find my environment less filled with warnings in the near future. I suppose I have to live with it, although I can still try to avoid it by buying a different brand of orange juice, taping over the message on my side-view mirror, and "throwing the bat into the woodpile" (Shulman, 1995).

RESISTANCE

Ironically, the only way I can imagine seeing the "danger-amplified environment" change is if a new social movement or advocacy group emerges to protect the environment from the overemphasis on frightening people with warnings. Sociologist Michael Goldstein (1992) suggests that such a movement might already exist, but on a very small scale. He calls it "an explicit antihealth promotion movement." This "movement" is rooted in a critique of the scientific claims of the health-promotion advocates. The antihealth promoters question the strength of the data that purportedly demonstrate a relationship between so-called risk behaviors and various health outcomes. A major object of skepticism is the Multiple Risk Factor Intervention Trial (MRFIT),

> The most sophisticated attempt to test the validity of the risk factors supposedly associated with coronary heart disease. MRFIT was financed by the National Heart, Lung, and Blood Institute at a cost of $115 million. The 250 investigators of 22 medical centers screened 351,662 men to get a sample of 12,886 who were at high risk for heart disease. The data from this test clearly show that modifying dietary, exercise, and other health behaviors has minimal benefits. . . . A similar overenthusiasm has characterized reports describing the relationship between diet and cancer. . . . More recently, controversy has erupted regarding the possible value of reducing cholesterol in the diet. (p. 153)

One critique of ubiquitous warnings that may be gaining some ground is the observation that warnings ignore differences in populations. Thus, warning people that if they drive when drunk, they are likely to end up, tragically, confined to a wheelchair, is offensive to people who use wheelchairs for other reasons. Similarly (Daykin & Naidoo, 1995),

> Telling women not to smoke without examining the pressures that lead to the desire for a cigarette is problematic, in the same way as is counseling women to adopt safer sexual practices without recognizing the unequal power relationships that construct sexuality. . . . [In addition] nutrition campaigns are often targeted at women in the role of food provider for families. However, this may trigger conflicts for women, who end up balancing health education messages with other priorities, such as providing food which is familiar and liked by other family members, and buying food within tightly constrained budgets. . . . All too often, the impact of health education campaigns has been to make women feel guilty because they cannot respond positively to the health education message. . . . The overall outcome may then be increased stress and ill health for women. (p. 63)

It is difficult to imagine a public space that does not tell me that I have to fear theft, suffocating others, becoming ill, or being blown to pieces, unless I join with others to demand such a space. I can only imagine succeeding if I can demonstrate scientifically that the current environment is making me sick and I can find someone to sue!

I don't want to give the impression that I don't care about people's troubles, public safety, and personal health—I do. I don't want to aggravate anyone's health by wearing perfume, or having a cat nearby, or doing anything that's troublesome. God forbid that I should smoke or breathe in anyone else's smoke. I'm not advocating recklessness or selfishness. Instead, I'm suggesting relaxation and pleasure.

These observations bring to mind a wonderful memoir—Alix Kates Shulman's *Drinking the Rain* (1995)—concerning a woman at midlife who has decided to spend time alone on an island. On her first night, she blows out the candle, snuggles under two sleeping bags, and

> the night fears fly in . . . leaking gas that may explode, embers flying up the chimney to ignite the roof, accidents, illness, lightning, hurricanes, tidal waves, the deadly nightshade surrounding the cabin, beasts, rodents, and worst of all that roaming hacker who, one moonlit night, seeing a humble shack set high on a lonely point, will walk across the beach, climb the stairs, throw open the door, and hack us all to death. I've been expecting him for years. . . . For comfort I lift the baseball bat Jerry keeps as a weapon beside the bed. . . . It's a long time before I fall asleep. (pp. 10-11)

A few pages later, after numerous nightmares,

> I pick up the bat from beside my bed, carry it out on the back deck, and with both hands heave it onto the woodpile. . . . If one day I should hear the hacker's slow, booted step on the stair, perhaps I'll suggest a cup of tea and try to get the story of his life. (p. 23)

NOTE

1. Reprinted with permission of Human Sciences Press, Inc. (1997).

REFERENCES

Bordo, S. (1993). *Unbearable weight: Feminism, Western culture, and the body.* Berkeley: University of California Press.

Daykin, N., & Naidoo, J. (1995). Feminist critiques of health promotion. In R. Bunton, S. Nettleton, & R. Burrows (Eds.), *The sociology of health promotion.* New York: Routledge.

Flora, J., & Cassady, D. (1990). Roles of media in community-based health promotion. In N. Bracht (Ed.), *Health promotion at the community level.* Newbury Park, CA: Sage.

Goldstein, M. (1992). *The health movement: Promoting fitness in America.* New York: Twayne.

Heller, K., Price, R., Reinharz, S., Riger, S., & Wandersman, A. (1984). *Psychology and community change: Challenges of the future.* Chicago: Dorsey.

Klein, R. (1996). *Eat fat.* New York: Pantheon.

Reinharz, S. (1992). *Feminist methods in social research.* New York: Oxford University Press.

Shulman, A. K. (1995). *Drinking the rain.* New York: Penguin.

CHAPTER 5

Earn as You Learn[1]
Connections Between Doing
Qualitative Work and Living Daily Life

CLINTON R. SANDERS

As a professed symbolic interactionist and qualitative researcher, I often find it difficult to maintain a relatively impermeable boundary between my occupational life and my everyday experience. This feature of being a qualitative sociologist occasionally presents something of a problem while, at other times, offering distinct advantages. The problematic consequences are most apparent when conflict, fear, and other painful (but instructive) elements of the field have direct impact on my life outside the confines of the research setting in which I am currently working. The primary advantage of this merger of life and work has been brought home to me most clearly when I have been drawn into issues and worlds that excite me because they encompass my immediate personal interests and strike me as of significance in building a disciplined understanding of the basic processes of social life (Prus, 1996, pp. 141-172). In short, doing fieldwork has allowed me to call "work" involvement in the kinds of activities and interests with which I would likely be engaged were it not the way I pursued my profession.

The liabilities involved in having troublesome features of the field experience slip over into my "private" life first struck me a number of years ago when I was involved in a study of narcotics enforcement. Since this was the late 1960s and most of the people with whom I associated rarely said "no" to drugs, I was not entirely unaccustomed to using illegal substances for recreational purposes.

My days were spent hanging out with narcs and drug lawyers or observing cases in the major narcotics court in Chicago. While I was rather circumspect about revealing certain aspects of my private life to those I was studying, the daily encounters with key workers in the official drug enforcement world did ratchet up my paranoia level a few notches. I had my shoulder-length hair cropped down to "respectable" length, donned a coat and tie when appearing in court, wore an American flag lapel pin, and scraped the peace sign decal off of the back window of my battered VW. Still, the pleasure the narcs obviously got from hunting people very much like myself made me uneasy despite my disguise. When leaving court, I routinely checked in my rearview mirror and took a variety of circuitous routes back to my apartment. Having gained considerable practical knowledge about issues of search and seizure in the course of my research, I was careful to secrete my small personal stash in a spot that had "public access" so that it would not be in my possession were the worst to happen.

My fears during this time were not solely related to my own casual involvement with the drug scene. I was also collecting considerable information about routine features of drug enforcement that were overtly illegal. It was fairly common, for example, to see lawyers slip money to police. These payments, I soon discovered, were in return for services rendered. Defendants I interviewed frequently told me that after they were taken into custody the arresting officer had given them a lawyer's business card and advised them to contact that particular attorney because "he got everyone off." Of course, the arresting officer eventually received a "finder's fee" from the lawyer for having provided this service. An even more questionable transaction involved the lawyer giving money to a police officer in exchange for his "forgetting" important details of an arrest during the preliminary hearing and thereby opening the way for the defense attorney to claim that the arrest was not properly conducted. This was "data" that could have caused me considerable personal trouble had it become known that I was systematically collecting it. While I was careful in my field notes not to specifically identify the parties in such illegal activities, I did go to some pains to protect my notes and myself. After typing the notes, I would destroy the original "jottings" made in the field, and I convinced a reliable acquaintance to store my data in a safe place.

As Herbert Blumer (1969, pp. 21-24) stressed, research is, most importantly, a way of interacting with the world. Given the annoying, conflictual, and dangerous way in which the world often works, it is hardly surprising that research immersion in it may draw trouble and anxiety into the investigator's extra-work life. Pain can be instructive, however. My encounter with narcotics enforcement provided invaluable lessons about key experiences of the recreational drug users in whom I was interested and reinforced my understanding of the importance of the "protective techniques" that were a central element of subcultural lore (Schaps & Sanders, 1970).

This exchange between work and life can flow the other way as well. One of the real advantages of being a qualitative researcher is that I have found that the "trivial" interests I pursue day-to-day can be turned to productive ends. After moving from Chicago to Philadelphia to take on my first full-time academic job, I found myself to be somewhat less than satisfied with my current situation. Philadelphia seemed to hold all the disadvantages of living in a city but few of the advantages, my partner's time was primarily devoted to finishing her dissertation, and I had yet to find any of my colleagues to be people with whom I had much in common. I responded to my plight by watching large amounts of television. One sunny Saturday afternoon I was mindlessly viewing my second or third horror film of the day and feeling guilty about wasting my life. Suddenly, the realization struck me that I wouldn't have to feel guilty about watching crummy horror films if I simply began to take notes on them. I could turn a waste of time into work and, once again, begin to feel that I was moving in a potentially productive direction. Although this project eventually resulted in only minimal professional returns (Sanders, 1991), it did help to get me out of my doldrums and brought home to me the fact that doing qualitative sociology offers the unique opportunity of turning casual interests to account. The trade-off, however, was that I did find that focusing in a more analytic way on these causal interests tended to decrease some of their immediate sensual pleasures. Work is rarely as pleasurable as leisure.

Few of the projects in which I have been involved brought home the intimate overlap between work and everyday life, and the way in which the former may have an impact on the latter, as did my research on tattooing (Sanders, 1989). I entered the world of tattooing with little knowledge of the practice or the range of products available. My initial entry came rather serendipitously as I happened to visit the Tattoo Art Museum in San Francisco. At this point, I had a fairly stereotypical view of tattooing as a craft activity that entailed the exercise of only minimal skill and was primarily practiced on those on the margins of the conventional world. At the museum, I was struck by the historical and cross-cultural roots of tattooing and the striking beauty of some of the images. This appreciation prompted me to impulsively purchase my first tattoo and to seriously consider launching a study of the subculture. It seemed, at this point, a natural focus for my preexisting academic interests in both deviance and the sociology of the arts.

I spent the next few years in a variety of tattoo studios. Like most of us who do fieldwork, I found it impossible to devote so much of my time to interacting within a social world and not participate directly in the activities that were central to that world. Initially, I added a couple of "pieces" to my tattoo collection that I chose from the "flash" sheets displayed on the walls of the local "street" shop in which I was collecting data. Like many people who become more and more involved with the "tattoo community," I eventually felt dissatisfied with these rather mundane images. Although they had been inscribed by the tattooists with adequate technical skill, I came to realize that these tattoos were not representative of the unique and visually exciting work being done by the most renowned artists in the field—practitioners with whom I was now coming in contact as my research access moved up the status ladder of the tattoo world. I also realized that those who were most centrally involved in collecting tattoos disdained the "badge motif" form in which various tattoos are placed here and there on the recipient's body and little or no thought is given to continuity of design, style, and image. I consequently had my initial tattoos covered with "custom" tattoos done by one of the most skilled artists on the east coast and worked with him to design a "full sleeve" that covered my right arm from the wrist to the shoulder. Being much taken with the classical Japanese style of tattooing, I chose oriental images—dragons, chrysanthemums, and a floating lotus—and had them bound together with "fill work" done in the traditional Japanese style of whirlwind, water, and fire.

In a literal way, my research involvement in the world of tattooing had transformed me. I was now a "serious collector" with work that afforded me some measure of status in the tattoo community. In the "real world" outside the boundaries of this community, however, I had become an object of curiosity, at best, and derision, at worst. What had in the past been routine and casually considered decisions, such as how to dress and what to reveal about myself, now became far more important. My personal identity had been sullied by my intimate involvement with the world in which I did research. Though I was able to hide the stigmata I had voluntarily acquired, when learning about my research interests, casual acquaintances in the university would frequently reveal that they found tattooing "disgusting" and would sometimes speculate about the pathologies that induced people to "mutilate" their bodies in that way. Like other tattoo collectors, I found responses such as this to be rather annoying, but they did prompt me to appreciate, and eventually explore at length, the symbolic importance of the tattoo as a "mark of disaffiliation." The often negative experiences I had outside of the tattoo world due to the fact that I was tattooed also provided immediate information about, and prompted me to explore, the key issues of how tattooees deal with being stigmatized and the sources of "tattoo regret."

My current research most directly illustrates the way in which everyday commitments and interests give rise in a more positive way to professional involvements. Since childhood, I have lived with and had considerable regard for companion dogs. Much of my youth was spent in the company of a beagle named Beepo, and when he passed on during my first year in college my mother acquired a Saint Bernard of whom I became quite fond and who was largely responsible for my attraction to large representatives of the "working" breeds. My second full-time academic job allowed me to move to rural Connecticut and I finally found myself in a position to include dogs in my household. At about the same time my research on tattooing was coming to an end, I adopted two Newfoundland puppies. Having finally read enough about dog ownership to realize that adequate bonding with these new members of my "pack" required me to spend most of my time in their company, I started taking them to school with me, walked with them in the woods near my house, and regularly took them along when doing routine errands. Watching the dogs interact with each other and the various members of the human public with whom we came in contact and attending to my own developing relationship with them sparked the beginnings of a sociological interest. Initial exploration of the literature related to human-animal interaction revealed that, while there was a considerable body of practical writing directed at the intricacies of dog rearing, there were no serious sociological discussions of this extremely common and emotionally involving type of relationship. In fact, what passing references I could find to dogs, and people's relationships with nonhuman animals generally, discounted these social exchanges. In essence, dogs and other animals were conventionally presented as mindless and human relationships with them as being on the par with one's relationships with cars, computers, and other nonsentient objects (Cohen, 1989; Mead, 1962, pp. 180-184, 1964, pp. 154-187). This lack of attention to, or overt discounting of, what I was experiencing as such a central social exchange struck me as indicating a considerable gap in the sociological understanding of everyday life. Since I was in an excellent position to explore canine-human relationships, I embarked on a research project that started first with my collecting autoethnographic (Hayano, 1979) field notes about my daily experiences with the dogs and with other people when I accompanied them in public. From here, I moved to broaden my observations by taking field notes in the puppy kindergarten in which my growing companions were enrolled. My search for yet another setting in which people routinely interacted with dogs soon led me to doing fieldwork in the large, mixed practice veterinary clinic in which my own animals received medical care. Eventually, my interest in canine-human relationships prompted me to gain research access to a guide dog training program in which I could systematically observe more focused and specialized examples of this type of association.

Research, as Michael Flaherty (1996) has recently observed, is a felicitous combination of curiosity and opportunity. Being in the daily company of my dogs offered a unique opportunity to experience and observe human-animal interaction, and my sociological curiosity prompted me to take advantage of this opportunity. My encounters with other people when in the company of my dogs, for example, led me to focus on how dog owners attempt to make amends when their animals misbehave and disrupt the more or less smooth flow of public interaction. Employing what I came to refer to as "excusing tactics" (Sanders, 1990) was clearly of significance since I routinely found myself utilizing them. Similarly, the intense sorrow I felt when forced to euthanize one of my dogs, combined with the trauma I observed when people in the veterinary hospital had their own pets "put to sleep," led me to explore the clinical encounters surrounding the purposive parting of the human-animal bond (Sanders, 1995a). Once again, personal experience moved me beyond the objective issue of whether or not I had the "right" answer. I was forced to confront the more important subjective and intersubjective issues: Did I have the personal experience to adequately grasp the emotional elements of the situation, and was I able to use this experience to persuade others that my evidence and analysis were sound (Flaherty, 1996, p. 295)?

Some time ago (Sanders, 1977), with reference to Cooley's concept of the looking-glass self, I wrote about how doing fieldwork places the investigator into a social hall of mirrors in which he or she is exposed to a variety of self-reflections. Dealing with the contingencies of the field setting and the relationships within it offer lessons that go beyond and may be, in the final accounting, of more importance than what one discovers about the more abstract workings of the social world. The process of doing qualitative work opens us up to situations that test our personal abilities and, in so doing, instructs us about who we are.

No matter whether it has impact on our everyday lives or its focus is shaped by our extracurricular interests, doing fieldwork is, to say the least, a mixed experience. As when most of life's experiences are retrospectively constructed, we tend to forget much of the pain and accentuate much of the pleasure. I am typically struck anew by the anxiety that is central to the experience when entering a new field setting. Clearly, field research is not something everyone should do or could do adequately. The pain of being a stranger, the ambiguity of not working with the "net" offered by a preconstructed hypothesis, the confusion of not knowing what is important or how it all fits together are experiences that our nonqualitative colleagues have rarely, if ever. It is understandable that many sociologists favor working with purchased data sets. While many of these same sociologists sometimes offer the opinion that qualitative work requires few specialized skills since it most basically involves employing the everyday practices of social interaction, I am certain that most of them would be abysmal failures were they to be required to move into the world outside the safe confines of their offices and classrooms and collect real data from real people. While I think John Lofland (1976, pp. 318-319) romanticizes and somewhat overstates the case when he writes that successful field-workers have "the gift," I do think that intimate qualitative work does require special skills, sensitivity, and a certain taste for adventure.

Furthermore, the interactionist perspective that informs our work—unlike more overtly abstracted, scientistic, macro-oriented, and mathematically modeled perspectives—touches directly on everyday experience. This means that the analytic lens through which qualitative researchers view the social world is also a useful tool we can use to orient ourselves as we move through the encounters, situations, and relationships that constitute our daily lives. It seems unlikely to me that neofunctionalists, mathematical modelers, or even rational choice theorists find this sort of practical, day-to-day utility in the theoretical orientations that shape their own sociological outlooks. This is also one of the complaints I have about the currently popular postmodernist turn in certain interactionist circles. A perspective that doubts the existence of an obdurate reality and holds such a radically flexible view of "truth value" offers little in the way of guiding one along the path of everyday life (Prus, 1996, pp. 203-243; Sanders, 1995b).

I have found that, ideally, qualitative sociology demystifies social life both as I live it as an individual in society and in my role as a professional opportunist exploring the social world. Unlike most of my colleagues in the academy, I live in and am part of my subject matter. While at times inconvenient and anxiety producing and at others the source of intimate pleasure and self-knowledge, doing qualitative work affords me the unique opportunity to appreciate and learn from the connections between my life and profession.

NOTE

1. Reprinted with permission of Human Sciences Press, Inc. (1997).

REFERENCES

Blumer, H. (1969). *Symbolic interactionism.* Englewood Cliffs, NJ: Prentice Hall.

Cohen, J. (1989). About steaks liking to be eaten: The conflicting views of symbolic interactionists and Talcott Parsons concerning the nature of relations between persons and non-human objects. *Symbolic Interaction, 12,* 191-214.

Flaherty, M. (1996). Some methodological principles from research in practice: Validity, truth, and method in the study of lived time. *Qualitative Inquiry, 2*(3), 285-299.

Hayano, D. (1979). Auto-ethnography: Paradigms, problems, and prospects. *Human Organization, 38,* 99-104.

Lofland, J. (1976). *Doing social life.* New York: John Wiley.

Mead, G. H. (1962). *Mind, self, and society* (C. Morris, Ed.). Chicago: University of Chicago Press.

Mead, G. H. (1964). *On social psychology: Selected papers* (A. Strauss, Ed.). Chicago: University of Chicago Press.

Prus, R. (1996). *Symbolic interaction and ethnographic research.* Albany: State University of New York Press.

Sanders, C. (1977). Entering the hall of mirrors: Social research and self-knowledge. In A. Shostak (Ed.), *Our sociological eye* (pp. 395-403). Port Washington, NY: Alfred.

Sanders, C. (1989). *Customizing the body: The art and culture of tattooing.* Philadelphia: Temple University Press.

Sanders, C. (1990). Excusing tactics: Social responses to the public misbehavior of companion animals. *Anthrozoos, 4*(2), 82-90.

Sanders, C. (1991). The armadillos in Dracula's foyer: Conventions and innovation in horror cinema. In P. Loukides & L. Fuller (Eds.), *Beyond the stars: Studies in American popular film, Vol. 2* (pp. 143-159). Bowling Green, OH: Popular Press.

Sanders, C. (1995a). Killing with kindness: Veterinary euthanasia and the social construction of personhood. *Sociological Forum, 10*(2), 195-214.

Sanders, C. (1995b). Stranger than fiction: Insights and pitfall in post-modern ethnography. In N. Denzin (Ed.), *Studies in symbolic interaction, 17* (pp. 89-104). Greenwich, CT: JAI.

Schaps, E., & Sanders, C. (1970). Purposes, patterns and protection in a campus drug using community. *Journal of Health and Social Behavior, 11,* 135-145.

CHAPTER 6

Real-Life Sexual Harassment

CHRISTINE L. WILLIAMS

> *Science is meaningless because it gives no answer to our question, the only question important for us: What shall we do and how shall we live?*
> —Tolstoy (as quoted in Weber, 1946, p. 143)

If you study sociology long enough, you are bound to encounter this passage. This quote from Tolstoy is cited by Max Weber in an essay lamenting the fact that science does not provide guidance on moral issues. Science can clarify the facts, organize our thinking, and identify courses of action and their likely consequences, but it can never solve the basic moral dilemma of the human condition: "What shall we do and how shall we live?" (Tolstoy as quoted in Weber, 1946, p. 143).

Most of us, however, get into the business of sociology because we want to change society for the better. I certainly did: I was drawn to the study of gender discrimination and sexual harassment because I wanted to help solve these persistent social problems. Twenty years later, confronted with a case of real-life sexual harassment, Weber's lament seems particularly poignant and true. Understanding an issue sociologically does not tell you what you should do about it.

I am not just referring to the failure of our legal system and work organizations to devise appropriate remedies for gender inequality, although these are

AUTHOR'S NOTE: I am grateful for the comments and suggestions made by my colleagues.

important barriers to social change. Rather, the focus of this chapter is the ongoing dilemmas faced by what Weber (1946) calls the moral striving of the autonomous individual. In dealing with an actual case of sexual harassment, I was confronted by moral dilemmas every step of the way. Although my extensive research on this topic helped me to understand what was going on, it never helped me to decide what I should do next.

One such moral dilemma is the very decision about whether or not to even discuss the case. The pressure to keep quiet is palpable. Interestingly, however, this pressure emanates almost entirely from the top down: Senior colleagues and administrative officials urge restraint and silence, whereas junior colleagues, graduate students, and undergraduates want to talk more, not less, about the issues. This is often how power works in bureaucratic organizations: Those who manage and run bureaucracies rely on secrets and silence to advance their objectives. Loyal subordinates are not supposed to leak information to outsiders or to openly criticize the organization. This silence typically is rewarded by those in power because it upholds the authority system (Williams, Sjoberg, & Sjoberg, 1983).

This silence imperative confronts individuals on both sides of sexual harassment complaints—both accusers and accused. Jane Gallop, a professor who was charged with sexual harassment and wrote a book about it (Gallop, 1997), claims that her accusers demanded that she never discuss the charges against her or use her experiences as an object of intellectual inquiry. Ultimately, she was exonerated from the charges of sexual harassment, and the university decided not to forbid her from discussing the case. Her case, however, illustrates the potential power of organizations to silence their members.

I have decided to write about my experiences with a case of sexual harassment, but I will not use the names of the individuals involved, and I will discuss only information available in the public record. The case was a simple and familiar one: A colleague was charged with sexual harassment by a student. An internal university investigation found the professor guilty. He was required to attend a sexual harassment sensitivity training course, he was prohibited from advising female students for 1 year, and a letter of reprimand was to be placed in his personnel file.

Although I did not have any direct involvement in the case, I was drawn into it by the attorney representing the student. He called a press conference to publicize what the student believed was an overly lenient punishment, and he invited all the tenured women in the department to attend and issue a statement about the failure of the university to adequately protect students from sexual harassment.

This is not a decision I took lightly. What should I do? There were only 3 women among a tenured faculty of 28. (The ratio among the assistant professors was skewed in the opposite direction—5 of the 7 were women—but no one considered asking untenured faculty to participate.) The fact that there are so few tenured women professors is a legacy of gender discrimination and bias in academia; if we all participated in the press conference, that in itself would make a powerful statement. Excluding our male colleagues from participating was troubling, however, because it might send the message that sexual harassment is an issue that only concerns women, when in fact many of the men in the department were equally concerned about eradicating this behavior.

This dilemma—to speak "as women" or to include men in our statement—is an example of the postmodern paradox of identity politics. Gamson (1995) describes this paradox as a conflict between the essentialist and the deconstructionist strategies to promote social change. The essentialist tactic is the demand for rights and dignity for all who share a common collective identity (in this case, women) on the grounds that members of the identity group face similar, if not identical, experiences of exclusion and discrimination. The deconstructionist tactic, however, argues that socially produced categories (in this case, man/woman) are themselves oppressive, and that the key to social liberation is to challenge these categories by forming alliances across identity-based groups. Those who endorse the deconstructionist tactic maintain that the essentialist tactic creates a false unity out of heterogeneous experiences and treats as outcasts those members of the group who do not share similar experiences or who have different interpretations of their situation.

I was ultimately persuaded that the essentialist tactic was appropriate in this case because of an argument made by a philosopher, Susan Bordo. Bordo maintains that, despite the heterogeneity of women's experiences, there are moments when "women may find themselves discovering that despite their differences they have many things in common by virtue of living in sexist culture" (Bordo, 1993, p. 237). She argues that this is precisely what happened during the Senate confirmation hearings of Clarence Thomas, a nominee to the Supreme Court in 1990 who was accused of sexual harassment by an Oklahoma law professor, Anita Hill. As a result of these hearings, women from all different walks of life came together to question our cultural tolerance of sexual harassment, bolstered by the essentialist conviction that men "just don't get it." Although Thomas eventually was confirmed, and now sits on the Supreme Court, the essentialist tactic was successful in spotlighting national attention on the problem of sexual harassment. I decided that the real-life sexual harassment in my department was another such "moment" requiring an "essentialist" response.

At the press conference, the three tenured women in the department issued a statement condemning the sexual harassment and the weak institutional response to it. As a concession to the limits of identity politics, however, we mentioned that several of our male colleagues are also aware of the problem in our department.

All the local media, including the television stations and newspapers, covered the event. Reporters addressed most of their questions to the student. They wanted to know the following: What did the professor do? Did the student indicate her discomfort to the professor? Did she tell him to stop? Did she suffer any ill effects?

This focus on the objective facts of the case does not surprise me. Most reputable reporters are trained to consider only the "who, what, when, where, and how" of any news event. Objective facts—not the subjective interpretation of those facts—determine whether a news story is "true." In sociology, this approach to learning about social reality is known as "positivism." Ironically, at the time of the press conference, I was revising a paper for publication that criticized positivism in sociological research on sexual harassment.

In my paper (Williams, 1997), I point out that the legal definition of sexual harassment is vague and difficult to operationalize using positivistic methodologies. The Equal Employment Opportunity Commission, the government agency that monitors workplace compliance with the law, defines sexual harassment as follows (Tamminen, 1994):

> Unwelcome sexual advances, requests for sexual favors, and other verbal or physical conduct of a sexual nature constitute sexual harassment when: submission to such conduct is made either explicitly or implicitly a term or condition of an individual's employment; submission to or rejection of such conduct . . . is used as a basis for employment decisions . . . ; or such conduct has the purpose or effect of unreasonably interfering with an individual's work performance or creating an intimidating, hostile, or offensive working environment. (p. 44)

The law does not state what specific behaviors constitute sexual harassment—only that the acts must be "unwelcome," "unreasonable," or that they cause "an intimidating, hostile, or offensive working environment." These are subjective interpretations that can vary a great deal depending on the social context and on the individual's definition of the situation. Nevertheless, several researchers who are trained in positivistic methods have devised their own lists of what they consider proscribed behaviors to measure the frequency of sexual harassment in a statistically reliable manner. These lists of behaviors vary considerably among researchers: For example, one 1994 study asked respondents to report on how frequently they were stared at and referred to as a "girl, hunk, doll, babe, or honey," whereas another study included only acts of intercourse or genital stimulation in its definition of sexual harassment (Arvey & Cavanaugh, 1995).

Even if researchers could agree on a single list, focusing on objective behaviors is problematic because what researchers define as sexual harassment, an individual respondent might view as a harmless flirtation, a temporary lapse of good manners, or even a legitimate requirement of the job (as in the case of so-called "Hooters Girls," the scantily clad waitresses at the Hooter's Restaurant chain; Giuffre & Williams, 1994). Most positivistic research also ignores the ambiguity and ambivalence that individuals experience in interpreting sexual interactions (Fiske & Glick, 1995; Hollway & Jefferson, 1996). Sexual behaviors rarely have unambiguous meanings, and they typically evoke ambivalent responses. This is particularly true for college students, who are often confused and flattered by a professor's sexual attention (Paludi & Barickman, 1991).

There is no place for subjectivity, ambiguity, or ambivalence at the press conference, however—only victim and harasser, unlawful conduct, and the resulting harm. The careful attention to context that I urge researchers to embrace in their studies flies out the window in the presence of lawyers and news reporters (Chamberlain, 1997; Glasser, 1992).

I also noticed that at the press conference, most of the questions focused on the sexual nature of the professor's behaviors. This focus also does not surprise me: When most people hear the term sexual harassment, they think first and foremost about the "sexual" part. Many have the misunderstanding that sexual harassment is illegal because it is sexually degrading or intimidating. In fact, sexual harassment is against the law only insofar as it is a form of gender discrimination. According to Mane Hajdin (1997),

> From the viewpoint of the law, even the fact that a victim of sexual harassment has suffered harm is not in itself a ground for providing a legal remedy, no matter how grave the harm might be. . . . The ultimate question that a court dealing with [a sexual harassment] case needs to resolve is not "Has the plaintiff suffered harm?" but, rather, "Has the plaintiff, in suffering the harm, been discriminated against on the basis of sex?" The evidence of the harm suffered by the victim is legally relevant only insofar as it can contribute to answering the latter question. (p. 123)

In a court of law, the victim of sexual harassment must show that she (or he) was treated differently than were men (or women) who were similarly situated, and that she (or he) consequently suffered a loss of opportunities or benefits. The question, Was the student discriminated against on the basis of gender?, was not asked at the press conference.[1]

The press conference resulted in several newspaper and television reports, which were followed several days later by reports telling the professor's side of the story. According to these reports, the professor, who denied the charges, claimed that the student was driven to falsely accuse him of sexual harassment because she feared receiving a low grade. Moreover, he was quoted in one article as saying that the student had filed her complaint because she had come under the influence of women professors who are "teaching women to hate men."

The essentialist strategy had backfired. The women who issued the statement at the press conference were portrayed as "a small number of antagonists" with a personal vendetta against the professor because of his unconventional theories. Perhaps I should have insisted that our male colleagues be invited to participate in the press conference after all. The backlash worsened: The confidential report on the internal investigation was leaked to a conservative student newspaper on campus. The fledgling paper (this was the first issue of Volume 1) featured the case on the front page, with the gripping headline, "Salem Revisited: Academic Witch Hunt in UT Sociology Department." In an astonishing inversion of the historical analogy, the article vilified the female faculty who supported the student. One of the reporters wrote, "Just because a few intellectually intimidated feminists with low self-esteem and inferiority complexes were challenged by the unorthodox ideas expressed by [the professor], there has been a dangerous infringement upon academic freedom." Speaking out against sexual harassment had been transformed into speaking out against academic freedom.

This is certainly not the message we intended, but it is a predictable response to feminist activism. In fact, much scholarly literature on gender discrimination and sexual harassment had prepared me for this response. Adrienne Rich (1983) argued that any effort to resist men's control of women's sexuality is usually dismissed as "the meaningless rant of a manhater" (p. 195). At the Senate confirmation hearings of Clarence Thomas, his accuser Anita Hill was portrayed variously as "the dupe of left-wing political activists or white feminists, a vengeful lesbian feminist herself, or just an evil person bent on unwarranted revenge to ruin her former employer" (McKay, 1992, p. 286). Knowing about the typical consequences of feminist activism made the backlash easier to endure, but nonetheless it was demoralizing.

Because of the publicity generated by the press conference, a second student decided to contact the attorney and file a separate charge of sexual harassment against the professor. Ten months pass before the university announced that it found the professor innocent of the second charge. A second press conference was held; more newspaper stories were printed.

These newspaper stories reveal that in the period of time since the decision in the first sexual harassment case, the university dropped its demand that the professor attend a sexual harassment sensitivity training course; the letter of reprimand, however, and the prohibition on individual instruction of women students are still implemented. Officials from the university decided to drop the course requirement because they believed that the professor had received sufficient exposure to sexual harassment training since his attorney was an expert in this area of law. The professor still maintained his innocence of all charges, however, and said to reporters that he feels harassed.

Universities often react with leniency toward professors found to be in violation of their sexual harassment policies. In fact, it is not unheard of for professors accused of sexual harassment to be placed on paid leave by their universities. Hawkesworth (1997, p. 115) describes a particularly egregious case in which a faculty member who was found guilty of sexual harassment was given a semester of paid leave and transferred to an administrative job at a higher salary.

Why would a university respond so leniently to a violation of its sexual harassment policies? Hawkesworth (1997) provides two possible interpretations: First, she points out that universities, as complex bureaucratic organizations, have a great deal of inertia built into them. Change is always slow, and it tends to proceed chaotically because competing constituencies within the organization have opposing interests. University officials are often forced to balance the interests of their students and their employees (in this case, the faculty) while at the same time protecting the institution from the threat of lawsuits. Leniency toward those found guilty of sexual harassment can be seen as the sort of compromise bureaucratic decision that satisfies no one to shield the institution from the greatest liability.

A second interpretation of lenient punishment draws on the theory of gendered organizations. Hawkesworth (1997) defines a gendered organization as one in which "organizational hierarchies, processes, practices, images, ideologies, and distributions of power contain deeply embedded assumptions about gender that limit women's opportunities and enhance men's occupational success" (p. 112). The university is a paradigm case of a gendered organization in that men dominate the top academic and administrative positions, control the decision-making process, produce the scholarship accorded the highest prestige, and receive the highest pay. Hawkesworth argues that sexual harassment of women is one of the means that men have used to maintain their power. Feminist efforts to rid the university of sexual harassment typically provoke institutional resistance because they are seen as a threat to this male dominance. Of course, administrators rarely explain their leniency to offenders in this way. Typically, they claim to be acting in the best interest of the university or out of a commitment to academic freedom and due process. They neglect to acknowledge that such gender-neutral principles often serve to maintain gendered power relations in practice.

Certainly, it is the case at my university that men are in control of the most powerful positions on the faculty and in the administration. It is also true, however, that several people who have been involved in the case have struggled to respond ethically and professionally to the crisis. Almost everyone agrees that students should not be subjected to sexual harassment, but not everyone agrees on the tactics that should be used to fight against it. Unfortunately, there are no easy solutions to the problem. No law, policy, or set of procedures can guarantee that all cases will be handled fairly and justly. The most anyone can do is to strive to do what they think is morally best, keeping in mind the complex power dynamics in organizations that privilege some groups while silencing others.

What advice can I now give to students who are confronted with real-life sexual harassment? Because students are relatively powerless in universities, I believe they must seek allies—other professors, administrators, and lawyers— to assist them through the often labyrinthine process of filing a sexual harass- ment complaint. Without such assistance, students' complaints probably will be ignored. It is also important to rely on friends and family for emotional support and empowerment through the process. Students must talk openly about their concerns with others, including those who have had similar experiences. Un- fortunately, I now believe that the "easiest" solution to real-life sexual harass- ment in the university is to drop the course or transfer to another one. Because entrenched organizational interests are threatened when students charge their professors with sexual harassment, pursuing a formal complaint can result in even greater misery for the student than that caused by the original harassment.

Of course, this is not what I think students should do. I think students who are sexually harassed by their professors should file complaints. As Weber (1946) points out, however, I have now overstepped the boundaries of sociology. Sociology can clarify the workings of society and identify the likely conse- quences of our actions, but it can never tell us what we should do. Taking a stand and suffering for a cause is (and should be!) a personal, moral choice.

NOTE

1. In March, 1998, the U.S. Supreme Court issued a ruling that will permit a heterosexual man to bring charges of sexual harassment against his heterosexual male coworkers. However, this same ruling affirmed the principle that all litigated sexual harassment cases must involve gender discrimination. According to Justice Scalia, the male plaintiff must still prove that his coworkers' behavior toward him was "not merely tinged with offensive sexual connotation, but actually constituted discrimination be- cause of sex" ("High Court Ruling," 1998, p. A17).

REFERENCES

Arvey, R. D., & Cavanaugh, M. A. (1995). Using surveys to assess the prevalence of sexual harassment: Some methodological problems. *Journal of Social Issues, 51,* 39-52.

Bordo, S. (1993). *Unbearable weight: Feminism, Western culture, and the body.* Berkeley: University of California Press.

Chamberlain, E. M. (1997). Courtroom to classroom: There is more to sexual harassment. *NWSA Journal, 9*(2), 135-154.

Fiske, S. T., & Glick, P. (1996). Ambivalence and stereotypes cause sexual harassment: A theory with implications for organizational change. *Journal of Social Issues, 51,* 97-115.

Gallop, J. (1997). *Feminist accused of sexual harassment.* Durham, NC: Duke University Press.

Gamson, J. (1995). Must identity movements self-destruct? A queer dilemma. *Social Problems, 42,* 390-407.

Giuffre, P. A., & Williams, C. L. (1994). Boundary lines: Labeling sexual harassment in restaurants. *Gender & Society, 8*(3), 378-401.

Glasser, T. L. (1992). Objectivity and news bias. In E. D. Cohen (Ed.), *Philosophical issues in journalism* (pp. 176-185). New York: Oxford University Press.

High court ruling says harassment includes same sex. (1998, March 5). *New York Times,* p. A17.

Hajdin, M. (1997). Why the fight against sexual harassment is misguided. In L. LeMoncheck & M. Hajdin (Eds.), *Sexual harassment: A debate* (pp. 97-163). Lanham, MD: Rowman & Littlefield.

Hawkesworth, M. (1997). Challenging the received wisdom and the status quo: Creating and implementing sexual harassment policy. *NWSA Journal, 9*(2), 94-117.

Hollway, W., & Jefferson, T. (1996). PC or not PC: Sexual harassment and the question of ambivalence. *Human Relations, 49*(3), 373-393.

McKay, N. Y. (1992). Remembering Anita Hill and Clarence Thomas: What really happened when one black woman spoke out. In T. Morrison (Ed.), *Race-ing justice, en-gendering power* (pp. 269-289). New York: Pantheon.

Paludi, M., & Barickman, R. B. (1991). *Academic and workplace sexual harassment.* Albany: State University of New York Press.

Rich, A. (1983). Compulsory heterosexuality and lesbian existence. In A. Snitow, C. Stansell, & S. Thompson (Eds.), *The powers of desire* (pp. 177-205). New York: Monthly Review Press.

Tamminen, J. M. (1994). *Sexual harassment in the workplace: Managing corporate policy.* New York: John Wiley.

Weber, M. (1946). Science as a vocation. In H. H. Gerth & C. Wright Mills (Eds.), *From Max Weber: Essays in sociology* (pp. 129-156). New York: Oxford University Press.

Williams, C. L. (1997). Sexual harassment in organizations: A critique of research and policy. *Sexuality & Culture, 1,* 19-43.

Williams, N., Sjoberg, G., & Sjoberg, A. F. (1983). The bureaucratic personality: A second look. In W. Boyd Littrell, G. Sjoberg, & L. A. Zurcher (Eds.), *Bureaucracy as a social problem* (pp. 173-189). Greenwich, CT: JAI.

PART II

Family Spaces

CHAPTER 7

A Conversation About Parenting

NAOMI GERSTEL
ROBERT ZUSSMAN[1]

We met at Columbia University in 1970, when both of us began graduate school in sociology. Three or 4 years later—we kept track less carefully in those days—we began living together. Although neither of us would quite say that sociology brought us together, it has certainly been a part of the field on which a 25-year relationship has played itself out. We have both worried about writing dissertations, finding jobs, publishing, and getting tenure. Although for many years we taught in different departments (Naomi at the University of Massachusetts-Amherst and Robert at the Columbia Medical School, then at Stony Brook), we have shared colleagues and friends. More important, we have been colleagues and friends. Although we have never before written together, we routinely read each other's work. We also have a long-standing habit of talking to each other. Sociology is not just part of what we talk about. It is how we talk.

Seven and a half years ago, we adopted our daughter, Kate Zussman Gerstel, when she was 1 day old. We talk less to each other now than we did before there was a kid in our house, but we do still talk. What follows are some of the things we say to each other when we're trying to make sense out of parenthood.

> **NG:** I thought I was prepared to be a parent. I teach a course on "The Family." I read lots of books about parenting. I thought endlessly about the decision to adopt.

61

Before Kate, I was perfectly happy to tell my friends who were parents how to do it right, typically around gender issues. I also spent a fair amount of time talking to my woman friends without children about how we could come to terms with the absence of children in our lives. But I was still unprepared.

RZ: I wasn't prepared for parenthood either. Some of our lack of preparation, I think, is because we adopted. Pregnancy is a kind of liminal state, part way between childlessness and parenthood. Whatever else, it gives you a chance to get used to other people reacting to you as parents. Because we hadn't told a lot of people about our plans before we picked Kate up, we made the transition all at once with even less preparation than most people have.

NG: I was unprepared for the way parenting completely transformed all domains of my life—work, language, my relationship with you, relatives, and friends—and that would happen with adoption or birthing. Most obviously, I spend a lot less time on paid work. I just don't have the time and can't focus late at night, early in the morning, or over weekends the way I used to. Sometimes I miss it (although equally often I find myself awed by mothers in jobs with less autonomy and flexibility). I also see friends less often—especially those who don't have kids and seem bored or overwhelmed by children. Sometimes, I miss adult-centered friendships. And my involvement in the community is more likely to be with parents and teachers at Kate's elementary school than at some women's studies event. I think worrying about field trips and public support of children may be a kind of identity or life-course politics. Each is divisive, and at meetings these days I find myself insisting on ways to encourage taxpayers to recognize that children are a collective responsibility.

RZ: Katie does take up a huge amount of time. But I'm not sure it's just the time that's the critical issue. Parenthood is a real master status. It determines what movies we see: Disney has replaced John Sayles as the must see. [And I suppose it's to the point that John Sayles is probably nearly a decade out of date as a must see.] It determines when we eat, how regularly we eat, what we eat. It makes an opera singer or a foreman at Amtrak or a radio station sales manager—the parents of Katie's friends—as familiar as sociologists without kids.

I do think, though, that parenting does involve a very concrete set of activities. Before we adopted Katie, I had some very abstract ideas about what it involved to be a parent. I did not particularly like kids and I was hostile to the *idea* of parenthood. We also both worried about how we would respond to having an adopted child instead of a birth child. I remember a friend of ours, who had also adopted, telling us that the everyday activities of taking care of a kid would wipe out any difference between adopting and birthing. He was right. Dealing with food and diapers at first, then with day care and school and after-school activities and getting Katie up and out in the morning and all the rest is a practice that requires a whole lot of activity but not a whole lot of reflection. I don't have a relationship with kids in general; I have a relationship with Katie. I don't think much about the *idea* of parenthood except for those very occasional moments when something pulls me up short and makes me reflect on what I've been doing. My relationship with Katie isn't the least bit abstract.

NG: I know what you mean. But I'm still struck by how people who have kids—relatives, friends, most of them progressives—seem to have such strong theories about parenting. Not only do they have theories about whether a mother should "work" (almost all think she should), but they have ideas they happily share about eating, sleeping, crying, pooping, hugging: "If she doesn't go to sleep, just leave her there. You'll see, it's good for her;" "Just be consistent." Well, I don't and can't just leave her in her bed and I am sure (or at least am pretty sure) this won't distort her. I include the "pretty" before the "sure" because I'm not immune to the theories even if I try to be analytical about them. And what's so good about consistency? In any event, it isn't very clear, even if you accept the idea that you should be consistent, which specific behaviors this applies to and which it does not.

For some time now, I have wanted to explore these questions: Who holds which theories and where did these theories originate? Sure, some come from those parenting experts who write for middle-class parents, sometimes far from relatives, who seem to need a recipe for parenting. Especially when Kate was younger, I worried and read and read and read, primarily looking to see that this development or that was okay, at least not outside somebody's acceptable range. But those sources explain neither what appears to be the wide range of theories (let her get up; make sure she stays in bed) nor the intensity with which most people I know seem to hold to them. That intensity is likely a result of their use as a justification for some concept—of self, of childhood, of "the family?"

Are these theories socially structured—by gender, by class or social circumstances, for example, in the way Kristin Luker [1984] found views on abortion were or Sharon Hays [1996] suggests views of maternal employment are? Do women and men hold different theories? Are women more likely to be prone to arguments for consistency, for example, or just more likely to be affected by parenting theories—any parenting theories. In some ways, middle-class mothers today resemble those nineteenth-century middle-class mothers who found themselves anxious all the time after their exposure to elite reformers and experts who kept telling them how to manage all the details of child rearing from toilet training to the expression of emotions. Just a couple of decades ago, LaRossa and LaRossa [1981] found that mothers-to-be were much more likely than fathers-to-be to read books about parenting. But they found that it was such reading that made women seem more prepared, more at ease with parenting than men.

RZ: I don't think I have theories about parenting so much as I have a whole lot of vague dispositions that I project onto parenting. For example, I don't much like rules and, as a result, I'm inclined to exercise as little parental authority as I can manage. I have, to be sure, experienced more than my share of shocks in this regard. I say "no" a whole lot more often than I ever thought I would. I'm more insistent about bedtimes and noise levels than I would have expected. What's striking, though, is how thoroughly I'm prepared to resist the evidence of my own behavior. No matter how convinced I am in the particular that my judgment is not only better than a seven-and-a-half year old's [a plausible conviction] or that my taste should be privileged over Katie's [a less plausible conviction], I seem entirely unwilling to move from the particular to the general. I seem perfectly happy both to make up rules and to claim that there's no need for them.

There's more, too. When I'm being sensible, I know that my convictions are just convictions—a loose mix of habit and taste. In more rhetorical modes, I'm inclined to make all sorts of claims: that my objection to a strict time limit on television is based on a Kantian respect for the autonomy of the subject or that television actually contributes to developmental goals. Leaving aside the kind of conceptual overkill that's an occupational hazard of academic types, I have no idea if I'm right. I've never read anything about developmental processes in kids or about the effects of television [and probably wouldn't believe anything if I read it]. What I have done is adopt a language of developmental goals, a child-centered language, as a means to justify the way I live.

NG: I don't know that a "language of developmental goals" is really a child-centered language, unless you mean by that a language that is centered on, rather than for, children. I think these get confused a lot. The behavior I insist on for Kate, like not watching "too much" TV [or our compromise on that], probably isn't meant to help her in some unspecified developmental goal in childhood so much as to help in her adulthood [even though I have little idea about what adulthood in the twenty-first century will look like]. I don't know how much I should think about these years as Kate's formative years, in terms of what this or that will do to and for her later, and to what extent I should think instead about her experience today, in childhood. I keep in mind Barrie Thorne's [1993] argument that children are not just the next generation's adults nor simply preparing for later life. The here and now is important, too.

RZ: I think the distinction between what's good for Katie now and what's good for her in the long run makes good sense. There's no reason they should be the same. But my point is that I don't really think about what's good for Katie—or any kid—in either sense. I just have a set of general dispositions that I'm prepared to impute all sorts of causal significance to without any evidence.

NG: Whatever we're doing to Kate, I do know that our life is different. We eat at home more often so as to feed and create a certain kind of family [DeVault, 1991]. But it's not exactly domestic bliss. Disagreements about what kind of meal to have are disguised disagreements about what kind of family to have. And you aren't exactly delighted when I refer to you as "dad." There may be a new bond between us, but it's one that speaks to the centrality of Kate rather than the centrality of our relationship. We speak in a new language—from pooping to play dates. There are new words, maybe new identity, but we've lost some of our old language; we talk less and we spend less time taking care of each other. We disagree about matters that we never cared about before: Does it matter if Kate watches TV or when she does her homework? Should we sit and share a family meal at the table and do we all have to eat vegetables? How often does Kate really need a bath?

I've read [and taught about] studies that show there's a decline, and sometimes even a crisis, in couples' relationships with the entry of a child. Ways we used to compliment each other now turn into routes to conflict because another person is implicated. A dyad becomes a triad and that's a far less stable form. That data and theory are both oddly distant and clarifying. I do think a little, "Oh good, other people feel this too" or "It's not me, it's structure."

RZ: I think you're right. Parenthood may have been good for us individually but it's been hard on us as a couple. I also think you're right that the key thing is that we've gone from a dyad to a triad. In fact, having a kid isn't just any example of going from a dyad to a triad. It's the classic example. A bunch of things happen. First, we now have a mediated relationship. I don't just have a relationship with you [or with Katie]. I have a relationship with you mediated through Katie and with Katie mediated through you. That makes things a lot more complicated. Second, there's a possibility for alliances. Maybe, once upon a time, parents always presented a united front to kids [although I doubt it]. We certainly don't. Sometimes we do present a united front. But sometimes you and Katie gang up on me and sometimes Katie and I gang up on you. I think it's a new experience for both of us to get outvoted at home.

NG: I'm also not sure you're right about adoption. I think you're right that the everyday experience of parenting is no different with an adopted child than with a birth child. But there are some differences, mostly having to do with the ways other people respond to adoptive parents. While it is parenthood rather than adoption that has transformed my life, adoption has forced me to rethink parenthood. Adoption is stigmatized. There is an article with a title something like this that I cannot bring myself to read, but I routinely encounter numerous indicators of stigma. When some crime against a parent is committed by an adopted child, journalists report that fact as though it helped explain the crime. The language attached to adoption certifies the normative state of parenthood. One of Kate's friends recently asked me who her "real parents" were. I answered, a little defensively, that we are. I explained that we changed her diapers, hug her, and read her a story every night. Still, the very term "real" parents says a lot about the power of biology and the weakness of social ties. I think this even shows up in the new "openness" around adoption. Now that I am a participant, I am not afraid of losing Kate's love; I even want to help her find the woman who gave birth to her [if she's interested]. I look forward to talking to Kate about her response. But the insistence on openness underscores a central social fact: Biology becomes the undeniable, real, natural, even essential. Biology is so central to the way most people think about childhood. So, when strangers see me with Kate, they often say "she looks like you." [I wish I looked like her, but I don't.] Or strangers see her with my elderly father, who only vaguely resembles what I know him to be, and say to him "she has your hair and eyes." Do they mean this as a compliment? Should I say, "Funny thing how we manage to impose biology even where none exists." At the same time, I feel a little ashamed about participating in a social system—expressed in both official policy and private adoptions—that invokes oppressive hierarchies, often justified in biological terms. Not only affluent, but also heterosexual, coupled, and white: We stood first in line for adoptions. We took advantage of prerogatives that, in other contexts, I criticize.

RZ: Maybe. The biology is tricky. Some of it is real and, if we're being honest, we have to acknowledge that, even if biology doesn't determine anything, it does make a difference to what Katie looks like, some of what she's good at and some of what she's not so good at. I think we also have to acknowledge that the claims that parenthood is social are as ideological as the claims about biological parenthood. Claims that parenthood is fundamentally biological or fundamentally social aren't exactly true or false. Parenthood isn't a thing. It's an idea, and claims about biological and social elements in parenthood are ways of staking out different ideas about parenthood.

That said, you're certainly right to distinguish the experience of parenting from the response to parenting. But even the attributions to biology are complicated. You're prepared to talk about helping Katie find her birth mother but leave out her birth father [as does almost everybody else]. Katie knows a bunch of kids who were adopted from China, including a girl who lives down the street. One day, after we had run into Angelica, Katie asked if she were "different" from us, the way Angelica is different from her parents. I don't think Katie just wanted to know if she is racially different from us. I think she was groping for a set of categories she could use to make sense of differences. In effect, she was asking whether race was a critical category, even though she doesn't yet have the conceptual apparatus to ask that question. Biology is real but it's not fixed. There's an obvious temptation to treat the difference between adoptive and biological parenting as a dichotomy. But, as with a lot of other things, the categories are probably a lot more complex. For people who do not know us well, the absence of any obvious racial differences between Katie and us means that most people probably don't realize Katie is adopted. For those who know us better, it probably makes a difference that we adopted her when she was a newborn. Grandparents and uncles and aunts who parent create ambiguities, too. We might push parenthood into a dichotomy, but the dichotomy is forced. Adoption becomes one more arena in which different ideas about the biological and the social, and the differences between them, get played out.

NG: I worry that all this makes parenthood seem oppressive. Somehow it doesn't quite take account of Kate. I remember a piece by Adrienne Rich [1976], "Motherhood and Ambivalence," about how mothers feel both strong love and hate. When I assigned it to my undergraduates, most despised it. I thought that was because they could not admit that their parents, especially mothers, hated and loved them. But, gosh, now I sometimes experience intense impatience, anxiety, or even anger toward Kate. But not hate. It is, though, much easier to write about the stresses and a little embarrassing to write about the almost overwhelming love. And that is really what I was unprepared for. Is it the public and private intimacy—holding hands and hugging? Is it her dependence—"Mom I need you; I cut my knee"—or my power—"Go wash your hands, now?" Is it the social reproduction—my mother is so proud? Or is it just Kate—proudly announcing as she walks in the door: "I'm home."

RZ: I feel a lot of ambivalence about parenting. Some of it's interesting and fun: I like reading kid books and meeting Katie's friends; I don't much like cooking macaroni and cheese or waiting for her to fall asleep. I also get annoyed with Katie: She takes much too long to get ready in the morning [and in the afternoon and in the evening]. But I'm amazed by how little ambivalence I feel about Katie herself. I'm sometimes sad for her; I'm rarely sad because of her. I'm amazed by how much I love her. But I don't think that love was instant. I think it comes from identification in a very literal sense. When you change a kid's diaper, if you do a lousy job, you pay the consequences in tears, noise, and more work. If a kid is unhappy, you suffer for it. And if a kid is happy, it's much more fun.

One of the things I've learned from being a father—and from Katie—is to think about people in terms of relationships instead of attributes. I'm not generally objective about Katie. Sure, some of what I love about Katie has to do with qualities she has that show up everyplace. But much more of it has to do specifically with my relationship to her. It matters to me that she's my kid. I don't want to hug kids in general; I want to hug her. I'm not proud of kids in general for learning to swim; I'm proud of her. I wind up understanding particularism, in its good sense, in a way I never have before. I suspect this has come as much less of a surprise to you than to me. Women, if we're to believe what we read, have a morality and emotional tone that's much more rooted in relationships than in more or less objective evaluations. Gilligan and Chodorow claim this makes women better parents. My guess is that it goes the other way, too, and that the acts of parenting make both men and women more sensitive to the particularities of individuals and relationships.

Still, I think that the love itself has to go unanalyzed. Maybe psychologists have something to say about parent-child love, but I don't and I'm not sure that I want to have anything to say. Love is consequential for social structure. Romantic love is dangerous because it constantly threatens to cross boundaries. Parental love is probably necessary to make sure that kids get taken care of. I also suppose there are social structures that encourage love. We know that romantic love is probably a pretty recent phenomenon as is the sentimentalization of children. But I'm not sure that, as a sociologist, I have anything to say about the phenomenon of love itself.

NG: I like that—your reversal of Chodorow and Gilligan—parenting is formative for parents. Parenting has given me a new reading of Chodorow, too. When I first read *The Reproduction of Motherhood* [1978], I remember asking my women's group, some of whom had children long before I did, whether they reacted, as Chodorow theorized, with a double identification—with both mother and child—or identified instead with only one or the other. Some said both; a few said neither. But, without child, I read it as a daughter, only partially individuated [and sometimes struggling with it] from my own mother. Now I again find that the issue is my individuation, not Kate's. She is only 7, but she's already trying to establish her independence, even if it's just by dialing her own phone call, getting her own juice, losing another baby tooth, spending the night at a friend's, or wearing clothes of her own choosing. I'm both pleased and upset by each step she takes away. I'll get back [I think] my time, my focus, my friends, and our relationship, but I will surely miss her childhood, even some of the demands. And I wonder how it would be different with a son.

RZ: Well, that's just one more thing we'll never know.

NOTE

1. The order of authors does not indicate greater contribution, power, or love. It is simply alphabetical.

REFERENCES

Chodorow, N. (1978). *The reproduction of motherhood.* Berkeley: University of California Press.

DeVault, M. (1991). *Feeding the family.* Chicago: University of Chicago Press.

Hays, S. (1996). *The contradictions of motherhood.* New Haven, CT: Yale University Press.

LaRossa, R., & LaRossa, M. (1981). *Transition to parenthood: How infants change families.* Beverly Hill, CA: Sage.

Luker, K. (1984). *Abortion and the politics of motherhood.* Berkeley: University of California Press.

Rich, A. (1976). *Of woman born: Motherhood as experience and institution.* New York: Norton.

Thorne, B. (1993). *Gender play: Girls and boys in school.* New Brunswick, NJ: Rutgers University Press.

CHAPTER 8

On the (Re)Production of Social Class

Living In, With, and Beyond Elementary School

SUSAN E. BELL

> *The concrete plan for realizing the curriculum for a given grade level and its realization as a practical matter over the school year are carried out with a given group of children, in a given budgetary context, and under given school policies. A given school interprets the curriculum in particular local contexts, with a particular group of teachers, with particular numbers of children, with ratios of children to teacher that are set by the board and that determine what personnel resources are available to the principal, and with a particular collection of children coming from particular families. Decisions about allocating teachers to children, allocating children to classes, creating different kinds of mixtures, setting curriculum objectives for the year for a given class, coordinating the products of the classes of one year, and so forth are made at school level.*
> —Smith (1987, p. 202)

As I reflect on the origins and development of my interest in sociology, and my decision in graduate school to take my first course in sociology, what stands out are several moments in time during which I questioned everyday practices in

AUTHOR'S NOTE: I acknowledge the work of Philip Hart, my partner in parenting, decision making, and constructing this account. I also thank Lynne Miller and Sara Dickey for propping us up and for reflecting back on the process of placement through their readings of and responses to this chapter.

the educational institutions I attended because these practices seemed unfair to me. The practices reproduced inequality of race, of gender, and of nation. At these moments, I found myself understanding the logic that lay behind the practices, how these practices reproduced inequality, and simultaneously the connection between these local, everyday practices and the historical and institutional settings in which they were embedded. In a rudimentary way, I had begun to use what I now call "the sociological imagination." Therefore, it is not surprising that for my contribution to this collection of essays about sociology and everyday life I would choose to write about how I self-consciously used my skills as a sociologist to question and make choices about everyday practices that I believe are unfair in the elementary school attended by my children.

The sociological imagination, according to C. Wright Mills (1959), "enables its possessor to understand the larger historical scene in terms of its meaning for the inner life and the external career of a variety of individuals" (p. 5). It provides a framework for understanding everyday practices (such as going to work, attending school, making a meal, and fighting with your lover) beyond the immediate settings in which they occur and seeing how, by the fact of living them, people contribute "however minutely, to the shaping of this society and to the course of its history, even as [we] are made by society and by its historical push and shove" (p. 6). The sociological imagination can be used to think through the social and political consequences of particular choices. Therefore, instead of simply being an individual "self" at the center, trying to get what he or she wants, it can be a way for its possessor to understand the sources and to envision the consequences of many people similarly situated making similar choices. It can become a framework for remaking, and making, social structure.

In the example that follows, I show how in the course of trying to understand what we perceived to be an unfair elementary school classroom assignment for our son, my husband and I began to see the everyday practices of inequality in a public elementary school and thus also to see how our inclination to resist the placement, our ability to know that resistance was possible, and our individual decisions in response to our son's placement fit with and grew out of those practices. By enabling us to think through the social roots and consequences of our individual actions, it also opened up a range of choices to us. This understanding helped us to place ourselves differently in relation to the principal and teachers in the school. Most simply, the sociological imagination helped to point us in a direction that we felt "right" about, both for our son in the here and now and for our vision of what public school should be like.

In addition to helping us to see the situation clearly, the sociological imagination also helped us to see how limited our power is and was. Without trying to change how teachers, the principal, and other parents acted, our own individual decisions about our own child, even though they were very important to us, could not have far-reaching or long-lasting effects even at the level of the school. This tension haunts much of sociology: the extent to which individual actions simultaneously do and do not shape social life, and thus the extent to which individual actions can be simultaneously the basis for both stability and social change.

Finally, in retrospect, the sociological imagination enables me to reflect on the extent to which my husband and I assumed that what we meant by a "better" or "worse" teacher was shared by all parents; that when parents made requests, it was only for teachers we identified as better, and that placement of students in the classroom of the worse teacher reflected a lack of agency among (working-class) parents. Our assumptions about meaning and agency guided our interpretation of the situation; these assumptions were formed from our ongoing discussions with other parents, most of whom were also professionals. At the time we made a decision about how to respond to our son's placement, we were less aware of these assumptions than we are today. This lack of awareness was a reflection of our limited interactions with working-class parents, itself one of the consequences of the assignment of individual children into individual classrooms and the accompanying parent-parent relationships that developed in and in relationship to those classrooms.

The way my husband and I constructed our understanding of what was "wrong" and how to "fix it" in this case is consistent with what I believe about the construction of knowledge in general—that it is always embodied and positioned, always partial, and always situated. Our task as sociologists is to continually attempt to explore the particular ways in which our knowledge is situated.[1] In my own case, I would have had an understanding of what working-class parents believed to be better teaching and how they negotiated placement of their children—and how these meanings and actions might have varied or been similar to mine—if I had talked with them during the course of my everyday life in the school and in this particular situation. The everyday practices of the school fostered separations between us.

Most of the approximately 400 children who attend school with my children are white. Of the 19 full-time teachers, all are white, and all but 2 are female. Class differences are more pronounced than racial or ethnic differences. One third of the children come from professional families and another third from military families. Approximately 24% of the children qualify for a free or reduced-cost lunch program, and the school itself qualifies for Title 1 funds. Title 1 provides the school with funding for compensatory educational programs designed especially for children from low-income households. The school has a policy of inclusiveness; although its resource room provides services to about 25 children with special needs, these children spend most of their time in mainstream (regular) classrooms.[2]

For the public elementary schools in the New England town in which we live, the last week of August is when parents and children are sent postcards informing them of the names of their teachers and their classroom assignments. In theory, children are placed in mixed groups, with each classroom in each grade containing children who performed at all levels the previous year. In practice, such heterogeneity does not occur. Parents can take it upon themselves to request a specific teacher or to request that their child is placed with (or without) a specific other child. Parents and children talk with one another and, as with all social systems, a culture develops. Parents "know" which are the better teachers and which are the worse ones and which are the students with problems and which are those without problems. As with other systems, this one works in class-based patterns. Children with professional parents are more likely to end up with the better teachers and with a "higher-achieving" mix of students; children with working-class or poor parents are more likely to end up with the worse teachers and with the "lower-achieving" mix of students. The cause of this is that professional parents are more likely to know how to work the system and are more able to put the time and energy into working it. Their jobs are likely to be more flexible, and their lives in general are more likely to provide them with the resources they need to advocate for their children.

Decisions about allocating children to classes and creating a mixture of children within each classroom could be based more on a balance in the mix of children if the principal and teachers chose to make it this way or if parents demanded it. Some schools in nearby school systems are more democratic than the one my children attend. In the school described here, however, when parents make their wishes known, their wishes are often (but not always) granted; the consequence of this practice is class-based tracking.

This particular year, we had believed other parents, our child's teacher, and the principal when they told us that all three of the teachers were "just fine" and that any placement would be "okay." We did not make a teacher request. The consequence of our silence was that our child was placed in a classroom with more lower-achieving students, with more children from families with fewer resources. None of his good friends was placed in the same classroom, even though students from all of the previous year's classrooms had been assigned to it. All of his friends were placed in one of the other two classes.

What had happened? We constructed an account between the first and second day of school, once placements were not only public but also visible. (On the first day of school, children had lined up on the playground in grades and classrooms after the first bell had rung, with each line headed by the teacher in charge of that particular class.) We spoke with other parents, the teacher our son had had the year before, the teacher to whose classroom he had been assigned, and the principal.

School policy is to identify and assign a balance of high-, middle-, and low-performing students to each classroom from each of the classrooms from the previous grade. Although there is no written record of this policy, the practice is publicly affirmed by the principal and teachers when parents ask about how placement decisions are made. In addition, there is another school practice related to classroom assignment that is neither formally nor publicly stated. This informal and implicit practice is to listen and respond to parent requests. Parents learn about this informal practice from other parents. If asked about it, the principal and teachers explain that parents can make requests, which are taken into account when assignments are made, but these requests cannot necessarily be honored. In our experience, parent requests that are made firmly are frequently met. Teacher A (the person to whom our son had been assigned) had developed a reputation among parents we knew for being a nice but unimaginative and unchallenging teacher. By contrast, Teacher B had previously taught in the now defunct program for gifted and talented students and thus parents we knew believed that she would be a stimulating and challenging teacher for high-achieving children, and Teacher C was known for being well organized and challenging. Because so many parents of high-achieving boys requested either Teacher B or Teacher C, our high-achieving son was the only boy in this category who "could" be assigned to Teacher A's classroom.

Having constructed this account, we then had to decide what to do about it. One of our options was to cry "foul," refuse to accede to the placement, and have our son moved into another classroom. Choosing this option—removing our son from the classroom he was in, thus removing the one high-achieving boy from it—would put us into the same position as that of other professional parents and would help to perpetuate or even exacerbate the tracking already in place. By removing our child from the teacher's classroom, we would also be placed in the position of publicly questioning a teacher's competence to teach. (Note that in this school, it is a common practice to resist classroom assignments and thus implicitly to contest the competence of teachers and the principal. This is typically done privately, in a letter to the principal before assignments are made or during the week between the time parents are notified of the assignments and the start of the school year.)

Choosing the other option would have more complicated effects. First, it would be a way for us to resist tracking. Second, it would be a way for us to signal to our son that there are many lessons to learn in school beyond narrowly defined academic ones, including valuing different kinds of achievement and differences among people (presumably values that even the school itself gives lip service to through its policy of mixed placement).

What did we do? Our first strategy was to try to move our son. We met with the principal and firmly requested a different teacher. We told the principal our interpretation of what had happened, describing in detail how we thought our son had ended up in this particular classroom and how the uneven mix of children in all three of the classrooms had occurred. My husband used the metaphor we had seized upon to describe the situation: Our son had been "cut from the herd." We were articulate and angry. We acted just like the professional parents who had made similar requests earlier in the process. The principal said "yes." We emerged from his office victorious.

We had not yet spoken with our son about any of this. We had simply responded to him sympathetically when he had become upset after finding out who was his teacher and who were his classmates. Our son was unaware of the flurry of activity surrounding the assignment, both in our household and in the school. He did not know that we had met with the principal or that word of our meeting with the principal had circulated among the teachers. Nor did he know that he had been reassigned to another classroom, and that I would be attending a parents' meeting with Teacher C that evening—not an individual conference with his new teacher but a previously organized meeting with all the parents of children in her classroom to introduce them to her teaching strategies and to one another.

I attended that meeting, but felt like an outsider. The teacher was neither friendly nor welcoming to me, signaling in multiple ways her knowledge of the reasons for my presence, her disagreement with my choices, and her support for Teacher A. The other parents, who guessed that my son was a late addition to the classroom, either ignored me or made supportive gestures. One of them, a teacher herself in another school system, said she believed every one of us must "look out for our own child."

My husband and I did not sleep that night. At first, neither of us could articulate why we felt so uneasy. Over the course of the night, it became clear to us that by moving our son, we would be undermining the values that had led me into becoming an educator, my husband into designing public school buildings, and the two us of to send our children to public school and to become actively involved as volunteers in their classrooms. By moving our son, we would support a system that responded to pushy, middle-class parents who defined good teaching in narrow ways; and contribute to the class-based assignment and education of children. By moving our son, we would be taking our labor at home and labor in the classroom with him, enriching his receiving classroom and depleting his sending classroom of productive resources.

The organization of schooling, individual schools, and classrooms within those schools all presuppose the availability of parents' (mothers') labor in the home. The school depends on the labor of parents: "The homework process loops through the home, is somehow managed there, and returns to school to be inserted into the classroom work process as part of what becomes the child's documented performance" (Smith, 1987, p. 203). Parent labor (especially mothers' unpaid labor)

> has been a major support to the level of functioning of schools . . . particularly of middle-class schools. If this work is not done by women it has to be done by someone

[a teacher or other person paid to do it]. If it is not done or is not done at the same level, then labor is withdrawn from the school and the school cannot function at the same level. Teachers cannot teach the way they have learned to value themselves and each other for. (pp. 203-204)

Differences in the amount and type of work done by parents at home create differences not only between schools, as Dorothy Smith and Alison Griffith found (Smith, 1987), but also between classrooms. By withdrawing our son and moving him, we would also be withdrawing our labor from that classroom so that the classroom could not function at the same level as it would be able to if we left him there. We would be adding our labor to another classroom.

Because both of us have flexible work schedules, we had begun volunteering at the school when our son had entered kindergarten, and as volunteers one or both of us had worked with individual children in our son's classrooms since then. Usually, teachers asked us to work with pairs or small groups of children. Our work varied and consisted of listening to or reading to them out loud, editing brief essays with them by hand or on computers, and giving them practice tests in geography and social studies. Sometimes, we accompanied the class on field trips. Through our engagement in the everyday life of our son's classmates, and through our work with him at home doing homework, we learned how parents are expected to supplement teachers' work in the class-rooms. These expectations take no account of the realities of parents' lives (that many of us work full-time, have more than one child in the school system, or are single parents) or of differences in parents' ability to meet these expectations (Smith, 1987, p. 205). We also saw firsthand the uneven ways in which parents were able to manage homework because we were often asked to work with children identified by the teachers as those whose parents could not provide as much support for them at home.

After much agony, my husband and I decided that we would leave our son in the classroom to which he had been assigned. We did not tell him that we had contested the placement, that he had consequently been reassigned, and that we had reconsidered and subsequently withdrawn our request. As a result of the flurry of activity surrounding our son's first few days of school, Teacher A singled him out for special attention. We had pushed just as hard as had other professional parents; the only difference between us and them was the outcome of our pushiness. Teacher A was simultaneously shamed and angry that we had contested her expertise, relieved that we had not moved him and that this choice had been enacted relatively discreetly (we had not told our son), intimidated by our strategic and assertive actions, and resolved not to disappoint us. Our son flourished that year. He continued to be a high achiever, and in conferences and informal conversations with us his teacher identified him as the "top" or "near-top" student in the class. He was not as challenged academically that year as he had been the previous year; he was at or near the top of the classroom filled with lower-achieving students. Teacher A supported and nurtured him, as she did the other students. At the end of the year, we could tell that our son was happy and more certain about his ability to be a "good student" than he had been at the beginning of the year.

The agonizing experience we had at the beginning of that year did not change our views of a better teacher. When it came time for students to be assigned to classrooms for the following year, Teacher A recommended the better teacher, and we agreed with her recommendation. We wrote a letter to the principal requesting this teacher, and the principal honored our request. Our son was placed in a classroom with some of his higher-achieving friends from professional families whose parents had requested the same teacher. This experience also did not lead us to try to change the organization of the school or the school system. Although we shared our concerns about classroom and school dynamics with the principal and a few other parents, we did not try to organize a group of parents to resist these dynamics nor did we actively try to change them beyond our own individual decision and our subsequent involvement inside and outside of our son's classroom.

In the example of everyday life I have examined here, I have shown how the sociological imagination enabled my husband and me to see the ways in which our understandings of and responses to our son's classroom assignment were embedded in and reflective of a class-based school system. It also enabled us to see the ways in which parents and teachers and home and school are linked together through schools' dependence on parents' unpaid labor. By seeing these dynamics, we could make a decision that "fit with" our values and sort through some of the social consequences of this decision for the everyday lives of our son and ourselves. For us, it opened up the meaning of the term right—we were able to identify a different solution to the problem of classroom assignment from that of other professional parents. Whereas we began the process by "knowing" what we wanted, in the course of the process, we began to "know" something different. Finally, reflecting on the example in retrospect reveals that acts of resistance do not necessarily result in resistant consequences.

NOTES

1. I realize that this view of knowledge is not what Mills (1959) had in mind. His text exemplifies modern sociological theory, whereas my view that all knowledge is situated and partial draws inspiration from Donna Haraway's (1988) postmodernist essay, "Situated Knowledges," and Smith's (1987) concept of "bifurcated consciousness."

2. To protect our son's privacy, as well as to preserve the anonymity of the school and its teachers, I have changed or removed some identifying details throughout this chapter in my description of the teachers and the school.

REFERENCES

Haraway, D. (1988). Situated knowledges: The science question in feminism and the privilege of partial perspective. *Feminist Studies, 14,* 575-599.

Mills, C. W. (1959). *The sociological imagination.* New York: Oxford University Press.

Smith, D. E. (1987). *The everyday world as problematic: A feminist sociology.* Boston: Northeastern University Press.

CHAPTER 9

The Personal, the Sociological, and the Intersection of the Two[1]

LYNN DAVIDMAN

I began my career as a sociologist exploring people, places, and issues that have great valence for me personally. Throughout my academic life, beginning with my undergraduate course work, I have engaged in intellectual work at least partly as a way to better understand my own life. I pursued several fields of inquiry—psychology and religious studies—before coming upon the sociological lens, which provided me with the most satisfying ways of asking questions and seeking answers. By placing individual experience within larger contexts, and by tracing the linkages between self and society, biography and history, sociology offers a broad perspective in which to understand individuals' lives and the factors that shape us.

The issues that have been most central to me, given the facts of my biography, revolve around the themes of meaning, identity, and gender. While I was growing up, I experienced two major biographical disruptions. The first was that my mother died of cancer when I was 13 years old, leaving me in a

AUTHOR'S NOTE: I have been blessed, in my life and in my work, with wonderful friends and colleagues who generously read and offer feedback on my writing. This chapter has benefited from the helpful comments of Phil Brown, Anita Garey, Mary Jo Nietz, Saul Olyan, and Shelly Tenenbaum.

patriarchal Orthodox Jewish home with my father and two brothers. The religious certainties with which I had been brought up immediately dissolved; if the rabbis my parents had consulted had assured them that everything would be fine, obviously the religion made no sense and there must be no God. Six years later, my lack of religious beliefs led my father to disown me, and I was thrust into the world on my own to build a new life. These two experiences produced in me an ongoing passion for studying issues of gender equity, the quest for meaning, the construction of identity, and the intersection of all three.

Sociology teaches us that the various ways individuals create a sense of self and build their lives are shaped by numerous social factors, such as gender, race, ethnicity, social class, religion, education, and the general cultural norms and values of the time. I was drawn to the discipline precisely because I found that highlighting these broader influences helped me to better understand my own life and those of the people around me. For example, one source of the conflict between my father and me had to do with his upbringing in an immigrant Eastern European family and my coming of age and being educated at a time when the ideas of the contemporary U.S. feminist movement were widely available. His family had warm memories of the *shtetl*;[2] I grew up in a secular, pluralistic society in which traditional religious norms were no longer taken for granted. By seeing our individual life choices in the context of these larger historical patterns, I was better able to comprehend the nature and sources of our differences. Although I was still unable to resolve these differences, the application of a sociological perspective was liberating; it enlarged and transformed my own understanding of myself and others by seeing how our lives are molded by wider social and cultural patterns.

Since the sociological questions about which I am most passionate concern the ways that people make sense of their lives, seek meaning, and construct identity, all of which are ongoing processes, I was particularly attracted to interpretive, qualitative sociology. This methodological approach allows for an in-depth, focused, and subtly nuanced exploration of individual and group experiences, within the context of the local, particular settings in which they are lived. Interviews and participant observation allow the researcher a more direct and nuanced understanding of the processes through which meaning is created and transmitted.

I have sought to answer my own questions about my disrupted biography, in particular the break from Orthodox religion and the premature death of my mother, by understanding how these personal issues are reflections of, and shaped by, broader social processes. My research projects have brought me into contact with people who struggle with the same issues as I do, or ones that are closely related. I seek to interpret and comprehend our experiences through a continuous movement back and forth between my own memories, feelings, and responses and those of my respondents. This process of digging deep into my psyche in order to develop a subtly nuanced, rich, and empathetic understanding of their lives, and simultaneously using these insights to better comprehend my own life, deepens the sociological interpretations and analysis yielded by this research.

My two major studies, *Tradition in a Rootless World: Women Turn to Orthodox Judaism (1991)* and *Motherloss* (1999), both focus on how people make sense of and rebuild their lives after experiencing a major, unanticipated disruption in their biographies (Bury, 1982). In using the term "disrupted biographies" I do not mean to imply that anyone has a smooth, seamless biography without interruptions. In fact, postmodern thought points out that the overarching metanarratives through which groups of people had understood their lives no longer exist.

Instead, I mean to highlight those particular, major disruptions that shatter people's culturally derived expectations of their life course, such as the death of a mother at an early age (which might have been more common in preindustrial societies but is relatively rare in the contemporary United States) and the adoption of a religious way of life that is quite different from ones' parents'. People who live through these sorts of experiences are uniquely situated to engage in the narrative production of identities, which is a central focus of ethnographic interviewing.

My study of newly Orthodox Jewish women enabled me to explore the role and nature of traditional religion in a modem world, and especially its attraction to contemporary women. Since I had rebelled against and left Orthodoxy for feminist, theological, and lifestyle reasons, I sought to understand why, in the 1980s, there was a pronounced revitalization of traditional religious groups (Jewish, Christian, and Muslim) that define women largely in terms of their roles as wives and mothers in nuclear families. I and my other feminist colleagues and friends were genuinely puzzled by this phenomenon, and I decided to explore it through participant observation and in-depth interviews in two distinct institutional contexts, in which contemporary women are attracted to and resocialized into Orthodox Judaism. Early on in this project, I learned that I had to struggle to separate my own assumptions and worldview from those of the women I was meeting. Since this was a self-selected group, it became apparent that they did not have the same feminist struggles with Orthodoxy I had; otherwise, they would simply not be there. The intrusiveness of my own blinders became crystal clear to me one Saturday morning at beginner's services in one community, when the rabbi (whom I had known for most of my life) looked at me and shouted "Sing!" In my mind's eye, at that moment, I could see myself pulling down a shade in front of my face to protect me from the enthusiastic rabbi's attempts to pull me into the community. As I saw the shade come down, I realized then that no one else in that room was pulling down such a shield and that as long as I did so, I would never be able to understand, much less make sensible to others, the meaning of this choice for the women who embraced it.

Since a central goal of the project was to convey, as best as I could, the women's attraction to Orthodox Judaism from the perspective of their life experiences and social locations, and not from mine, I knew I needed help sorting out my personal reactions. Otherwise, these feelings would prevent me from seeing and hearing realities that differed from my own and my research project would be a failure. I worked for over a year with a therapist to separate out my memories and feelings of being forced by my father to attend services and observe Jewish laws and practices from the realities of the women who made a conscious choice to be in the synagogue every Shabbat morning. By making visible, grappling with, and doing my best to set aside my own biases, I was able to more clearly hear, comprehend, and represent to readers the experiences of the women who were adopting Orthodoxy.

Through participating with these women in their worlds, I came to a better sociological understanding of the nature and attraction of traditional religions in the modern context. Orthodox Judaism offers several important dimensions of life that the women found missing in secular society: a clear sense of roots and identity, membership in a community, a meaningful framework in which to locate one's role and place in the world, clarity about gender, and assistance in forming stable, nuclear family relationships. Conducting this research also taught me a great deal about the research process, about myself, and the integration of the two. Whereas at the beginning of my project I had framed my inquiry in terms of the question, "Why in the world would anyone do this?," I learned that allowing myself to become open to and immersed in the setting produced more suitable research questions, such as "What is the meaning of this experience for the people who choose it?" and "How can I better understand—and thus render comprehensible to others—their attraction to Orthodoxy in terms of the larger social contexts in which they made this choice?" Although I never would have recognized it when I began, I came to see that this project gave me a way to place myself, as an adult, back into those contexts I had left so rebelliously as a teenager and make a different sort of peace with them. Through the process of developing an empathetic analysis of the women's turn to Orthodoxy, I was better able to integrate my biography, not in the sense of returning to the Orthodoxy I had left, but in terms of better comprehending and appreciating religion's place in my life and its role in shaping the person I had become.

Tradition in a Rootless World was written largely as a "realist tale" (Van Maanen, 1988), a conventional ethnography that attempted, through extensive quotations from respondents and lengthy extracts from my field notes, to convey an impression of what happened in the settings, who the members were, and what they were about. Although I strove to let my participants "speak for themselves," I knew that the book was indeed an interpretive work, shaped by the particular interactions between me and my respondents, each of us with distinct biographies and self-understandings. Nevertheless, I wrote about myself only enough to broadly inform my readers where I was coming from. I did not probe deeply, throughout the narrative, into the specific ways my own biography shaped how I saw, heard, and interpreted the women's actions and life stories.

For me, writing this book was a way of coming to terms with my disrupted relationship with my father, an issue that was central to the way I understood and presented myself to others. Completing it allowed me to move on, both in my psyche and in my research. My current project, on growing up motherless, forces me to probe my memories and confront my feelings about my mother's death and its impact on my life, a subject that has been deeply repressed by me and my family. The silences around my mother's sickness and death began when she took ill. I was not told what was wrong with her, and when I guessed it was cancer, since what else was unnameable in the late 1960s, my father and aunt denied it. This made me terribly confused about why my mother continued to be ill, recited Psalms all day, and clutched a piece of rock from the Western Wall in Jerusalem, from the time of her surgery in September until her death in March. Needless to say, I was shocked when she died. The silences surrounding her illness and death have continued until very recently in my life; my brothers and I have almost never discussed our mother, nor was it a topic I brought up even with my closest friends.

An example of how deeply I sought to avoid talking about this issue can be seen in my self-presentation at my first appointment with the therapist I sought out when I was struggling with the blocks I faced in my dissertation research. When I told her my life story and got to the part about my mother dying when I was 13, she immediately said, "That is a very tough age at which to lose a mother." I breezily replied, "Oh, it would be tough at any age," thereby making clear that I didn't like to talk about this experience, and instead tried to normalize it as best as I could.

It has taken me over 10 years since then to feel ready to deal with and probe into my experience of growing up motherless. I had known for years that I would eventually have to write a book on this subject, as a way of compelling myself to break the silences and better integrate this powerful piece of my biography. Nevertheless, I felt unable to take on this challenging, potentially painful task until I had the sense of stability in my life that would allow me to take this plunge. At the age of 39, I had a tenured appointment and a house of my own; I knew that the time had come. I was already older than the 36 years of age that my mother had been at her death.

My goal in this project is to write a book exploring the various ways that early motherloss, as it is experienced within particular social contexts, shapes the narratives people construct about their lives. My central question is: How do individuals create a sense of meaning and identity after losing—at a young age—the person who generally provides the basic caring and nurturance in their lives? For the past 2½ years, I have engaged in intensive conversations with 60 women and men from a variety of class backgrounds whose mothers died when the children were between 10 and 15 years of age—a time period I selected because 10 is old enough that people are likely to have memories and young enough that the child still has significant growing up to do. Also, my own mother had died when I was 13: I was particularly interested in the experiences of early adolescent motherloss. Through these interviews, I have engaged in the co-creation of narratives about motherloss, using others' experiences to better illuminate my own and developing an empathic understanding of their experiences by digging deep into my own psyche for memories and feelings about my own mother's death and its impact on my life.

As I work on this study, I am more informed than in my first project by the postmodern turn in ethnography which has led to the production of more critical, experimental forms of fieldwork narratives, particularly within the discipline of anthropology (Behar, 1993, 1996; Geertz, 1988; Wolf, 1992). It has become less plausible to present material on others' lives that rests on the naive assumption of the authority of a researcher who goes to live among "others," discerns what manner of lives they lead, and simply reports these findings back to an audience of outsiders. Instead, contemporary ethnography rests on the assumption that all knowledge in the field is produced through the interactions between a researcher, who is a socially situated self with particular life experiences, and her respondents, who bring to the dialogue their own embedded assumptions and meanings. Analyzing the ways in which these conversations we call interviews create and shape the narratives produced is as essential to our comprehension of the subject matter as are the actual words of our interviewees. Thus, I plan to write a more searchingly self-reflexive book this time, one that seeks to balance and mediate between the inside and the outside, self and others, individuals (including myself) and the social.

My interviews for this project provided a context in which I participated with my respondents in creating narratives that make sense of their disrupted biographies and tie together the diverse parts of their lives, while doing the same for myself. Narratives, like memoirs, are constructed ways of making sense of a life. People tell stories and/or write memoirs to say something about who they are as individuals and the combination of personal experiences and social/cultural contexts that shaped their identities. Our stories root us, give us identity and grounding, and a guideline for action. The particular linkages and connections people make in these narratives—such as "I can't nurture, because I had no mother"—help them account for their life choices and constitute the primary basis for my analysis.

Throughout this project I have learned a great deal about myself as well as the larger social and cultural factors that shape people's experiences of motherloss. For example, in my conversations with others about their mothers' death and its aftermath, the theme of silence repeatedly surfaced.

Over and over again I heard stories of how the mother's illness was kept a secret (the large majority of mothers had died from cancer), with the child not being informed about the cause for the major disruptions in the household. From this secrecy, the children, of course, sensed that something awful was going on and further, that it was taboo to bring it up and inquire about it. This silence continued after the mother's death and was reinforced in subtle and gross ways, such as the removal of the mother's pictures from the house when the father remarried. And because they had learned early on, when their mothers first became sick, that the subject was taboo, my respondents, like me, rarely discussed their mothers with anyone, from the onset of her illness and throughout their lives.

My own visceral understanding of the devastating consequences of these lies, secrets, and silences helps me to break these silences in my life and those of my respondents' and ultimately, I hope, in the wider culture and society. By realizing how commonly the experience of motherloss has been silenced, normalized, repressed, and long-buried, I have become interested in understanding those factors in U.S. culture that shape our attitudes toward serious illness and death. In general, death is a taboo subject in our society and even grave illnesses are often perceived as shameful (Becker, 1973; Sontag, 1978). Maternal death results in an "abnormal" family structure, setting motherless children apart from their peers, at a time when they are most eager to fit in. Many of my respondents, like me, learned to normalize and even deny the reality and impact of motherloss, thus avoiding being "different" and being singled out for sympathy and extra attention. The cultural taboos about this subject, and people's—those who are motherless as well as most others'—inability to openly discuss it, produce a lifelong habit of silence, which further deepens our sense of biographical disruption. There are no cultural scripts available within which to think about and make sense of this experience. I and my respondents struggle to find ways to create our own scripts, to produce narratives that help us cut through the taboos and integrate these painful experiences into new and more complete understandings of ourselves and our social worlds.

While this research has taught me a great deal about numerous dimensions of social life, it has also engaged my whole being, from my conscious actions, such as having my mother's picture on my desk as I write; my conversations, in which I now am more likely to talk about my mother, what she was like, and what her death meant to me; to my subconscious life as well. Repeatedly while working on this project my dreams have given voice and image to my suppressed memories. Over a year ago, I found myself quite depressed by all the pain and emotional devastation revealed by my respondents and the ways these feelings echoed in my own psyche.

I felt paralyzed, unable to proceed any further. I discussed these feelings with some of my closest colleagues/friends, and together we decided that I should simply drop the project, that it was too deeply painful for me to stay with for the remaining 2 to 3 years that it would take to complete the book. And yet, right when I thought I had reached a clear decision about this, my mother began to appear in my dreams, something that had only rarely happened before. I knew then that I could not give up; my mother had come to help guide the way.

There was a pattern to my dreams about my mother. Typically, she would reappear after being gone (dead?) for a while, and would once again be living with me, my father, and brothers in my childhood home. And yet, she somehow was not properly fulfilling her old roles, especially the task of feeding us, one of the key functions of women in families in postindustrial America (DeVault, 1991). In most of these dreams, I and sometimes my older brother were quite concerned about planning meals, purchasing and putting food on the table. In some of these dreams I would confront my mother, or complain to my father, about her failure to properly feed us. These dreams revealed not only how tough it was for me, as a young adolescent, to have to take on maternal roles, but also provided insights that shaped parts of my interviews. In fact, nearly all of my respondents described the disruption in daily meals that resulted from their mother's illnesses and death. These conversations helped me understand how critical the mother's feeding her family is, not only for its nutritional value, but as a symbolic manifestation of her caring. And indeed, the social organization of gender, and the assignment of caretaking roles largely to women (DeVault, 1991), is another structural factor that shapes individuals' experiences of motherloss and its consequences, a subject that emerged in all my interviews and that I am further developing in my book.

More recently I have had dreams about some form of paralysis afflicting me. In some, I am walking and suddenly find myself simply unable to move my legs; in others, my vision is impaired, and I can no longer see. To me these dreams reveal my anxiety about making my way through my own and others' repressed memories and feelings about motherloss, developing an analytic interpretation, and writing my book. And yet I also know that I will complete this task and emerge more informed about the subject matter, the nature of ethnographic research and writing, and, of course, myself. The discipline of sociology, with its habit of breaking silences by probing deeply underneath surface, taken-for-granted assumptions, and its emphasis on the interplay between the personal and intellectual, the self and society, has both prepared me for this task and provided me with a way to do it.

NOTES

1. Reprinted with permission of Human Sciences Press, Inc. (1997).
2. The small, tightly knit, bounded community in which Jews in premodern Europe lived.

REFERENCES

Becker, E. (1973). *The denial of death.* New York: Free Press.

Behar, R. (1993). *Translated woman: Crossing the border with Esperanza's Story* Boston: Beacon.

Behar, R. (1996). *The vulnerable observer. Anthropology that breaks your heart.* Boston: Beacon.

Chodorow, N. (1978). *The reproduction of mothering: Psychoanalysis and the sociology of gender.* Berkeley: University of California Press.

Clifford, J., & Marcus, G. E. (Eds.). (1986). *Writing culture: The poetics and politics of ethnography.* Berkeley: University of California Press.

Davidman, L. (1991). *Tradition in a rootless world: Women turn to Orthodox Judaism.* Berkeley: University of California Press.

DeVault, M. L. (1991). *Feeding the family: The social organization of caring as gendered work.* Chicago: University of Chicago Press.

Edelman, H. (1994). *Motherless daughters: The legacy of loss.* Reading, MA: Addison-Wesley.

Elli, C. (1995). *Final negotiations: A story of love, loss, and chronic illness.* Philadelphia: Temple University Press.

Geertz, C. (1988). *Works and lives: The anthropologist as author.* Stanford, CA: Stanford University Press.

Miller, N. K. (1996). *Bequest and betrayal: Memoirs of a parent's death.* New York: Oxford University Press.

Rich, A. (1976). *Of woman born: Motherhood as experiences and institution.* New York: Ballantine.

Rothman, B. K. (1989). *Recreating motherhood: Ideology and technology in a patriarchal society.* New York: Norton.

Ruddick, S. (1989). *Maternal thinking: Toward a politics of peace.* New York: Ballantine.

Sontag, S. (1978). *Illness as metaphor.* New York: Farrar, Straus & Giroux.

Van Maanen, J. (1988). *Tales of the field. On writing ethnography.* Chicago: University of Chicago Press.

Walker, A. (1983). *In search of our mothers' gardens.* San Diego: Harcourt, Brace, Jovanovich.

Wolf, M. (1992). *A thrice told tale: Feminism, postmodemism, and ethnographic responsibility.* Stanford, CA: Stanford University Press.

CHAPTER 10

"Are We Alone?"[1]

MARJORIE L. DEVAULT

Visiting my father in late summer of 1996, I began a meditation on the phrase, "Are we alone?"

How it happened:

In retirement from teaching, he's taken up astronomy. Over several days visiting, we'd chatted about recent *Nova's* and new discoveries about the universe. (I remember, as I write, my best childhood strategy for extending my bedtime: "Daddy, how did the world begin?") We'd mentioned the approaching millennium, noted a rising interest in paranormal phenomena (citing with stylish alarm the polling data from a recent "All Things Considered"), looked askance at a missive from Roswell, accessed from the Web (*http://www.art-bell.com*). And at some point (out of nostalgia or a puzzled concern for the present, I can't remember which), recalling childhood fascinations, we remembered awe, and the question, "Are we alone?"

The words—"Are we alone?"—slide easily into our discourse and organize a stretch of talk that follows. They also mark a moment in the conversation when my attention doubles: I listen, I talk, participating "normally." But I also enter a mental state associated with my work as an observer and analyst. "Are we alone?" jumps out, activating this state as if tripping a switch. I sense immediately that it is a peculiar construction, common enough that its peculiarity passes unnoticed, a phrase doing ideological work that interests me.

Asking the question, "Are we alone?" We mean by this construction, of course, to refer to various ways of taking an interest in scientific debate about the possibility and likelihood of life in other parts of the universe. That goes without saying.

Two aspects of this construction interest me. One is the going without saying. We use this phrase—"Are we alone?"—as shorthand, to refer to a discourse, a history of that discourse, a realm of investigation. It situates us, apparently instantly and seamlessly, as participants (members of an audience at least) in an ongoing, collective quest for knowledge. This question—filed in the everyday stocks of knowledge of innumerable individuals, no doubt acquiring subtle variations of meaning and networks of association for each—operates to coordinate our conversation on this day, as we drive down this street, to eat this food and continue our chat. Rather a marvel of verbal engineering, I think.

"We," however, is the hook that grabbed my attention. It is a small word, and one that comes so easily, entering speech almost unnoticed. Yet I have come to think of it as a word with surprising power, a word that often trips me up as I muddle through the everyday dilemmas of teaching and scholarship. "We" is a word that marks boundaries of belonging and exclusion. It can signal shared experience or empathic identification, invite coalition, impose perceptions of sameness and difference. As I lecture, facilitate, respond, advise, joke, and of course write, "we" sneaks up on me to announce my assumptions and prejudices.

"Are we alone?" A global, encompassing we. We humans? We life?

Flying home from this late-summer visit: *Are we alone?* Now I'm working on the phrase more seriously, wondering if I've found a topic for this essay. I let the phrase sound in my mind, feeling its resonance. We (that is, I, with my companion) arrive in the city and lug our bags into the subway, plopping down among the other riders. As always, I am painfully conscious of the economic divisions that become so obvious here. I look, knowing that many of these people have no other means of transportation. And endure their gaze, knowing that my bags mark me as one who moves easily, at will. I watch, in the urban not-watching way, the woman whose breasts, spilling out of a fringed leather halter, draw many eyes. I watch, also watching those breasts, the 9-year-old girl sitting on her mother's lap—Central American perhaps—and wonder where they are going so late at night. I'm aware of the tall black man next to me, African I think, because of body, posture, clothing. And I watch, slumped over in the corner, a disheveled white man who might be homeless, or just tired.

"We"? "Alone"? Suddenly, I feel my own tiredness. I close my eyes.

The phenomenologist Herbert Spiegelberg (1973) suggests that the construction "we" should, as a matter of both accuracy and morality, be used only in carefully limited ways. Providing both linguistic and phenomenological analyses, he distinguishes between the "we" of copresence and the "absentee we."

He points out that we-unions can be variably strong or weak, permanent or temporary, superficial or deep. The sticking point, for Spiegelberg, is the difficulty of checking to make sure that potential we-partners share the we-consciousness, especially in the absentee case. He proposes

> a maxim: Limit we-talk to occasions where you honestly believe that your we-partners want you to speak for them. Without good evidence for such an honest belief one had better speak only for oneself. This is a matter of social humility for humans who cannot know one another's hearts. It is a matter of respect for their dignity. It is also a matter of intellectual honesty and moral courage. (p. 154)

His essay is provocative, of course, precisely because the word is ubiquitous in social discourse, and so rarely examined with care.

Tuesday, August 6: My partner is cooking supper; I'm puttering in my study. In the background, as usual in our household, the ABC *Nightly News*. I am startled out of habitual half-listening when I hear, in that definitive, male TV-anchor voice, portentously framed by the network's opening fanfare, what I have come to think of as my question: "Are we alone?"

Scientists have been analyzing the composition of a 4-pound rock. They believe it is an asteroid that originated on Mars and landed in Antarctica 13,000 years ago. They have found tiny bacteria-like fossils and traces of chemicals nearby that could have been produced by living organisms. These are the details of the story as I eventually piece them together.

In the next week, I find myself surrounded by a robust discourse on the topic. It is a contrapuntal mix of very diverse "voices": the tabloids, the scientists, and many in between. Bacteria morph into Martians as the story circulates; the *Weekly World News* supplies its usual picture of an insect-like alien.

My work as an analyst is to pay careful attention—to language, to detail, to whatever is there. It is a craft: to notice and then to ask, Why this? What is it? and Where does it lead? Of course, my noticing is directed, disciplined—by my capacities, needs, history, interests. And of course, my asking and thinking about what I notice are social too. I ask and think about things I have been invited to notice: talk, power, membership and exclusion, science and technology, texts and embodied actors.

Spiegelberg's essay speaks to questions that worry me. Like most feminist scholars, I often invoke a "we" in my speaking and writing. It is a "we" that I have learned from, that I depend on, that I hope to make more durable. Jane Mansbridge (1995) suggests that this discursive "we" of feminism is "internally contested," "in turmoil," "self-transforming"; Chandra Mohanty (1991) speaks of an "imagined community" of third-world feminism. Both writers imply that this "we" is useful, but recognize that it is treacherous if unexamined: It can cover over differences and conflict, constructing flawed communities that ignore and exclude many who would and should be active members. Spiegelberg's cautions suggest greater attention to what happens when anyone deploys we-talk. I try to imagine, among feminists, a more careful discourse—particular strategies for talking, listening, writing, reading that allow for legitimate uses of we-talk. Considering the problem, I find that often I am content to speak as an "I" who is a member of a community.

———————————

August 9th is another "Science Friday" on NPRs "Talk of the Nation" call-in radio program. This week there is discussion with scientists involved in the Mars rock discovery. The host, Ira Flatow, pushes them to be interesting to the lay audience, urging them to address the big question. They mostly resist, adopting the cautious skepticism of their professional training. But occasionally they seize the opportunities afforded by the moment, and argue enthusiastically that we now see why we must increase support for basic science. A 14-year-old caller objects. She sees too many needs here on earth, and suggests, earnestly and with a surprisingly mature confidence, that money would be better spent on schools in urban neighborhoods. The scientists seem abashed for only a moment, and then talk her down with their arsenal of justifications. "Wondering," they finally explain, "is what makes us human."

The program ends, but this young girl's voice, so unusual on the radio, haunts me, a vivid memory of this listening. As I look forward to writing about it, I realize I can access it from the World Wide Web. With the aid of RealAudio, she might speak again and again, the same words, frozen and mobile at once.

———————————

In mid-September, I make a note. It's been weeks since I've heard anything about my question. The news has moved on, as it does. But of course, the story doesn't disappear. It is now part of a common world, a discursive resource to be invoked in ways we cannot yet see. On November 26, as I dress for school, I listen to "Morning Edition." The asteroid from Mars provides the foundation for a Thanksgiving-week essay: Is life a miracle, or just coincidence? I groan, expecting "miracle." But as I listen, I'm surprised that the essayist doesn't seem to be going in that direction. The Mars rock contains mere squiggles, hardly "life" as we understand it. What the scientists have discovered is merely a tiny—yes, coincidental—imprint of some complex material process that is far from miraculous. But then there's a last-minute about-face. The real miracle, it seems, is our kind of multicellular life, and the essay ends with the smug and rather revolting conclusion that even if there is other life in the universe, "most of it's just slime."

I realize I can access it from the World Wide Web. True. But it sounds so misleadingly effortless. My software isn't working; and I realize that, even if it were, I have inadvertently "thrown away" all my "bookmarks," as well as the RealAudio "reader" I once managed to download. I put the project on the list of things to do, where it sits for months. Eventually I try, not at home where I imagined hearing the young girl's voice, but in a borrowed office during vacation—way too hot for comfort—on someone else's machine. I spend an hour finding things, reading instructions, guessing how to access what I want. Finally, I arrive at the site (*http:christie.prognet.com/contentp/npr/nf6/aO9.html*). I click on a fragment of bluish text, and in a moment, the young girl I remember does speak again:

"Hi," she offers. "My point of view is completely different."

"Ahh," I think, sitting straighter in my chair, "I'd forgotten how she began."

I begin to take notes, and can't resist producing a transcript:

Laura: Hi, um, my point of view is completely different. I'm a 14-year-old trying to become educated in today's society. I feel frustrated at the amount of money being spent on NASA's expensive programs. Shouldn't our, our country's fu- ture—*not* answers to questions like "Is there life on Mars?"

[There's a pause here, 3.4 seconds.]

Ira: You don't think we should be looking for life on other planets, spending money on that?

Laura: Well, I do, but that expensive microscope that they looked, um, for, at the meteor [**Ira:** Right.] I think that that could've funded a school for about 5 years.

Ira: You think so?

Laura: Yeah, maybe.

Ira: Maybe.

One of the scientists (rather softly): Huhh, hhI guess I'll take a shot at that one. Heh heh.

Ira: Go ahead, _____.

The scientist: I think, I think, it's a, it's a quality of life issue. Essentially, one of the greatest things about being human beings is trying to understand the world around us, and trying to understand the world beyond the earth. And I think if we give up that goal we really lose what makes us human, our humanity. And I think that the amount of money that's spent is large, relative to a personal scale. But I think on a scale of the GNP of, of America, it's actually a very small fraction. And I don't think it's a large investment to be made, to understand something which really may open up a whole horizon, a whole view of the universe.

Ira: Laura, let me, let me also jump in. As someone who was your age in the 60s, there was a whole generation of children who went to school and studied science because of the search for, the aim to go to the moon. And money was not available, and the United States decided it would spend a lot of money on training people, on students, and sink it into science and technology. And suddenly the science school system got a lot better, because of the space race. Did you know about that?

Laura: Me?

Ira: Yeah.

Laura: Well, no, (laughing) not really.

Ira: So there are all kinds of spin-offs, uh. And in fact, finding an, uh, a meteorite in, in Antarctica, right there on the ice, means that we can explore another planet without even going there. You'd save a hundred billion dollars on that.

Laura: Yeah, that is true. Thank you very much.

Ira: You're welcome. Did I make the case at all there? Gentlemen?

Talk is fascinating, and its details seem immensely significant. Listening and transcribing, I notice how very long a 3.4-second pause can seem, in a radio conversation. I linger over tone, wondering how to convey, in a printed text, Flatow's tone of condescension as he speaks to Laura. Or her laugh when she answers his question ("Did you know about that?"). She seems to me to say: "I'm 14—how would I know about that?" I am bemused to hear Ira, seeking approval from his scientist guests, address them as "gentlemen." One is a woman, and I wonder if she notices. And I catch my own slip: Despite my interest in the details of this exchange, I forgot to go back and record the name of the scientist who speaks. I become extremely attached to this stretch of talk. I want to include it in my essay. But what will it mean? It seems that I will make Laura a hero of sorts. But I begin to feel sympathy for the scientists as well, speaking in this unfamiliar context. I pause to consider in which "we" I want to position myself, in this writing. A "we" concerned with social issues? We women and girls? We sociologists, we scientists?

Leaving the borrowed office, I stand in the hallway and stare vacantly at a collection of academic notices intended for others. One catches my eye: It announces a conference, titled "Text/Archive/Trace" (or was it "Archive/ Text/Trace"?). Like so many other things, it seems a part of my essay. I want to take it home, as "data," but I'm unwilling to steal it from a community I am only visiting. I could find the information elsewhere, I think, imagining visits to reference rooms. I walk into the cold outdoors, chatting with my friend but also conscious of a lingering mantra as I hold the words in my mind: text, archive, trace; text, archive, trace.

I live not exactly alone, but in the alternating alone-and-together rhythms of an academic commuting relationship. Often, I am alone in my three-bedroom, second-floor flat in Syracuse. For near-constant companionship, I have NPR, ABC, and the local "all-news" radio station. Many mornings, I work at the computer, then pace. I stand by the window, sipping coffee and watching the squirrels—some brown and some black, in this neighborhood (a few blocks over, they are all black, and a bit farther in another direction, all brown). Sometimes I ponder the various "I"'s that put words like these on my screen. Sometimes I worry about imposing a sociologist's "we" on my students. And sometimes, now, I try to conceive a "we" that includes me, the leather-clad woman in the subway, the squirrels, and the squiggles on a rock from Mars.

As an ethnographer, I live in the world, observe it, and write about it, delicately positioning self and others, "I," "we," and "they." Always, there are decisions, about what to see and what to reveal. Here, for example: I did not set out to write about the internet, but it has become part of the world I inhabit. I imagined a more explicitly theoretical lesson, but the pleasure of writing led me elsewhere. And I tried to write about my father as an anonymous "friend," but it didn't seem right. Some say it doesn't matter, who I am or where I live. Who cares about these details, or about life on Mars? But I would suggest that these should be empirical, not rhetorical questions.

I wonder how an audience of sociologists will read this essay. Some, no doubt, will see it as mere indulgence, a selfish frivolity; some will take it as an experiment with form, or an exercise in reflexivity. And some, I hope, will read it as a brief for ethnography that extends across local sites, following connections that lead through both texts and a material world.

Leaving one home for another, I wait on the platform, gazing idly at the fragments of text that organize an urban system of comings and goings:

4 STOPS TO AIRPORT
NO TRESPASSING
DANGER THIRD RAIL

I board the train, settling myself and luggage. Watchful, as usual, I notice, this time, how I slump in the seat.

DO NOT LEAN AGAINST DOOR

And I enjoy an inward smile at the odd instruction produced by a small act of vandalism:

DURING AN EMERGENCY
PLEASE FOLLOW THE INSTRUCTIONS OF THE OPERA

I walk through Terminal B, aware of the double row of telephones, each in its cubicle, floating through snatches of urgent talk, selves connected to others, busily organizing their movement from here to so many theres, just as I do. I board the plane, and as we taxi toward the runway, scan the notes I made in the subway, attending to the obvious and wondering at obscure details:

B
2

W
A
T
C
H

Y
O
U
R

S
T
E
P

Watchfulness, yes: The pleasure, purpose, and means of my craft.

NOTE

1. Reprinted with permission of Human Sciences Press, Inc. (1997).

REFERENCES

Mansbridge, J. (1995). What is the feminist movement? In M. M. Ferree & P. Y. Martin (Eds.), *Feminist organizations: Harvest of the new women's movement* (pp. 27-34). Philadelphia: Temple University Press.
Mohanty, C. (1991). Cartographies of struggle: Third world women and the politics of feminism. In C. Mohanty, A. Russo, & L. Torres (Eds.), *Third world women and the politics of feminism* (pp. 1-47). Bloomington: Indiana University Press.
Spiegelberg, H. (1973). On the right to say "we": A linguistic and phenomenological analysis. In G. Psathas (Ed.), *Phenomenological sociology: Issues and applications* (pp. 129-156). New York: John Wiley.

CHAPTER 11

Five Minutes[1]

PETER K. MANNING

Studies of everyday life, biography and case studies, have taken a personalistic, narrative turn, even though the featured performers are often obscure voices,[2] the role of the narrator problematic, and the stories' analytic purposes unclear (Cullum-Swan and Manning, 1998). The premise of these narrative analyses is that while life shapes stories, stories also shape life. A corollary of this is that families are shaped and sustained by talk that produces shared meanings (Berger & Kellner, 1970). Families talk themselves into collective memories, just as we are said to "uncouple" from them via subtle symbolic processes (Vaughan, 1984). Families and generations are connected by stories, oral narratives that weave fortunes, ensnare some, free others, and suspend time like a clinging spider's web. Perhaps modern stories are surrogates for history, religion, and extended family interactions.

Or, perhaps the absence of compelling stories lodged in a mini-collective memory stimulates a normative and even nostalgic reaction. Sophisticated modern fiction displays fragments, time telescoping, -blindness, and aporia, and rarely tells a simple story. The free-floating textual play manifested in the writings of Cortazar, Barthes, Delillo, Calvino, and Eco reflects the simultaneity of perspectives struggling to emerge in modern experience. This culture validates the question "who says so?" and considers "standpoint" a source of theory. If stories weave cultural fabric, then a faded remnant of stories also exists.

AUTHOR'S NOTE: I thank Rosanna Hertz for editorial advice and detailed comments on earlier drafts and Norman Denzin for sharing his Carver-like essay on a similar subject.

[I was once told that like Richard Ford, I spoke as if everything I said were in quotes, I spoke metaphorically (as if I were speaking metaphorically?)].

The tangled green woody vine shading the porch had overwhelmed its once tidy space and now drooped, visible through the window under which the gray haired man sat. Morning light penetrated the white frame house, possessed it, tripping across the rugs and collapsing in the corners of the room. The television was cornered, gray and eyeless. While three people wandered in the house, the fourth sat, a newspaper spread on his lap atop two quilts. It was a cool Oregon morning in May.

In the nook adjoining the kitchen, silently, stood a large picture showing some 60 family members. Stacked against each other, standing on risers, they posed at a family picnic in some small Oregon town after World War One. Bent and discolored now, its cardboard backing warped and rotting, it perched limply on the brown plastic vinyl seat surrounding the red formica kitchen table.

The nook once held happy breakfasts, but the formica table, now gritty and sticky with abandoned crumbs, hosted no recent gatherings. Plastic bottles for recycling were jumbled in latticed yellow milk boxes, while old newspapers filled torn brown grocery sacks. Signs of years of eroded domesticity were visible everywhere.

Circling the kitchen and using almost random, anticipatory movements, she and her son arrived awkwardly before the picture. She was neither a linear thinker nor walker, she skipped, slid, and fussed, twisted and spat out fragments of talk like shards of glass shattered on a concrete floor.

"Some were Catholics, we think."

"They had a lot of children, . . . 13 or 14 . . ."

"Here he is . . . we think." She gestured to a small, dark and intense boy seated cross-legged on the ground in the front row.

Her small feet in white canvas running shoes pawed the ground, as she made obsessively the same semicircles on the lino as she did at the beach. She jammed her hands in her pockets, looked at the picture and then glanced sideways at him. He seldom looked at anyone directly, preferring to appear to be sought not seeking. He preferred to observe rather than to be observed.

"I'd like a copy of that. I've never seen it; I didn't know it existed."

[Why was I never told anything, or so little, about my family? Have I "forgotten" what I was told? I don't remember if I have forgotten or if I was never told.]

The street outside was silent. No children played, no cars rushed by going to work. The leaves on the Maple trees were heavy. It was so quiet that the hiss and whirr of the oxygen compressor in the corner drew attention, even if one did not notice the thin life lines, the clear plastic tubing, running from it to the small hospital bed shoved far in the corner of the dining room. Outside, dogs barked, howled, then commenced a pitiful, lonesome chorus with no protagonist to guide them, to cheer them, to focus them. They crashed against the back fence, and shoved their noses hopefully against it, but no one in the house responded to them or each other. Nor did those in the house reveal their own silent cries.

He looked at the paper—then turned it up to read the lower half, his lustrous thin gray hair straight and shining, his eyes blue to slate gray. His now depleted frame was wrapped in a far too large woolen robe of black watch plaid. It had been made for him in the room around the corner. The robe hung loosely and fell open at the front. His right arm above the wrist had a red shunt secured by a resilient plastic tape. Some medical instruction, perhaps orders signifying some past crisis, was scrawled on the tape. He bore the scars of hospitalization, although he was nominally home. His left arm was equally thin and had been skewered repeatedly. His long and delicate fingers were attached to hands with outstanding blue veins, not unlike those of the man standing quietly across from him.

"Do you guys need me to drive you to the airport?" He offered this, 3 days after his dance with death.

"Thanks, but I think we can make it ourselves. I'd agree to let you do it, but Mom does not drive and if you felt tired, she would not be able to drive me. It's a matter of not having a 'back-up driver.' "

[I guess I should not have lied, denied that he was too sick to drive. Oblique remarks have always served me well. My time in Oxford had sharpened my ability to slide by awkwardness with a distracting phrase].

In some nuanced fashion, aging sets centripetal-free forces in a family. Moral burdens, once carried by life's rituals and routines, tasks and roles suffused with energy and purpose, shift within the family. To where had it been shifted in the last year or so? Other routines, rational and institutional, would now have to suffice. New agents, hired nurses, doctors, social workers relegated to bar stools near the nurses station, could only simulate, not convey the style, the purpose, the purity of exchanges once featured in my parents' mutual drama. No others could fully assume the burdens they had accumulated through their more than 60 years together.

His body had served him well, even though he admitted to his son-in-law later that his body was "failing" him. Ever balanced and coordinated, his feet now wandered astray, his ears filled with something, and produced pain and annoying buzzing, and his hands seemed under someone else's command. Grace of movement remained, a shadow of the old forms and actions, briefly revealed in the hospital corridor as he was rehearsed for home ambulation. He held the bar, turned, an awkward emulation of his granddaughters learning to walk years before, sidestepped and crab-walked, and paced slowly on reddened, swollen, and twisted feet. They had not forgiven years of service.

"He was a professional baseball player." Almost 60 years later, this singular identity was fixed in her mind. Mom smiled, proud of him, and chirped at his side speaking to no one while hoping everyone would hear and respond. The two handsome therapists, dressed in purple, holding his arms as he struggled to walk, his hair messy and uncombed as it never was, smiled. His face showed concentration, oscillating with pain and determination, and both drained down the halls with his strength. It was a painful scene, something of an annuciation, and his son, in part to avoid watching it, walked to an adjacent hall and listened to the morning prayer over the loudspeaker.

When they returned to the house, he noticed that on the mantle were cards sent by those who comforted themselves as they fashioned their messages. One was typed in a style mocking a sermon: "Our thoughts are with you we went to the lake the other day. . . ." Beneath the cards in the drawer were the several bills she dare not examine, statements from Blue Cross and Blue Shield, the *billets-doux* of high-tech medicine, a crumbled insurance policy in an old manila envelope, tablecloths now never to be used again, napkins, and napkin rings. Ivory, wooden, plastic, they were signs of years of domesticity, fraught and anxious meals, collapsed occasions, and tearful Sunday lunches. They bore silent testimony.

The younger man showered, packed a few things, drying his hair inefficaciously with an already damp towel, and wondered what to say in these last fleeting moments.

A few minutes, perhaps five, remained. He cogitated but knew quickly that he had lost the struggle for words long ago.

[I am somewhere else. No, you're here! In this room you once knew well.]

He was now standing before his father with his mother and the younger woman.

He placed his hand gently on his Dad's shoulder, feeling the bones, seeing the translucent skin, and the heavy leaves of the overgrown maple trees out the window on his right. The room was alight. His eyes were now a muddy gray blue, intelligent and pained, and he looked up hopefully. Something between a hug and a squeeze passed between them. His arms when raised revealed the darkened blood coagulated in the veins of his hands and his long graceful fingers.

"I'll get up."

"No, please don't bother."

He struggled to rise, hesitated, seized the blankets and replaced them around his legs as he recognized that his effort was insufficient. His body visibly relaxed and he sat back down. He had risen about an inch from the surface of his favorite chair.

She watched, moving uneasily, unspeaking, bending to hug him, and moving to the door. This awkward physical closeness at leaving was unusual, and not typical in the family. It was a simulation, an allusion, a gesture to what might have been.

"Thanks for coming, you guys." His voice had some emotion, a rare gift to them in these mordant days.

"We are happy we could come and glad we could be here."

He had been unable, while visiting home, to penetrate the fog of everyday chat, the binding talk about now dead relatives and their survivors, the bustle of meal preparation, planning, and deciding, and listening to nurses, doctors, therapists, and clerks. He had done practical things—bought a socket for a three-pronged plug, medicines, and a heating pad, fixed the screen door; shopped for groceries.

He sought a nonexistent clarity and intensity, a factual exchange, or man to-man talk. They had tried; sparred with a direct conversation when they were alone 2 days previously in the hospital. His dad sat by the window and said, "I think they [the drs.] think I'm going to die." He was asking for something. I had said, "Well, that's their job, Dad, they speculate about life and death" And then, thinking of himself, he asked his dad if a priest had come to see him, or if he wanted a priest to come. "I haven't been to church in years."

[I had successfully changed the subject or had he? I think he wanted me to tell him that he was going to be alright. But he is going to die, perhaps shortly.]

Now, he put his head down, shifted, looked at his feet and at the luggage he had brought into the room, and bent over. He grabbed two and lunged out the door, banging the heavy wooden screen. He made another trip from the living room to the car. He got in and as he did, suddenly, the trip to the airport commanded his attention. He did not look up, back or sideways, or at the house as he reversed the car down the drive, cut the wheel to his left, and put the car in first gear. It spilt the trees on the maple-coffined street.

SECOND THOUGHTS:
A PHONE CALL

After my visit to dad, I wrote eight loosely connected pages about the experience. It was an unsatisfying intellectualized catharsis. I buried it somewhere on a disc. I was struck while writing by the paucity of meaningful communication during 3 days of virtually constant nonconversation. I concluded as others had that people die much as they lived.

At 9 p.m. on a Thursday spring night, I answered the upstairs phone. The caller introduced herself as my father's doctor. She had called to explain that my dad was in the hospital, the result of a chronic, incurable blood disease that had "blasted" in the previous 24 hours. She carefully explained the dynamics of kidney and pulmonary function and their relationships to the heart and blood pressure. I recalled teaching medical students for 25 years, discussing "Focal problems" on congestive heart problems, high blood pressure, and kidney malfunction, the dynamics of left-right congestive heart failure, and the ethics of treatment. I struggled, trying to think medically, gather and analyze the facts, and thereby understand his present condition. I wanted to penetrate the emotion and uncover the bare bones of the matter.

"It sounds to me as if I'd better come out there."

"Yes, I think so if you can."

Monday morning, now in Oregon, we visited the hospital to see him. In the following 3 days we went several times, each time finding my father surprised and pleased to see us.

My brother said, "We didn't tell him you were coming. We thought he'd think he was dying if we told him you were coming out!" This was said over a huge Chinese meal in the afternoon after our first hospital visit. The detritus, shells and claws of a gutted lobster, lay unceremoniously on the table.

After he had spent 6 days in the hospital, we made arrangements for hospital equipment to be delivered, drove together to the hospital, and brought him home in my brother's van.

That night, we had something like the last supper, which he ate happily while we watched. We perched on chairs, eating off TV trays as we had in the late 'fifties.

FRAGMENTS

Death stories, of course, vary in content, form, and style. Death narratives are shaped by the sociocultural era in which death is experienced. In postindustrial societies, death disappears, is concealed in new spaces, symbolized rather than visible, and even more rationalized than the ceremonial practices of preindustrial societies.

In a postmortem world, one has glimpses of, windows into, death and dying, rather than direct experiences. Windows are a function of standpoint: They display perspectives and angles of vision. Here is a series of windows.

Windows

Literary. Tolstoy's "The Death of Ivan Ilyich" was mentioned by Arthur Frank in a moving presentation on chronic disease and dying this summer. Because Ivan Ilyich fails to grasp the meaning or meaninglessness of his life, he also denies the imminence of his impending death. He cries out before he dies, "So that's what it is!" Recognition strikes. Death so easily shifts one's attention, Tolstoy notes, to the complacent acceptance of the fact that it is the other who is dead or dying, not I. We live with the fact of our ultimate death, even as it is an unacceptable thought. But the fear and trembling go on apace.

Family Ties. My youngest daughter, an MD, traveled West and reported back without medical details that Grandpa was "doing fine." My son, Sean Peter, and his fiancee reported after driving up the coast from San Francisco that he was doing well, "Really, Dad, much better than I . . . He went out to eat with us . . . and we all went over to the Mannings and ate Chinese food." A friend, Wye, says flatly to me at night after hearing my worries about my feelings of powerlessness and being unable to help my Dad: "There is nothing you can do. There is nothing you can do." I explain to my silent son at lunch about my insurance, my growing retirement fund, and my joint agreements with Wye. "I don't even know if my father has a will." After about 10 minutes of this obsessional talk, S. P. quietly asks, "Are you telling me this because you are worried about Grandpa, Dad?"

Pragmatism. I am on the phone with my mother encouraged by several beers. She says merrily "I should go get him; he will wonder who I have been talking to for so long . . . !" She puts down the phone and goes to ask him to walk over to the phone. I wait, hearing distant disturbing background noises. I hear a cry, nearly a scream, from the distant reaches of the house, from another room, and I wait. Soon she comes on the phone and says "I'll have to call you back, your Dad fell." She hangs up. She calls back 15 minutes later to say he fell rising from a chair, the chair collapsed on him, and he is hurt. I infer from her tone of voice that the fall is serious and doubtless painful. A neighbor, a nurse, came over, she says, and helped her pick him up and bandage him. Meaning comes in the completion of the attitude: The following morning I bought a cellular phone, tested it, repacked it, and mailed it to them. That was something I could do.

These windows or fragments are only tacitly connected by the narrator's string. They reveal quite different facets of the ongoing drama of death. They take the form of ill-shaped vignettes containing family conversations, medical diagnoses, psychological defenses, especially denial and reaction formation, emotional distress, and bits of personal history. They do not, it seems to me, "add up," or communicate a fully connected story. They fail to connect me solidly with the past, but make the past problematic. Yet, the past colors the future and the here and now. The stories do not recoat social bonds and renew moral obligations because they are made obscure by being cast in varying perspectives.

STORIES

What is the story here? Is there a story here? Does the study of everyday life enable one to weave a narrative tapestry?

Clearly, Americans share little consensus on death's meaning—the loss of the "great narratives" of religion and progress, the vast mobility of families, the enormous impact of the visual on our own sense of lived experience, the deterioration of courtesy and rituals in American life, the commodification and commercialization of death, the pervasive presence of images of death in all forms of visual entertainment, and the display of entertaining, crime-related, often adventitious death on television news and feature programs, must serve to wither our sensibilities. Perhaps the rise of the visual contributes to transformations of experiences of death and the dying into abstractions and simulations.

This transformation of experience is one concrete translation of how hyperreality is mingled with everyday life.

Tolstoy's brilliant story, "The Death of Ivan Ilyich" (1960), is told from Ilyich's perspective (even though an unknown narrator—Tolstoy?—recounts it in the third person). The unity of the experience, emerging as Ilyich accepts the emptiness of his life, is in fact a literary construction. Death happens on the pages. Ilyich, in a sense, is too close to his own experiences, his now past life, to fully understand it.

In the same sense, the field-worker may "overlook" the realities of intimate others. Certainly, we imagine death. But our images vary, shaped by dreams, collective memories, stories, I can imagine death, but my repertoire of images has little value to me because they lack detailed, reciprocated contexts.

Writing this is revelatory. I know precious little about what my dad thinks, feels, or imagines about his own imminent dying, or for that matter, how he might sum up life.

[How shall I arrange this thought iconically? What spacing, what fonts, what margins shall I use?]

As I have done most of my life, or at least since I was 4 or 5, I seek to mentally construct the various possibilities that "death" means to him. I write myself here. I try to fill in the visible spaces, the conversational gaps, and the missing words, letters, and calls. I substitute for the absent. And this is one root of sadness. But the spots of which I am aware and "fill" may be a product of my own blindness. One is severely limited in trying to do fieldwork among one's family or even in similar family systems. The self-as-field tool is compromised, made problematic, when the self one sees is reflected by intimate others who share historic and collective bonds. One lives at least in part in the web of others, but not always in their thoughts and feelings. Conversely, old ties and feelings produce important traces in the text. They cling to materials based on the accumulation of memory and its hidden tricks. My immediate family, all college-educated, including several attorneys and doctors, an MA, and a couple of PhDs, developed no shared discourse around his dying, only a network of exchanges and weak speculations.

Abstract thinking, distancing oneself from the messiness of everyday life, under these conditions may have modest value. Concepts like "illness" and "disease" suggest the mind-body problem, and the limits of linguistic constructions of change. Disease works structurally and functionally, while illness works phenomenologically. The network of roles and statuses that form a family are but the fragile infrastructure for potentially rich, dense, spatially located interactions. Illness, as both a consequence and antecedent of such familial interactions, may provide little understanding of past experience. What turning points in an "illness career" arise when multiple unconnected stories fail to converge? The value of therapeutic stories is certainly incontestable, and telling one is incontrovertibly valuable. Perhaps the limiting cases, the "outliers," also illuminate the claims of the narrativists and those trying to reconstitute modern life.

EPILOGUE

The phone rings, and at first I fail to hear it. It seems to be ringing in a dream. It rings again a few minutes later and I reach over and switch off the bell on the side of the phone. I decide to answer it. My brother is on the phone. He reports that the doctors tell them that it looks bleak. "He's a pretty sick guy," said the renal specialist. I listen half asleep and preoccupied with the evening's vicissitudes.

My mother calls the following day and cheerfully reports improvements.

Meanwhile, I have left messages on several answering machines, hoping for a response and some news of my dad.

My daughter Kathleen, visiting her grandparents with a new grandchild, calls me on my sister-in-law's cellular phone. She is calling from just outside the intensive care unit. Kathleen gives me a succinct medical status report. It is doubly rewarding because it is a factual summary from someone I love and who loves me. I trust her judgment. "He is better." she says.

He goes home in a day or so.

That Wednesday night, I slept restlessly and then awoke, a 55-year-old white male in good physical condition, reporting chest pains. I am sweating. I feel a damp patch on the left side of my forehead and turn onto my back and stare hopefully at the white ceiling. The green vines painted on the far wall glow green in the dim light. I am a bit short of breath, so I reach for the Proventil and take a couple of quick hits. Closing my eyes, flooded with thought, he lays there. (David Lodge, in *Therapy* [1995], claims that all narratives happen "now." Lodge is playing on framing conventions. This was then, this writing is now. Your reading is in the future? Isn't it?).

REFLECTIONS

This fragment is my story about how sociology illuminates everyday life. Only I possess this story, for I have no first- or second-person narrative available in which to recast its meaning. Who and what is the story about?

It seems to me that the bias of symbolic interactionism in respect to elevating the importance of the verbal, and seeing rational discourse as a source of significant symbols, is misleading if we are to understand the expressive and the unspoken, what Goffman (1959) called the "given off." (Of course, sometimes these cues are not "given" at all). Silences communicate, too. Silence was often my father's way of communicating. Symbolic interactionism presumes correctly that relationships develop via language. However, the salience of language, symbols, and discourse in relations are "variables," not constants. Meaning arises from communication about what is not verbally communicated.

Social distance and abstraction vary in this essay, as indicated by changes in the literary voice (Hertz, 1997). The distance from the events displayed in my writing is often inversely related to the intensity of my feelings. My feelings are encoded. Under what conditions does affective intensity develop from words? "Don't speak unless spoken to" is a child's rule in Protestant families. Does differentiated social structure produce refined emotional language? In America, the flight and perhaps extrusion of the ambitious from the home, their use of professional jargon and trendy abstractions, and the marginalization of the favored child as he or she succeeds, create social distance. The corrosive effects of American individualism are played out repeatedly in death scenes. They are not inscribed and embodied scenes, narratives encapsulating lengthy and deep family histories; they are glimpses of death. Can we see ourselves seeing ourselves and others die?[3]

NOTES

1. Reprinted with permission of Human Sciences Press, Inc. (1997).

2. *Editor's note.* Manning tries to convey, as best I can fathom, "voice" by means of spacing conventions, fonts, and margins. I discern a possible postmortem fragmentation being signaled in this awkward fashion, but as there would be no self to animate such meaning, this is probably not tenable. I guess I should raise my voice. If he had a self, and was trying to convey voice via these means, I suggest the reader attend to these analytic distinctions:

- Description—the "my father is dying" story—uses extracted text to set it apart.

- "Private author's thoughts" (how can they be private if he publishes them here?) are set in brackets.

- The occasional ambivalent writer's notes to the writer, the editor, the typesetter, or the proofreader are set in parentheses.

Fortunately, unlike Lodge, he does not tell us the result of each search for a word in the dictionary! Q.E.D.

3. On the night of December 2, 1966, in a cold, dripping penetrating Oregon rain, my father swung his feet onto the floor in the bedroom and walked, shaking with arrythmias, to my brother's waiting van. He was taken by my mother and brother to the hospital where he died the next morning. They cremated him. I flew out with my son for a sterile ceremony. No tears, no hugs, little drinking—just a few polite cliches and a couple of stand-up meals with the television on. His silence still speaks to me.

REFERENCES

Berger, P., & Kellner, H. (1970). The social construction of marriage. In H. P. Dreitzel (Ed.), *Recent developments in ethnomethodology.* New York: MacMillan.

Cullum-Swan, B., & Manning, P. K. (1998). Narrative discourses. In *Cultural studies.* Greenwich: JAI.

Goffman, E. (1959). *The presentation of self in everyday life.* Garden City, NY: Doubleday Anchor.

Hertz, R. (1997). *Reflexivity and voice.* Thousand Oaks, CA: Sage.

Lodge, D. (1995). *Therapy.* New York: Penguin.

Tolstoy, L. (1960). *The death of Ivan Ilyich and other stories* (R. Edmonds, Trans). New York: Penguin.

Vaughan, D. (1984). *Uncoupling.* New York: Random House.

PART **III**

Interior Spaces

CHAPTER 12

The Pleasures of Slowness

DAVID SILVERMAN

> *The degree of speed is directly proportional to the intensity of forgetting.*
> —Kundera (1996, p. 114)

Imagine an English movie of the 1940s: perhaps two lovers saying fond farewells in clipped upper-class accents, or, better still, two English gentlemen wearing bowler hats and pin-striped business suits (and carrying the compulsory rolled umbrellas) ignoring the clouds of war to chat about the latest cricket scores.

In both cases, the backdrop is a railway station. For some reason, in the 1940s, train journeys were synonymous with romance. Romance, as often as not, was not about the love of two people but about the love of a game.

Just after World War II, Dudley Carew (1950) wrote about the romance of a railway journey from London to Brighton to watch the south coast county Sussex play cricket:

> It did not need arrival at the ground and the sight of Sussex men batting or bowling to release the springs of enjoyment—it was enough to be at Victoria, to be taking a place on the Brighton Belle with its glass-covered tables, its Schweppes menu cards, its raffish collection of passengers. Sometimes the races would be on, but, even when they were not, a kind of genial, book-makerishness pervaded those glassy, tinkling pullmans. Whiskies-and-sodas were ordered at an impossibly early hour while, on the arrival platforms, hordes of office workers were streaming in to spend the June day with files and artificial light. Holiday was always aboard the Brighton Belle,

holiday with too much makeup and a hat tilted at a tipsy angle, but holiday unabashed and determined to make the most of its time. The cricket might be serious enough on Sussex grounds but there is about the game, whenever Sussex play it, the faint suggestion of sand-shoes, of a breeze off the sea, and of people inordinately enjoying themselves. (pp. 35-36)

Carew has caught something of cricket's appeal to the English. The ingredients are romance and humor but also a wackiness able to unite in pleasure everyone from the staid bank manager to the overly made-up floozy.

In 1948, the chronicler of English cricket, Neville Cardus, captured this in an essay titled "The Most Fascinating Game in the World." Cardus (1985) wrote,

Other games are as exciting, more dynamic, and as skilful as cricket. No game is richer in humour and fellow-feeling. That is why, I suggest, cricket wins the favour of most Englishmen and of many who are not English. For we are the world's most humorous people. We "give and take." . . . Other games, I say, can vie with cricket for cleverness, sensation, beauty. None is more capricious in its rapid reversals of fortune, none is more revealing of character—it lasts so long, the "exposure" is continuous for hours—none more picturesque, more elegantly poised, more liable to comic descents. None, in all the world, more English! (p. 15)

Allowing for Cardus's chauvinism ("we are the world's most humorous people. We 'give and take' "; Cardus, 1985, p. 15), he catches, like Carew, the essential "Englishness" of the game of cricket, or, rather, should I say, how cricket seems to fit familiar representations of Englishness. All that is missing is the London fog so beloved of Hollywood directors—regrettable, but then cricket is played in the English summer, which is more known for rain than fog.

I am not mainly concerned here with media representations, however. Like Cardus and Carew, I love cricket. Cardus (1985, p. 15) suggests one reason: "it lasts so long, the 'exposure' is continuous for hours."

To some of you, this reason for loving cricket may appear contrary if not bizarre. After all, we live in a world in which interest and excitement are linked to fast-moving "events." For example, motor racing in sport or, in television, think of the sated viewer with the remote control, forever zapping the buttons in search of a new, transitory pleasure.

Now compare this to a cricket game, which can last up to 5 days and involve 30 hours of play that often ends in a "draw." Surely, boredom rather than pleasure, one might believe, is the likely spectator's response to such apparently mind-boggling slowness.

This is not necessarily true, however. First, why should we assume that the only interesting things are over quickly? How much gratification do we really get from fast sport or fast food or fast sex? Second, why should we demand that our leisure activities should mirror the form of our working lives? Just because most of us spend the time from 9 to 5 rushing around at our jobs or studies (and perhaps the rest of our days rushing to work or to cook the meal or to spend "quality time" with our kids), does this mean that our free time should fit this pattern as well—even if, for most males, the rushing here is limited to the sport on TV while we lie on the couch with a beer?

Why must sport replicate society? If the world at the end of the millennium is a hyped-up, globalized, postmodern mess, does this mean that sport must take on these very features? Well, yes, of course it does if the sport in question is to have big audiences, big sponsorship, and to be big business.

Now I have to lay more of my cards on the table. Even cricket can be played in a hyped-up way. For instance, although the cricket I like is played in anonymous white clothing and lasts 4 or 5 days (including leisurely breaks for lunch and tea), some cricket is now played in colored outfits with (of all things) players names on their backs. To make matters worse, these games finish, with a guaranteed win for one team, in a mere 5 to 7 hours. Needless to say, the latter (debased!) form draws the large crowds. The cricket I like is played in near empty stadiums.

Of course, this is not surprising. Traditional cricket represents a society that is largely defunct. A society of country houses and cream teas on the lawn, of gentlemen and players, of "fair play," and so on. Indeed, it might be more accurate to say that this "traditional" society did not ever exist except as a set of representations. For instance, it is amusing to reflect that the archetype of traditional cricket, a large Victorian man with a beard called W. G. Grace, actually had little respect for the laws of the game and was mainly interested in a result in terms of a possible gambling coup.

Be that as it may, there is no doubt that the older version of cricket sits uncomfortably in a (post)modern world. Financially, it survives by drawing resources from the faster version of the game. Therefore, the kind of cricket I like is a minority interest in which the paying spectators are numbered in hundreds. Again, however, why should we assume that the only good things are popular?

Of course, we all know that there is nothing that the English like more than standing in line. Whatever is available at the line's end, they assume that, if a lot of people want it, it must be good. In the same way, people all over the world seem to be attracted by crowds. It is, I sense, that a person believes that a mass of humanity at the spot where one is standing confirms that one is in the right place.

Is there anything for you to learn from my (reported) idiosyncratic tastes, however? In particular, how can a taste for slow, minority activities relate to sociology?

After all, you might think, a lot of sociology wants to explain what people share in common by appealing to social structures that organize us into various collectivities: groups, genders, classes, and so on. Moreover, in the thriving sociology of culture, the focus is usually on popular cultural products (soap operas, chat shows, tabloid magazines, etc.). By contrast, minority interests (especially of the "highbrow" kind) are ignored or despised.

SOCIOLOGY AND NARRATIVE

The world narrated to us by the mass media demands immediate gratification in the form of simple narratives containing exciting "incidents." More specifically, Princess Diana's death held most of us enthralled by presenting images of simple contrasts between "good" (Diana herself) and "evil" (the press "ratpack"). In the O. J. Simpson and the British nanny trials, the same contrasts were present, although the distribution of good and evil was more contested. In this respect, we are talking about how all these events were understood as "fairy tales."

An obscure Russian book, written in 1928, gives us a deeper means of understanding this concept. V. I. Propp's study, *The Morphology of the Folktale* (1968), argues that fairy tales establish a narrative form that is central to all storytelling. The fairy tale is structured not by the nature of the characters that appear in it but by the function they play in the plot. Despite its great detail and many characters, Propp suggests that "the number of functions is extremely small" (p. 20). This allows him to attend to a favorite distinction of structuralists between appearances (massive detail and complexity) and reality (a simple underlying structure repeated in different ways).

Propp (1968) suggests that fairy tales in many cultures share similar themes, for example, "a dragon kidnaps the king's daughter." These themes can be broken into four elements, each of which can be replaced without altering the basic structure of the story. This is because each element has a certain function. This is shown as follows:

"A Dragon Kidnaps the King's Daughter"[a]

Element	Function	Replacement
Dragon	Evil force	Witch
King	Ruler	Chief
Daughter	Loved one	Wife
Kidnap	Disappearance	Vanish

a. Example adapted from Culler (1976, pp. 207-208)

Following the previous example, we could rewrite "A dragon kidnaps the king's daughter" as "A witch makes the chief's wife vanish" while retaining the same function of each element. Thus, a function can be taken by many different roles. This is because the function of a role arises in its significance for the structure of the tale as a whole.

Using a group of 100 tales, Propp (1968) isolates 31 functions (actions such as "prohibition," "violation," or, as previously mentioned, "disappearance"). These functions are played out in seven "spheres of action": the villain, the provider, the helper, the princess and her father, the despatcher, the hero, and the false hero.

Such functions and spheres of action constitute an ordered set. Their presence or absence in any particular tale allows their plots to be classified. Thus, plots take the following forms:

1. Development through struggle and victory

2. Development through the accomplishment of a difficult task

3. Development through both Nos. 1 and 2

4. Development through neither Nos. 1 nor 2

Thus, although any one character may be involved in any sphere of action, and several characters may be involved in the same sphere, we are dealing with a finite sequence: "The important thing is to notice the number of spheres of action occurring in the fairy tale is infinite: We are dealing with discernible and repeated structures" (Hawkes, 1977, p. 69).

Why this excursion into obscure literary theory? First, think back to a recent popular movie that you saw—for example, a thriller such as *LA Confidential*. How different was it from other detective movies you have seen? Didn't they all share the forms of development and spheres of action that Propp (1968) describes? This is why Propp's ideas are not so obscure.

Second, once we become aware of the discernible and repeated structures in popular narratives, something may or may not happen to our own cultural tastes. Growing awareness of the source of our addiction to, for example, soap operas or Oprah Winfrey may have as little impact as knowing why we are addicted to, for example, nicotine or alcohol. We simply crave another fix—the last Oprah is never enough. Alternatively, we bore of the endless (Proppian) repetition of so many popular cultural products and reach out for something different.

Compare the trite story line of *LA Confidential* (the usual closing shootout and the happy ending) with the surprises of the Coen Brothers' *Fargo* (a pregnant woman as sheriff). Think of how *Fargo* slows down its narrative by detailing the mundane lives of both sheriff and criminals in a small town quite unlike the usual big-city setting of such movies. Also, consider the positively ethnographic pursuit of the "boring" features of the world in Bertrand Tavernier's *L327,* a police story almost without arrests or car chases but with a strong focus on the routines of police work as we see Parisian drug cops spending most of the time sitting in their offices, "cooking" their official reports.

Such movies require a certain discipline from their audience just as scientific work is, in a dual sense, disciplinary. Therefore, the social scientist, like the moviegoer at a Coen Brothers or Tavernier film, must forgo the temptation to seek the instant gratifications trumpeted all around. This does not mean, however, that such movies are completely idiosyncratic or without form.

The pianist and music critic Charles Rosen (1976) tells us that classical composers at the end of the eighteenth century were able to develop their own identities and surprise their audiences by both respecting and playing with musical form. Similarly, directors such as Tavernier and the Coen Brothers delight their small audiences by the way they play with cinematic forms.

Necessarily, such films are for a minority. They are often slow and demand close attention to appreciate their artistry. Most people want something different: the quick fix of the familiar, the excitement of the car chase, or the satisfaction of the ending when all the pieces are tied together.

Of course, the distinction I have drawn between popular and minority storytelling is not always so clear. For instance, in a British TV detective series called *Inspector Morse,* I enjoy the attention it gives to the everyday incidents in Morse's life at work and at leisure. Unfortunately for me, after a little while, yet another murder is shown and the viewer is invited to follow the relentless pursuit of the murderer. At this point, *Morse* becomes like any other detective story and I lose interest.

So there we have it: endless repetition of the same that gives addicts what they think is "action" or, if we are prepared not to be frightened by slowness, the possibility of using our eyes and our brain to derive pleasure from observing a skillful play with the forms of cinematic representation.

THE RELATIVIST TRAP

In the prevailing cultural world, the very idea that any activity is "better" than any other is depicted as elitist, and slow, rule-governed activities give way to instant gratification. Therefore, in a sense, anything goes, just as Jeremy Bentham, the English utilitarian philosopher of the eighteenth century, once remarked about the contemporary form of bowling: Pushpin is as good as poetry.

Bentham's relativism extends today beyond contemporary media researchers and into much qualitative sociology. This is particularly the case in which the cry of "anything goes" leads to a total rejection of any appeal to "facts" or even "evidence." Just as cinema, music, and even cricket need their structures and rules, so does social science.

Unfortunately, anything goes has become a positive virtue in the eyes of many sociologists. A whole army of postmodern anthropologists (Clifford & Marcus, 1986) focus on narrative to deconstruct the subjects and objects of the field-worker's gaze. Such deconstruction sometimes leads to playful experiments in writing sociology, from the construction of social science texts as dialogues (Woolgar, 1988) to even replacing sober scientific papers by poetry(Richardson, 1994).

In part, my worries about these ploys relate to the image that we present to the world. A focus on the narrative construction of our texts may be an emancipating activity. When carried on too much or too far, however, it is difficult to resist outside critics who accuse sociology of navel-gazing and, thereby, producing the conditions for a dialogue of the deaf between itself and the community (Silverman, 1993, Chap. 8).

This is not meant to indicate that I want to downgrade the issues that arise from the narrative organization of social science texts. Rather, it expresses my sense that perhaps the reflexive card is now being played too regularly in the social sciences.

ON USING OUR EYES

Contemporary mores not only affect the place of rigor in scientific research but also influence matters of more specific sociological interest regarding how we use our eyes. In societies in which television is central to leisure, there are grounds to believe that, somewhat ironically, we have become lazy with our eyes. Thus, what we see is taken for granted and we tend to associate social research with what we can read (texts and statistics) or hear (usually what interview respondents say).

In this context, observation becomes a somewhat neglected art. Like the TV sports fan who, to judge from TV coverage, is less interested in the game than in prematch and postmatch team interviews, in sociology we are reluctant to use our eyes.

The ethnographic work that originated in the 1930s in the sociology department of the University of Chicago, however, tried to teach us something different. This work represented the first flowering of an empirical school of sociology concerned with observing what it termed the "subcultures" to be found in the buildings and the streets of the modern city and encouraging detailed, careful observation (Hammersley, 1989).

In the 1960s, despite taking a different theoretical tack, the ethnomethodologist Harvey Sacks found much to admire in the Chicago School's attention to detail. As he commented in one lecture (Sacks, 1992a), transcribed at the time,

Instead of pushing aside the older ethnographic work in sociology, I would treat it
as the only work worth criticizing in sociology; where criticizing is giving some
dignity to something. So, for example, the relevance of the works of the Chicago
sociologists is that they do contain a lot of information about this and that. And
this-and-that is what the world is made up of. (p. 27)

Like the older ethnographers, Sacks rejected the crass empiricism of certain
kinds of quantitative sociology, in particular, its assumptions that research is
based on finding some indices and explaining why they rise and fall by ex post
facto interpretations of significant correlations.

Sacks was convinced that serious work paid attention to detail and that, if
something mattered, it should be observable. For instance, in a fascinating
passage, Sacks noted the baleful influence on sociology of G. H. Mead's (1934)
proposal that we need to study things that are not available to observation—for
example, "society" and "attitudes." Sacks (1992a) comments,

But social activities are observable, you can see them all around you, and you can
write them down. The tape recorder is important, but a lot of this can be done without
a tape recorder. If you think you can see it, that means we can build an observational
study. (p. 28)

For Sacks, "observational study" meant putting on one side everyday assumptions of where "reality" is to be found. For instance, a popular activity in
everyday life is to wonder about people's motives. Indeed, in the case of talk
shows, the motives of the rich, famous, or just plain unlucky or deviant become
a central topic. In many respects, however, social science has picked up this
habit, taking as its task the revelation of other people's "motives" and "experiences." Elsewhere, I have noted this "Romantic" tendency in social science
(Atkinson & Silverman, 1997; Silverman, 1993).

Even in the 1960s, Sacks seemed fully aware of these issues. His kind of
social science always turned away from the insides of people's heads and toward
their observable activities. In this sense, Sacks was a self-proclaimed behaviorist who announced that his task was to elucidate how members (of society) did
whatever they did. He (1992a) stated,

For Members, activities are observables. They see activities. They see persons doing
intimacy, they see persons lying, etc. . . . And that poses for us the task of being
behaviorists in this sense: finding how it is that people can produce sets of actions
that provide that others can see such things. (p. 119)

As examples of such "sets of actions," Sacks offers "describing" and "questioning." These are interesting examples because each may be seen to be a resource
for social scientists—for example, ethnographers describe cultures and ques-

tion informants. Sacks wants to make both activities a topic, however, by examining them as forms of behavior that, through some methods awaiting inspection, are produced and recognized.

SACKS, CRICKET, AND MOVIES: IN SEARCH OF AN AESTHETIC

It seems to me that Sacks offers us a distinct aesthetic that inspires a range of contemporary social science extending beyond conversation analysis. Elsewhere, I have discussed some aspects of a contemporary aesthetic for qualitative research (Silverman, 1997). Here, I emphasize those parts of that aesthetic that, I believe, we owe to Harvey Sacks and link that aesthetic with the pleasures I derive from cricket and (certain) movies.

On Slowness

Milan Kundera's novel *Slowness* (1996) reminds us of a world that demands immediate gratification in the form of simple narratives containing exciting incidents. It has no time to gaze around, no desire to take pleasure in the unremarkable, and no ability to view without background sounds or to listen without distracting images. No time for cricket! Speed is all.

Like Kundera, Sacks speaks to us about the pleasures of slowness. He adopts what he calls "a counterstrategy" of choosing specifically uninteresting data (Sacks, 1992a, p. 293). In this way, he set out to try to make the unremarkable remarkable by "picking up things which are so overwhelmingly true that if we are to understand that sector of the world, they are something we will have to come to terms with" (Sacks, 1987, p. 56).

None of this, however, required indecent haste or overrapid elaboration of large claims. Indeed, Sacks (1992a) warned his students against worrying about the speed with which people do things:

> Don't worry about how fast they're thinking. First of all, don't worry about whether they're "thinking." Just try to come to terms with how it is that the thing comes off. Because you'll find that they can do these things. Just take any other area of natural science and see, for example, how fast molecules do things. And they don't have very good brains. So just let the materials fall as they may. (p. 11)

Sacks's preparedness to celebrate the natural sciences' study of molecules as a model for social science still has the power to shock contemporary Romanticists—perhaps in the same way as beginning sociology students are even today shocked by Emile Durkheim's (1982) nineteenth-century injunction to treat "social facts" as "things." In both cases, I believe, the sense of shock derives from the profoundly Romantic turn of contemporary cultural representations.

The kitsch world of the chat show (and the Romantic sociologist) depends on the valorization of "personal experience." In this context, Sacks's (1992b) observation that experiences are "carefully regulated sorts of things" (p. 248) comes as a shock. As Sacks shows, however, you are indeed only entitled to have certain experiences. For instance, on being told about someone's good experience, you can be "pleased for her" but there are sharp limits on how good you can feel about it and even sharper limits on the good feeling you can give to a third party with the story (p. 244).

On Smallness

Pursue truth, not rarity. The atypical can fend for itself. . . . And very often, when we are looking over several common truths, holding them next to one another in an effort to feel again what makes them true, rarities will mysteriously germinate in the charged space between them.

—Baker (1996, p. 24)

For Sacks, like the essayist Nicholson Baker, rarity was never the point. The mysterious germination of rarities out of the familiar to which Baker refers is matched by Schegloff's observation that, in Sacks's work, "previously unsuspected details were critical resources in [seeing] what was getting done in and by the talk" (Schegloff as quoted in Sacks, 1992a, p. xviii).

Sacks (1992a) rejected "the notion that you could tell right off whether something was important" (p. 28). He uses the case of biology to show how the study of an apparently minor object ("one bacterium") can revolutionize our knowledge. Why assume, for instance, you need to look at states and revolutions, when "it's possible that some object, for example proverbs, may give an enormous understanding of the way humans do things and the kinds of objects they use to construct and order their affairs" (p. 28).

Sacks was able to show us these things because of what, I believe, was his profoundly anti-Romantic aesthetic preference. When wedded to slow (and careful) pursuit of (apparently) small objects, described with clarity, I suggest that Sacks offers an inspiring path for any contemporary social science that is prepared to take a step away from the powerful messages provided by the prevailing representations of our time (Silverman, 1998).

CONCLUDING REMARKS

In the spirit of this book, I have been attempting to make some links between my personal tastes and the aesthetics of social science. Therefore, we have traveled a long way from my initial observations on cricket. The railway line from London to Brighton, mentioned earlier, has indeed taken a very circuitous route.

Of course, I have inevitably provided you with a rationalization of what may just be my own prejudices. In this sense, like any societal member, faced with some outcome, I have "rewritten history" to appear sensible (Garfinkel, 1967).

I will have achieved my purpose, however, if you are encouraged to think anew about the merits of a sociology that is not afraid to tackle "small" objects in a disciplined way, or, in the realm of your own leisure activities, if you think more about why you need fast-moving narratives or "authentic" personal accounts.

REFERENCES

Atkinson, P., & Silverman, D. (1997). Kundera's *Immortality*: The interview society and the invention of the self. *Qualitative Inquiry, 3*(3), 304-325.

Baker, N. (1996). *The size of thoughts*. London: Chatto.

Cardus, N. (1985). *A Cardus for all seasons* (M. Hughes, Ed.). London: Souvenir.

Carew, D. (1950). *To the wicket*. London: Chapman & Hall.

Clifford, J., & Marcus, G. E. (Eds.). (1986). *Writing ethnography: The poetics and politics of ethnography*. Berkeley: University of California Press.

Culler, J. (1976). *Saussure*. London: Fontana.

Durkheim, E. (1982). *Rules of sociological method* (W. D. Halls, Trans.). London: Macmillan.

Garfinkel, S. (1967). *Studies in ethnomethodology*. Englewood Cliffs, NJ: Prentice Hall.

Hammersley, M. (1989). *The dilemma of qualitative method: Herbert Blumer and the Chicago tradition*. Routledge: London.

Hawkes, T. (1977). *Structuralism and semiotics*. London: Methuen.

Kundera, M. (1996). *Slowness* (L. Asher, Trans.). London: Faber & Faber.

Mead, G. H. (1934). *Mind, self and society*. Chicago: University of Chicago Press.

Propp, V. I. (1968). *Morphology of the folktale* (L. A. Wagner, Ed.; 2nd rev. ed.). Austin: University of Texas Press.

Richardson, L. (1994). Nine poems: Marriage and the family. *Journal of Contemporary Ethnography, 23*, 3-13.

Rosen, C. (1976). *The Romantic style: Haydn, Beethoven, Mozart*. London: Faber & Faber.

Sacks, H. (1987). On the preferences for agreement and contiguity in sequences in conversation. In G. Button & J. R. E. Lee (Eds.), *Talk and social organization* (pp. 54-69). Philadelphia: Multilingual Matters. [From a lecture by H. Sacks (1970), edited by E. Schegloff]

Sacks, H. (with an Introduction by E. Schegloff). (1992a). *Lectures on conversation* (G. Jefferson, Ed.; Vol. 1). Blackwell: Oxford, UK.

Sacks, H. (with an Introduction by E. Schegloff). (1992b). *Lectures on conversation* (G. Jefferson, Ed.; Vol. 2). Blackwell: Oxford, UK.

Silverman, D. (1993). *Interpreting qualitative data: Methods for analysing talk, text and interaction.* London: Sage.

Silverman, D. (1998). *Harvey Sacks and conversation analysis.* Cambridge, MA: Polity.

Woolgar, S. (Ed.). (1988). *Knowledge and reflexivity.* London: Sage.

CHAPTER 13

It's Boring[1]
Notes on the Meanings
of Boredom in Everyday Life

PETER CONRAD

Boredom has long interested me. Reflecting on boredom stirs up several clear memories. As I child I remember complaining to my grandmother that I was bored, and she'd always answer (in German): "Take two little sticks and drum them on your belly." My parents often had friends over for Sunday luncheon and then sat around the table talking after the meal was done for what seemed like hours; why would anyone want to do such a boring thing when one could go out and play? As teenagers, we would hang out ruefully lamenting about the boredom of suburban life—there was nothing to do. As I got older, perhaps I was bored less, but I still thought about it.

In graduate school I read Colin Turnbull's (1961) enchanting book about the pygmies in the Ituri forest. These people lived, hunted, migrated, and (especially the men) sat around in the forest; their lives seemed calm and almost serene, yet I wondered, didn't they ever get bored? After all, by my standards, there is little to do in the forest and their life was simple yet repetitive. Was boredom part of their experience? I have taught in universities for 25 years and have frequently heard students grumble that a book, lecture, course, or professor was boring. What did students mean by saying something was boring? Or for

AUTHOR'S NOTE: My thanks to the students for sharing their boring experiences with me and to Phil Brown and Gary Alan Fine for comments on an earlier draft of this chapter.

that matter, what did my adolescent-aged children mean when we asked them to go hiking in the White Mountains and they responded, "We don't want to go hiking; it's too boring"?

What is this thing boredom? Being boring or bored? What might a sociologist make out of all this? I want to take the opportunity here to begin to explore the meaning of boredom in everyday life.

ON THE EMERGENCE OF BOREDOM

The idea of boredom emerged as a concept in the late eighteenth century. Surely people had experiences that are similar to what today we might call boredom, but the word first appeared in 1777 in the *Dictionnaire* of the French Academy (Peters, 1975). While boredom may be related to older concepts for alienation like *acedia* or *ennui,* it appeared late in English, without a certain etymological ancestry, and never shared the kind of rich spiritual or psychological connotations of *ennui* (Peters, 1975).

In her magisterial study of boredom through literature, Patricia Meyer Spacks (1995) traces the evolution of boredom into the modern notion with which we are now familiar. She suggests several factors may explain the increasing importance of boredom. In part, it is probably related to the development of the notion of leisure and the increase in what has been called leisure time; boredom is something more easily experienced when someone does not need to work all the time. Others have also recognized this connection to boredom (Brissett & Snow, 1993):

> The relative freedom from necessity, the growing reliance on consumer goods as a way of energizing ourselves, and the sense of liberation and emancipation felt by many Americans provide the conditions where boredom can so easily, and effortlessly, be experienced (p. 244)

Prior to modern times, according to Brissett and Snow (1993, p. 245), "mundane life was hard but not boring."

Boredom arose with the increasing emphasis on the individual, particularly the greater concentration on the self. This played itself out in several ways. "The intensification of concern with individual rights," including the right to happiness, led to more concern with boredom as an unpleasant state. The growing emphasis on the individual also encouraged paying more attention to one's subjective life, a greater focus on inner experiences, invoking all sorts of "feelings" including boredom (Specks, 1995). It seems likely that prior to increased leisure and affluence, it didn't much matter whether life was deemed interesting or boring. The importance of these kinds of distinctions may be a peculiarity of modern times.

Some evidence suggests that boredom is becoming a more common state in the twentieth century, or at least more writers have taken to commenting on it. Orrin Klapp (1986) argues that an increase in the use of the word boredom between 1931 and 1961 reflects an expansion of boredom in modern society. Other studies have suggested that a growing percentage of the population finds boredom a "great problem" in filling leisure time (Specks. 1995, p. 3). Numerous commentators have suggested that in some quarters at least, boredom is a significant problem at work (Fisher, 1993; Molstad, 1986).

WHAT IS BOREDOM?

We can think of numerous words that connote boredom: weariness, tedium, monotony, inattention, disinterest, dull, repetitive, and tiresome, to name just a few. Boredom can be defined more specifically as "an unpleasant, transient affective state in which the individual feels a pervasive lack of interest in and difficulty concentrating on the current activity" (Fisher, 1993, p. 396). Boredom is deemed a fundamentally negative subjective state where the individual experiences little interest in what is currently happening.

In our culture there are recognizable signs indicative of boredom, such as yawning or twiddling one's thumbs, along with more ambiguous signs, like daydreaming or turning one's attention to other tasks (e.g., doodling). These signs serve to signify one's boredom and relay the message to others.

There has been some sociological interest in the meaning of boredom, perhaps most notably in a recent thoughtful article by Brissett and Snow (1993). They conceptualize boredom as an interactional phenomenon directly connected to social rhythms:

> Boredom, in its most basic sense, is an experience of the absence of momentum or flow in a person's life. What is going on, and what the person is doing, seems to have lost impetus and life stands still. (p. 238)

They see boredom related to a disconnection from the future. Boredom thus occurs

> when what is going on has no, or too few, personally viable implications for the future of the bored person. Literally, boredom is the experience of "dead ending," of being someplace with nowhere to go, of being disengaged from the ebb and flow of human interaction. (pp. 240-241)

While Brissett and Snow's examination of boredom rightly contextualizes boredom in everyday life, it is not obvious that most people experience boredom as the absence of flow. Indeed, I wonder if many people actually experience momentum or flow as a regular feature of their life experience. Moreover, it is not clear to what degree forms of garden-variety boredom are related to "where the future isn't." If the meaning here is the immediate future, when this "boring" event or activity will pass, then Brissett and Snow are surely correct. But it may not be necessary to connect boredom to uncertain futures to understand its meaning.

Boredom is in part a function of social expectations. Spacks (1995) suggests that

> the category of boredom implies a set of expectations of the external world that apparently did not affect our remote predecessors. The detail of life in the distant past may sound boring to us; indeed, some may have imagined Eden as boring. Adam and Eve, before the Fall, found little occupation and no excitement. (p. 11)

It would be difficult to experience boredom unless we anticipated the possibility of something else. Psychoanalyst Otto Fenichel suggested boredom occurs when something expected doesn't occur and that "we have *the right to expect*" helpful stimulation from the social world (cited in Spacks, 1995, pp. 6-7). When this is not coming, in his view, we are "justifiably bored." While Fenichel sees this as resulting from an inherent "need for intense mental activity," it seems to me that boredom may be more situationally and culturally variable than Fenichel suggests. Boredom stems not from expectations rooted in our nature, but from failing to meet socially derived expectations.

Boredom is a social construction—an interpretive category that has common uses in everyday life. It is a term we use to describe a certain feeling of disinterest or our experience of a situation that is tedious. Thus, at the very least, it is a label we use to depict a feeling or situation that we find unpleasant or unrewarding. In our society, to call something boring attributes certain characteristics to it, at the same time discounting it or at least presenting it in a negative light. Boredom is an inclusive explanatory notion; boring has become an all-purpose term of disapproval, especially among the young. This is exemplified in the teenage appellation "bore-r-ring." Indeed, boring can be used as a powerful epithet. Who wants to meet a boring person, take a boring course, or read a boring book? In addition, boredom can be invoked as a vocabulary of motive, as in "I'm bored so I'm leaving" or "that was just too boring for me to do" (cf. Brissett & Snow, 1993). Whatever boredom is in our society, it has largely a negative designation.[2]

But boredom is also in the eye of the beholder. What may be boring to one person may be fascinating to another. Boredom is not a characteristic of an object, event, or person, but exists in the relationship between individuals and their interpretation of their experience. A baseball game may be an object of great interest to one, while being deadly boring to another. A chemistry course may be the epitome of boredom for some students, and a never-ending font of fascination for others. While there may be some activities that are nearly universally experienced as boring, this does not negate the insight that boredom is a relationship and is not intrinsic to any event or object.

Thus I believe that often when boredom is invoked as an explanation, it is a gloss. It describes only the endpoint, the interpretation of the situation. It is an indication that something is happening (or not happening) but says little of what that is. It doesn't tell us much about the event or object, or even what the person's evaluation of it might be. When someone declares, "it's boring" or "I'm bored," it may be useful to probe further. At the very least we can ask, what are you bored of or what is it that is boring? Or we might ask, what is really going on here; what is the term boring emblematic of in this situation? Simply depicting something as boring doesn't say very much.

To explore this notion of boredom further, I want to begin to unpack what is meant when boredom is invoked. I will use illustrations from my own experience and from 35 students who were asked to write about a recent boring experience and describe what was boring about it. As anyone who works in a university knows, students have well-developed "boredom detectors." While they sometimes may appear a bit cavalier in their designations, they often experience boredom as part of their college experience. As a caveat, I must say this is a most preliminary exploration of the meanings of boredom and as such presents only a sketch of the meaning of boredom in everyday life.

MEANINGS OF BOREDOM

If boredom is a gloss for what is going on, we need to look more closely at how people talk about boredom. Since I am relying largely on student responses for my investigation, the examples relate mostly to the students' immediate experience, including college courses and professors. While these surely do not exhaust boring situations, they allow us a certain window into boredom.

As a first cut, we can identify two meanings of boredom as experienced by students. Undoubtedly there are other meanings, but by focusing on these two we can begin to have some insight in what boring means in everyday life.

Boredom as Understimulation

When asked why they were bored, students' common response was there was "nothing to do":

Saturday afternoon when there is nothing on TV and I have no car to go anywhere with, I feel bored. I felt like I had nothing to do and no way to find something to do. (M, 19)

Of course, the claims of "nothing to do" didn't literally mean there was nothing one could do, only that there was nothing they wanted to do or that aroused their interest.

> One Friday night. There I was, I had my license, a car to drive, friends I could hang out with, yet there I was—bored. There was nothing peaking my interest on TV—I didn't feel like staying in either . . . simply had no interest in doing anything, but didn't want to sit there and do nothing. (F, 18)

On occasions, it seemed like they had done all they could in the situation and had nothing left to do, at least in terms of the tasks at hand.

> I was at the restaurant where I work late one afternoon waitressing and there was no one there. It was a rainy day and it appeared no one wanted to venture out. I had done all the prep work for the night shift and other little jobs—so there was nothing left to do. (F, 20)

Or that they had exhausted all their resources, and were left, again, with nothing to do.

> On an airplane [coming] home from Israel. . . . There was nothing to do after a movie, reading for hours, and listening to music. It was a really long plane ride (14 hours) and one will run out of things to do, eventually. (F, 19)

When people find themselves with "nothing to do" in a situation where they wish they had something to do—if only to occupy them enough so the time would seem to pass more quickly—the experience of boredom is likely. The absence of external stimulation when it is desired seems to engender boredom.

Sometimes, however, people can actually be involved in an activity and still feel bored. In this excerpt, a young man describes his boredom at the gym, a place he goes regularly:

> Sitting on the exercise bike yesterday, I felt like the 10 minutes that I was on it were actually 100; time just dripped by. The boredom I felt was immense, it made me feel edgy and gave me the urge to just go up off the bike and start my weights workout [I think I was bored because] the gym was empty. There was no visual or mental *stimulus* besides the *rote activity* of biking, I felt no stimulation. (M, 20)

Here it seems the immediate lack of stimulation, perhaps particularly interaction with others, led to his feeling bored. But lack of stimulation need not only be immediate, it can occur over long periods of time. Then the experience of boredom can become a regular feature of life.

My second semester of freshman year in college, I was extremely bored. For some reason, my course load just turned out to be too light. Even if I read every single article on reserve and took a whole week to write a paper, I never had enough to do . . . all of my friends had immense amounts of work and couldn't spend inordinate amounts of time with me. So besides boredom, I felt guilt that I wasn't doing work when they were. (F, 20)

The boredom attributed to too little to do made this young woman unhappy, so she remedied this with a more challenging workload the next semester.

The boredom described here is one of understimulation. For whatever reason, students experienced little stimulation from their social environs. This is clearly related to what they define as to "do," implicitly meaning what they would like to do.

As Fenichel noted, we come to expect stimulation from life. In particular, this takes the form of external stimulation, for it seems likely that internal stimulation (e.g., thoughts, imagination, and fantasy) could be available to all. One could blame the students for their own boredom; after all, there must be something that would stimulate them, or couldn't they be more imaginative, or why not go read a good book. Does the world really owe people stimulation? But this misses the point; understimulation is a situation that people frequently call boredom.

Boredom as Disconnection

As we encounter the everyday world, we continually engage and disengage in social interactions. When we are engaged, we feel interested and connected to the world around us. Sometimes disengagement is pleasant, as when we rest, relax, or just "chill out." But if the disengagement is a disconnection to what is going on, if the activity continues without our making a connection with it, we can feel bored.

For students, some course-related experiences are the quintessential boring situation. Some students said simply when they were not interested in a subject or because something was a "waste of time" they were bored. But "lack of interest" tells us little about the nature of boredom; it is unclear whether "lack of interest" or "waste of time" are causes or effects of feeling bored. There are of course things that are more or less interesting to different people, but the "intrinsic" interest of the subject does not by itself determine whether it will be deemed boring.

We can examine what the students say to identify some characteristics of situations that lead to feeling bored. Students reported boredom occurring while sitting in class and a professor was talking on a topic "that I have no knowledge about," "that had no point," "repeated what I already knew," or was "over my head." Too much or too little familiarity seem to make it difficult for students to connect to the interaction. This was amplified by some structural factors: large lecture classes, classes with no participation, and required courses. As one student noted: "I get extremely bored when I am in a class lecture, which is either repetitive or over my head . . . because I [cannot] connect with what is being discussed" (M, 20). Numerous students mentioned repetition as an aspect of boredom. What appears to students to be unnecessary repetition can lead to spacing out or disconnecting from the interaction. This listener feels they have already "got" it, so why stay engaged.

Disconnection can occur out of class as well. This student was in the library reading an assigned article for a class:

> The article discussed art forms and how they relate to optics. The feeling of boredom came after reading half-way through the article. . . . I can remember a feeling of frustration because I didn't feel confident that I was understanding the material. This feeling of not understanding the article made the boredom worse because it seemed such a waste of time. (F, 21)

The difficulty this young woman was having comprehending the article left her unconnected to her reading.

Students frequently blame teachers for "boring" classes. The one overwhelming characteristic they associate with boredom is the delivery of a lecture in a monotone voice. The lack of action makes it difficult for students to engage: "The professor never moved from his seat, spoke in a monotone voice, and seemed unaware (or uncaring) of this student's presence" (F, 22). Perhaps this is where disconnection and understimulation meet to create a particularly powerful sense of boredom. The lack of action is also reflected in students attributing boredom due to an absence of interaction or participation in classes.[3]

Disconnection can of course occur in other situations. A student wrote about his experience of boredom at a family gathering:

> At my mother's engagement party in a fairly fancy restaurant . . . We all sat in two tables and were there for at least 4-5 hours. It was boring because the conversation was repetitive and generally stupid . . . consisting primarily of where do you go to college, do you like it, and what is your major. It seemed endless, and at the end I felt I was replying [with] the same cliche answers. (M, 19)

We have all had such experiences, and worse, social occasions when the interaction seemed banal or repetitive or where we didn't know anyone and couldn't make interactive contact. There was just "nothing we could relate to"; or rather, a disconnection that we cannot name, and hence call boredom.

Several other sources of disconnection come to mind. One results from a "bad fit" between the individual and situation. A rock-only music lover at the opera or a nonsports fan at a baseball game might well experience boredom through an inability to connect. A second might be a lack of context; it takes a certain amount of knowledge and context to appreciate classical ballet or a game of cricket. Without these, engagement is difficult and boredom is likely. I experienced an extreme of this when at a professional meeting I attended a lecture that was entirely in French (which I don't understand), in a room I was unable to leave. There was no hope for connection in that situation, so for the hour I felt very bored.

CONCLUDING REMARKS

We have briefly examined some meanings of boredom, at least as articulated by students. What is clear is that "boringness" is not intrinsic to the object or event, but how it is experienced and attributed. Understimulation and disconnection can be pleasant if one wants to rest or meditate, but when not desired, they can be interpreted as boredom. There are factors that contribute to the likelihood of occasions being depicted as boring, such as repetition, lack of interaction, and minimal variation, but it seems that something else is a key trigger to becoming bored. These can be social, individual, or cultural.

Boredom has a temporal dimension and may be in part contingent on the social organization of time. Boredom may be more likely to occur in spaces where large blocks of time need to be filled. One is not often bored in 5 minutes, especially when one knows that something more stimulating or engaging will follow.[4] The experience of the slow passage of time, while perhaps also reflecting understimulation or disconnection, may result from the temporal structure of a situation. Situations that are particularly regular or stable—one's with little variety in action—can lack temporal oscillation and thus are more likely to be felt to be boring (Fine, 1990). Fine (1990) notes that an absence of temporal autonomy—a lack of control of temporal decision making or how to use time—in these situations can create a structure that amplifies the experience of boredom. Thus, boredom can be a function of the way time is socially organized and one's relation to it.

It is likely that individual characteristics such as mood, tiredness, previous experiences, personal interests, and the like also influence whether someone becomes bored in a particular situation. But even given these, it is the interpretation of situations that creates boredom. Sometimes a claim of boredom may serve to justify one's own withdrawal of attention and interaction. Other situational factors that we did not explore here, such as the inability to leave or ignore a situation, a kind of "entrapment," may well exacerbate feelings of boredom.

Boredom is sure to vary by cultural expectations. "Waiting" is often an occasion of potential boredom. By definition, waiting is referenced to the future until what one is waiting for arrives or one's turn comes. In waiting, there may seem to be "nothing going on" except the waiting, surely a recipe for boredom. But is this inherent to the situation? When I lived in Indonesia, people often had to wait for long stretches in the bank or in a government office; Americans would get bored and impatient with the waiting, while Indonesians would see it as something to be expected or as an opportunity to socialize.

One of the fundamental attributes of boredom may be misaligned expectations. It is possible that we would not be bored if we did not expect more from situations. In our society we expect stimulation and connections from certain situations and events and may feel bored when social occasions fall short of our expectations. These may be general expectations about social interactions, as well as specific expectations of college courses or forms of entertainment. Boredom is a failure of expectation. To reduce boredom, theoretically at least, one could just as well change one's expectations or interpretations of the situation or one's relationship to it. "Boringness" isn't out there; it is between there and us.

Fortunately, humans are not always stymied by boredom. We may complain about it, but many have learned ways of dealing with it. Adopting Hirschman's (1970) terms, we can choose exit or voice. By exit, we may learn how to deal with boredom by spacing out, engaging in other activities (from fantasy to doodling), moving into what Goffman called "aways," creating games to occupy oneself, leaving the situation, or any number of other ways of psychically or bodily leaving boredom behind. By voice, we challenge the sources of boredom individually or collectively, identify and grouse about it, or confront it directly. With boredom, exit seems the most common response. While it is always possible that some people relish the experience of boredom, most want to leave or change it.

Boredom may be a malaise of modernity, but in the pantheon of human problems it is a relatively minor irritation. It has become an "all-purpose index of dissatisfaction" (Specks, 1993, p. 249), a vocabulary of discontent, indicating a sort of alienation from the moment. It reminds us that the best we can do is endeavor to make our lives interesting.

NOTES

1. Reprinted with permission of Human Sciences Press, Inc. (1997).

2. While many have lamented boredom as a negative experience, the anthropologist Ralph Linton contended that "the human capacity for being bored, rather than man's social and natural needs, lies at the root of man's cultural advance" (quoted in Sparks, 1995, p. 2).

3. Students and others often lay blame on the object (e.g., teacher, book, movie, class, etc.) for boredom, but as I have tried to show the source of boredom is more complex. There is no guarantee that a more dynamic or less repetitive presentation would by itself eliminate boredom.

4. I am grateful to Gary Alan Fine for pointing out that boredom has temporal dimensions.

REFERENCES

Brissett, D., & Snow, R. P. (1993). Boredom: Where the future isn't. *Symbolic Interaction, 16,* 237-256.

Fine, G. A. (1990). Organizational time: Temporal demands and the experience of work in restaurant kitchens. *Social Forces, 69,* 95-114.

Fisher, C. D. (1993). Boredom at work: A neglect concept. *Human Relations, 46,* 395-417.

Hirschman, H. (1970). *Exit, voice and loyalty: Responses to decline in firms, organizations, and states.* Cambridge, MA: Harvard University Press.

Klapp, O. (1986). *Overload and boredom.* New York: Greenwood.

Molstad, C. (1986). Choosing and coping with boring work. *Urban Life, 15,* 215-236.

Peters, E. (1975). Notes toward an archaeology of boredom. *Social Research, 42,* 493-511.

Spacks, P. M. (1995). *Boredom: The literary history of a state of mind.* Chicago: University of Chicago Press.

Turnbull, C. (1961). *The forest people.* New York: Simon & Schuster.

CHAPTER 14

Memory and the Practices of Commitment

BARRY SCHWARTZ[1]

Eighteen years ago, I bought a book whose front cover is backgrounded by a raven, traditional bird of night, descending sun, and windblown sands—all symbols of the passage of time. I am looking at it now. At the foreground appear three children, the biggest of whom, a 7- or 8-year old, stands with a miniature sword beside a toy horse. Until this moment, I assumed the picture was taken in France during World War I. The book's author is French, which makes my assumption about the scene's location reasonable; nothing in the picture, however, suggests that it was taken in wartime. I supplied this assumption myself. My professional interests in collective memory, which account for my buying this book, have somehow become entangled with my personal experiences. This occurs commonly. Paul Valery observed, "There is no theory that is not a fragment, carefully prepared, of some autobiography" (Crane, 1996, p. 5). I recognize the truth of Valery's words in my own life and work.

I move backward, from present to past, beginning with the observation that late adolescence and early adulthood are "the formative years during which a distinctive personal outlook on politics emerges" (Rintala, 1968, p. 93; see also Mannheim 1928/1952, p. 300). Howard Schuman and Jacqueline Scott (1989) tested this observation by asking a sample of American adults to identify the two or three most important events of the past 50 years. They found that respondents tend to name events occurring during their late adolescence and young adulthood (Conway, 1997; Sehulster, 1996). That my experience deviates so markedly from Schuman and Scott's findings would be an uninteresting anomaly if age differences explained most of the variation among the events that their respondents named. Because the effect of age is much weaker, my case might contribute something to what they are trying to understand.

C. Wright Mills (1959, p. 6), writing about the "sociological imagination," observed that "no social study that does not come back to the problems of biography, of history, and their intersections within a society has completed its intellectual journey." The writing of this essay, an exercise that has led me to the meaning of my earliest memories, has been a deeply personal journey. As a sociologist, however, my aim cannot be self-discovery; it must be self-transcendence: the understanding of cultures, social structures, and mentalities that lie outside the narrow confines of my own life. As a sociologist, I must address phenomena objectively; I must sometimes draw on my experience, however, to make progress in my work. Because the fine-tuning of theory and of self-understanding are two aspects of the same thing, the aim of my essay is the illumination of both my personal memory and the sociological theory of memory. Self-discovery becomes sociological discovery when it suggests general ways of knowing the world.

The link between research and autobiography appears through "sociological introspection" (Ellis, 1991, 1993)—deliberate self-dialogue to determine how public events are privately processed and become objects of moral commitment and identity. The focus of my introspection is to determine why some events (a) are remembered better than others and (b) are more salient than others to one's identity and (c) why the most salient and self-defining events can be remembered least vividly.

The most important historical event for me is World War II, which occurred not between my late adolescence and early adulthood but between the fifth and eighth years of my childhood. To say that I remember these years of war is not enough. I cannot forget them and wish to repossess them, traumatic as they were. Something about them makes sorrowful their passing, more than the passing of any other years of my life. Although the term *hypermnesia*—the unexpected and involuntary amplification of memory, of seemingly forgotten contents erupting into consciousness (Terdiman, 1993, pp. 185-202)—relates to my situation, it does not describe it accurately. I can evoke or suppress my memories of the war years at will, but I cannot rid myself of them. If Schuman and Scott (1989) had included me in their sample, I would have named World War II as the most important event in American history and would have had difficulty naming a comparable second-place event. The reason I would have given for naming the war is its geopolitical significance, but I would have been unable to articulate its effect on my experience, which is also an important reason for my singling it out. This experience is worth talking about, I think, not only because I shared it with millions of other youngsters but also because no theory of cognition, personality, or socialization—including Karl Mannheim's, Sigmund Freud's, Jean Piaget's, Lawrence Kohlberg's, Erik Erikson's, or any other I know—throws much light on it.

PRACTICES OF COMMITMENT

As I look back in time, I find that "practices"—cooperative activities oriented toward the communal life they constitute (MacIntyre, 1981)—contribute to the memorability of events. Embodied in the routine performances of ritual and of social duties, practices are "habits of the heart" that connect culture, social structure, and personality. I am interested in practices of a particular kind, namely, practices of commitment—self-transcending activities whose purpose is to secure the social good. Practices of commitment establish webs of interconnection and shape identity by creating trust, joining people to families, friends, and communities, and making individuals aware of their reliance on the larger society. Practices of commitment enact obligations that keep the nation and its communities alive (Bellah, Madsen, Sullivan, Swidler, & Tipton, 1985, p. 154). I intend to demonstrate and explain the memorability of commitment practices, including practices undertaken at the very edge of "childhood amnesia" (Wetzler & Sweeney, 1986), and to extend this understanding to autobiographical memory in general.

The commitment practices undertaken by Philadelphia's first, second, and third graders in the early 1940s were utterly mundane: (a) the carrying of recyclable metal and newspapers to school; (b) the daily school ritual of pledging allegiance in a classroom filled with reminders of the ongoing war; (c) the acceleration of history lessons and their application to contemporary events during the days leading to school holidays (Columbus Day, Armistice Day, Lincoln's and Washington's birthdays, and Memorial Day); (d) purchasing of Savings Stamps (miniature war bonds) "for the boys," as soldiers and sailors were then called; (e) school-organized visits to historical sites, monuments, and shrines (including Independence Hall, the Liberty Bell, and gigantic statues of George Washington); and (f) Saturday afternoon movie matinees during which the president's image, backgrounded by the national flag and accompanying a message to buy war bonds, preceded and gave an almost ceremonial quality to the main attraction, which usually featured unblemished heroes dramatically conquering unredeemable villains.

These practices were supported by an infrastructure of play that took place in arcades, in which children shot at moving images of Hitler, Mussolini, Tojo, enemy paratroopers, and airplanes; in the home, in which toy soldiers, guns, tanks, planes, and cannons were arrayed against each other; and in the streets, where rifles, walkie-talkies, helmets, and uniforms simulated war and sacrifice. Play was not in itself a practice of commitment, but it socialized children into understanding what commitment entails. On the basis of sharp division of the world into good and evil, child's play moralized violence by defining the ends to which it had to be applied and dramatized morality by defining the lengths to which one had to go to sustain it. In the late twentieth century, war toys seem to many to be instruments of a mindless culture of violence; in the mid-twentieth century, the toys of war sustained a culture of commitment.

Salvaging

Edward Tiryakian (1997) asks,

> How is it that in the socialization process of the family and other primary groups (such as the school, the neighborhood, and the peer group), the person develops the same sentiments of belonging to and participating in something larger on which the nation depends? (p. 163)

I developed the sentiments to which Tiryakian refers through commitment practices and play. The activities I remember best, however, were neither the most fun nor the most entertaining; they were the most tedious—the gathering and depositing at school of wastepaper and tin cans. Like others trying to recall decades-old events (Pillemer, Goldsmith, Panter, & White, 1988), I remember no details. I am uncertain whether I carried trash from home to school or if I picked it up on the way to school. Tin and metal refuse, I recall, was more prestigious than paper, but I cannot say where I delivered either. I do not remember whether the papers I carried were tied or not, or whether the metal was bagged or boxed. I have never been without the memory of regularly bearing something heavy down Huntington Street from 33rd Street to my 28th Street school, however.

Recalling no single episode of gathering and delivery, I have assembled into memory a summary scene of the entire salvaging experience—one that probably lasted, for me, from the first to the third grade. This anomalous memory, vague but powerful and unforgettable, calls to mind the following observation by Maurice Halbwachs (1950/1980), a sociologist who conducted pioneering research on memory: In some instances, we know "beyond any doubt that a certain event occurred, that we were present and actively participated in it. Nevertheless, this episode remains foreign to us, just as if someone else played our role" (p. 24). Halbwachs is relevant to my effort to understand how some memories can be important but remain vague. Of the several commitment practices in which I engaged, however, why do I remember salvaging newspapers and tin cans above all others? The substance of the matter—carrying trash—is insignificant, but might it reveal something important about the general problems of memory and political socialization?

CULTURE OF MOBILIZATION

I grew up in the midst of total war mobilization. The purpose of mobilization was pictured on front pages of daily newspapers, which carried war news—only war news, day after day, week after week, month after month, year after year. There was no effective way to escape the presence of war: The radio, which carried the burden of home entertainment, conveyed war reports continually; comic books, a new genre whose volume of titles had peaked in 1941, saturated a generation of children, adolescents, and young adults with stories explaining the evil of the enemy and the moral purpose of the struggle against him; and in the movies, there were regular newsreels of the fighting, appeals to buy war bonds, and feature films concerning war.

War defined the meaning of everything. Everywhere, public information posters urged people to waste nothing and to use time efficiently. Above all was the summons to relentless work: "Every Day You Take Off Gives the Axis a Break," "Give 'Em the Stuff to Fight With," and "He's Betting His Life That We Stay on the Job." Students, like workers, were militarized. At the start of the school year, as I discovered after I began to write this essay, the *Philadelphia Bulletin* (1944c, p. 3) reported that "an army of 270,000 boys and girls started their march from . . . summer vacations to their battle stations in the classrooms." Parents having reason to fear polio were permitted to keep their children home, but all other pupils "are earnestly urged to take up their school books, as the most effective weapons by which to aid the Nation now" (p. 3). Three months after "The Invasion," the local War Manpower Commission chairman said, "The opening of school is your D-Day" (p. 3). At a time when "big government" has become a political issue, it is difficult to convey how comprehensive the role of government can actually become.

Most striking among my recent discoveries about the "home front" was the great paper shortage. "Wastepaper Goes to War," a cartooned announcement that children and adults could understand, appeared in every issue of the *Philadelphia Bulletin.* Because paper was necessary to package supplies, including weapons, its collection was imperative. More than 90% of Philadelphia's households, according to one survey, saved newspapers, most of which was collected by schoolchildren. Some schools gave awards to students for collecting the most paper, whereas the city gave school awards for per capita collection (*Philadelphia Bulletin,* 1944a, 1944b, 1944d, 1944e).

Chronic paper shortage and reliance on the school to collect wastepaper helps explain why I remember my part in the salvage effort, but it does not explain why I remember so little in detail. What I forgot about these years, however, was hardly idiosyncratic. Maurice Halbwachs (1950/1980) observed, "We appeal to witnesses to corroborate or invalidate as well as supplement what we somehow know already about an event that in many other details remains obscure" (p. 22; for recent evidence, see Fivush, Haden, & Reese, 1996). As I try to remember, I "recognize in myself many ideas and ways of thinking that could not have originated with me and that keep me in contact with it" (p. 24). Thus, memory is a social process: We appropriate most of our childhood recollection through the stories told us by others.

My witnesses were not the children with whom I went to school because I have seen none of them since I left. The school itself, however, was an important site of memory. If I had not attended school, I would have had an impoverished sense of what I was doing by salvaging and buying stamps; I would have had little conception of the war itself. I would have had no idea what the conversations at home meant or how to interpret the Saturday afternoon newsreels. The school, however, was not a source of vivid memories. This is because I remember not as an individual but by assuming the viewpoint and employing the conceptions of the group of which I am a part. If remembering is framed by witnesses, then forgetting must be an aspect of a change in my relation to the group (Halbwachs, 1950/1980, pp. 24-30). I forget most about events when the group in whose midst I experienced them no longer exists.

SOCIAL FRAMEWORKS OF MEMORY

Given the precariousness of memory, I wonder whether the war was actually meaningful to me as a child or whether I undertook my practices of commitment as would a robot and projected on them understandings of the war acquired as an adult. The more I think about the matter as an adult, however, the more certain I am that I knew the meaning of what I was doing as a child. I did not gain this knowledge, however, directly. Maurice Halbwachs (1992) was probably right when he asserted that, as children, "we knew nothing of the external world but the repercussions of outside events within the circle of our kin" (p. 61). Given the family's centrality in our early childhood, "family thoughts become ingredients of most of our [childhood] thoughts" (p. 61). This is because "the group to which the child at this age most intimately belongs, which constantly surrounds him, is the family" (Halbwachs, 1950/1980, p. 37). It is through the family that national history becomes a personal possession (Niemi & Sobieszek, 1977) and an object of knowledge.

My earliest family memories, unlike my memories of trash collecting, are abundant, vivid, and event specific. Many family memories are war related: sleeping in the same bed with a cousin wearing his olive drab (army) underwear; watching two cousins leaving for duty, their mother-in-law (my aunt) tearfully bidding them farewell; and receiving two photographs of a B-17 bomber that I had requested by letter from an aircraft mechanic cousin, and when he was home on leave, being carried about on his shoulders. Once, in an exuberant mood, I struck his head repeatedly with my little fists and remember his cheerful reprimand. He fixed radios and victrolas (phonographs), and I associate him alone with a 78-rpm Dick Haymes album. I remember the tune and most of the lyrics of my favorite record, "Why Am I Always Dreaming of Theresa?" even though I have not heard it in more than 50 years. I also recall pulling down the shades and sitting next to my mother during blackout exercises; examining my father's air-raid warden helmet and arm band; an elderly aunt exclaiming *Schiess far Amerika* (Shoot for America) as she shot her Casino hand; my grandmother telling me about her nephew giving chocolate to children in Burma; going with a pretty cousin, a sailor's wife, to see the movie *Objective Burma*; accompanying my mother to the corner barber shop (the neighborhood polling place) to vote for Franklin D. Roosevelt; believing that moustached Thomas Dewey, Roosevelt's Republican challenger, resembled Hitler; my mother's crying at the news of Roosevelt's death; banging together tin can tops to celebrate VJ Day; setting the bolt and clicking the trigger of the rifle that my sailor cousin brought back from Japan; going to the crowded homecoming, in a small row house like mine, of a cousin I never knew; and attending a double wedding at which one of the two grooms was civilian and the other was a fierce-looking soldier wearing boots. I forgot what the brides, two sisters, looked like.

Through these repercussions on the life of my family, I experienced the war's reality. What I learned in subsequent years, however, was disenchanting. I discovered that only a few of my cousins actually saw heroic combat, and none did what Errol Flynn or John Wayne did at the Saturday afternoon movies. This unpleasant discovery, however, had no effect on the vividness with which I remembered them. I remember them now because of what they were and not because of what they did. Of this matter, too, my understanding is dependent on Maurice Halbwachs. The family is unique, Halbwachs explained (1992), because its members perceive one another as "unique in kind," irreplaceable, and unsubstitutable. This image of distinctive individuals, condensed in our knowledge of their first names, is "deeply penetrating since it allows us to retrieve realities we have come to know personally through intimate experience"—even after the persons whose names we know have died (pp. 70-73), as have most of those who were young adults during my childhood. In other words, memories are stored as systems: "Some memories allow the reconstruction of others" (p. 53). What Halbwachs is saying is that public events and personal experience intersect in such a way that the objects of recall and the contexts of which those objects were a part are stored together in the mind (Brown, Shevell, & Rips, 1986). This is important for making sense of why vague memories are so salient. We cannot gauge "their relative strength and the ways in which they combine within individual thought unless we connect the individual to the various groups of which he is simultaneously a member" (Halbwachs, 1992, p. 53). The vagueness of my school memories is understandable in these terms. I recollect the names and faces of a few schoolmates but nothing more. Because I had no prolonged contact with them, I forget almost everything I did in their company. If the family is a carrier, a frame, for the retention of childhood memories, however, then why should not activities outside the family, including the salvaging of paper and tin, be forgotten? What was it about collecting trash that made it so meaningful, so worthy of remembrance?

MEMORY AND COMMITMENT

War feeds on obligation. I cannot recall feeling moral obligation any more than I recall experiencing material scarcity; I think of salvaging today as a practice of commitment, however, because it is associated in my mind with both. Obligations are satisfied through practices of commitment, whereas the sharing of these practices, in Bellah et al.'s (1985) words, "helps us identify with others different from ourselves, yet joined with us . . . by common ends" (p. 251). Practices of commitment are memorable because they are self-defining, and they are self-defining because they embody communal attachment. We remember best what we do when we act for the sake of causes that transcend our individual lives; we remember doing things imbued with collective purpose. Notwithstanding residual ethnic, religious, and racial bitterness (Adams, 1994), the meaning of the war for me, as for others like me, is rooted in the fact that "the war years provided the last great collective social experience in the country's history" (Perrett, 1973, p. 12). I have never been plugged into the society as directly and totally as I was while this event—the event I now consider to be the century's most important—was transpiring.

The activities I have described did not have the same meaning for all children. As far as I can remember, Jewish children like myself made no distinction between Germans and Japanese. We had somehow come to believe that both wished to win the war to kill Americans—all Americans. This belief was manifest in my imagination by foreign soldiers assaulting my street and shooting all its residents. Somehow, I had overgeneralized German hatred for the Jews—a hatred that most Jewish children, I believe, could vaguely realize but not accurately attribute.

Memory's "critical period," then, may not be entirely developmental, as Schuman and Scott (1989) believed; it may also be social—the period in which individuals feel society most deeply within themselves. My critical period affected not only my perception of past events but also my vision of the present and future: my strong support for liberal domestic policies and the Democratic Party; my contempt for defeatist policies, such as that of Henry Kissinger, which assumed that America could best survive by becoming part of an "interdependent" world; my support for the Vietnam War long after most Americans had turned against it; my strong support for the Gulf War; my dismay at the Smithsonian Institution's proposed Hiroshima display, which would have presented Japan's suffering and its viewpoint more elaborately than that of America; and my many disagreements with colleagues on the academic Left. My memories have been models for, not reflections of, my current experiences.

Some events are memorable because of their objective significance, regardless of when they occurred in the life of the individual—or even if they occurred before the individual was born. Many people, however, remember events that concretely affect their late adolescent and young adult lives. Schuman and Scott (1989), for example, demonstrate that people who passed through World War II as young adults remember the period not because of its moral or geopolitical significance but because of the personal hardships it caused. Whether Schuman and Scott's short telephone interviews succeeded in capturing deeper layers of their respondents' feelings and thoughts, however, is open to question. No one can deny the age cohort effect that Schuman and Scott document; yet, in some cases, this effect is accompanied by other influences.

In describing the effect of World War II on the residents of "Yankee City," Lloyd Warner's (1959) observations are similar to mine: "Verbally and superficially [Yankee City's residents] disapprove of war, but at best this only partly reveals their deeper feelings" (p. 274). It is in time of war that the average resident "gets his deepest satisfaction as a member of his society" (p. 274). Various organizations, instead of undertaking their usual activities, turned to work that was vital both to them and to the men fighting overseas. Traditional antagonisms between ethnic, religious, and racial groups never disappeared but lessened, and as everyone gave up something for the sake of the common enterprise "there was a feeling of unconscious well-being—a euphoria" (p. 275). The daily newspaper listing of young men injured and killed infused significance in all acts to help win the war no matter how small. That war is the great unifier is also evident in the fact that the local organizations most likely to draw members from all class levels and religious, ethnic, and racial groups were patriotic associations (pp. 276-277).

Many social scientists have, for understandable reasons, become skeptical, even hostile, to any manifestation of patriotic sentiment, but its constructive aspects must be recognized. Patriotism, the readiness to renounce one's own interests for the sake of one's country, is distinguishable from nationalism, the cultivation of national consciousness and invidious veneration of the nation and its history (Lowenthal, 1994). Because sacrifice for the sake of a cause reflects greater commitment than do verbal assertions alone, patriotism exemplifies the reasons why social scientists focus more on practices than language as conveyers of meaning (Swidler, 1996, p. 2). Gertrude Himmelfarb (1997) acknowledged this when she described patriotism as "an ennobling sentiment, quite as ennobling as love of family and community. It elevates us, invests our daily life with a larger meaning, dignifies the individual even as it humanizes politics" (p. 37). Himmelfarb's words explain why memory of patriotic efforts makes the nation a permanent object of one's sense of self.

Patriotism ennobles, elevates, dignifies, and humanizes as long as it enables us to transcend our narrow loyalties and tribalisms and motivates us to preserve practices of commitment in remembrance. Emile Durkheim (1915/1965), the great teacher of Maurice Halbwachs, asserted that in modern societies only patriotism is capable of overriding society's internal divisions:

> There are periods in history when, under the influence of some great collective shock, social interactions have become much more frequent and active. . . . Because [the individual] is in moral harmony with his comrades, he has more confidence, courage, and boldness in action, just like the believer who thinks he feels the regard of his god turned graciously towards him." (pp. 241-242)

This same current of collective arousal probably accompanied the events commonly named by Schuman and Scott's (1989) respondents—President Kennedy's assassination, the civil rights movement, and the first landing on the moon. To suggest that arousal helped make these events memorable is not to deny their objective importance. On the contrary, the intrinsic salience of crisis determines why certain events create a state of collective arousal and others do not. Our sharing of this effervescent state, however, is what we remember most directly and what induces some of us later to learn and to write about the events that caused it.

Paul Valery's belief that theory is an elaboration of biography has merit, but the concept of biography itself might be more complex than Valery believed. Biographical memory, in particular, is to be understood as a social process and not the result of "human development" (the unfolding of life stages given in human nature itself). As we reflect on our lives, we find ourselves remembering our lives in terms of our experience with others. This is why the content of what we remember and forget is a sociological puzzle—one that becomes less daunting when the insights of qualitative sociology are brought to bear on it. The past, it is true, is stored in individual minds, but what is stored and how it is stored are determined socially.

NOTE

1. The author thanks Howard Schuman and this volume's editors for useful comments on an earlier draft.

REFERENCES

Adams, M. C. C. (1994). *The best war ever: America and World War II.* Baltimore, MD: Johns Hopkins University Press.

Bellah, R. N., Madsen, R., Sullivan, W. M., Swidler, A., & Tipton, S. M. (1985). *Habits of the heart: Individualism and commitment in American life.* New York: Harper.

Brown, N. R., Shevell, S. K., & Rips, L. J. (1986). Public memories and their personal context. In D. C. Rubin (Ed.), *Autobiographical memory* (pp. 137-158). Cambridge, UK: Cambridge University Press.

Conway, M. A. (1997). The inventory of experience: Memory and identity. In J. W. Pennebaker, D. Paez, & B. Rime (Eds.), *Collective memory of political events: Social psychological perspectives* (pp. 21-45). Mahwah, NJ: Lawrence Erlbaum.

Crane, S. A. (1996). Not writing history: Rethinking the intersections of personal history and collective memory with Hans von Aufsess. *History and Memory, 8,* 5-29.

Durkheim, E. (1965). *The elementary forms of the religious life.* New York: Free Press. (Original work published 1915)

Ellis, C. (1991). Sociological introspection and emotional experience. *Symbolic Interaction, 14,* 23-50.

Ellis, C. (1993). There are survivors: Telling a story of sudden death. *Sociological Quarterly, 34,* 711-730.

Fivush, R., Haden, C., & Reese, E. (1996). Remembering, recounting, and reminiscing: The development of autobiographical memory in social context. In D. C. Rubin (Ed.), *Remembering our past* (pp. 341-359). Cambridge, UK: Cambridge University Press.

Halbwachs, M. (1980). Individual memory and collective memory. In M. Douglas (Ed.), *Collective memory* (pp. 22-49). New York: Harper. (Original work published 1950)

Halbwachs, M. (1992). "The localization of memories" and "The collective memory of the family." In L. A. Coser (Ed.), *Maurice Halbwachs on collective memory* (pp. 52-83). Chicago: University of Chicago Press.

Himmelfarb, G. (1997). For the love of country. *Commentary, 103,* 34-37.

Lowenthal, D. (1994). Identity, heritage, and history. In J. R. Gillis (Ed.), *Commemorations: The politics of national identity* (pp. 41-60). Princeton, NJ: Princeton University Press.

MacIntyre, A. (1981). *After virtue.* London: Duckworth.

Mannheim, K. (1952). The problem of generations. In K. Mannheim (Ed.), *Essays on the sociology of knowledge* (pp. 276-322). London: Routledge, Kegan Paul. (Original work published 1928)

Mills, C. W. (1959). The promise. In *The sociological imagination* (pp. 1-17). New York: Grove Press.

Niemi, R. G., & Sobieszek, B. (1977). Political socialization. *Annual Review of Sociology, 3,* 209-233.

Perret, G. (1973). *Days of sadness, years of triumph: The American people, 1939-1945.* New York: Coward, McCann, & Geohagan.

Philadelphia Bulletin. (1944a, February 22). p. 3.

Philadelphia Bulletin. (1944b, May 17). p. 3.

Philadelphia Bulletin. (1944c, September 17). p. 3.

Philadelphia Bulletin. (1944d, September 19). p. 3.

Philadelphia Bulletin. (1944e, September 20). p. 12.

Pillemer, D. B., Goldsmith, L. R., Panter, A. T., & White, S. H. (1988). Very long-term memories of the first year of college. *Journal of Experimental Psychology: Learning, Memory, and Cognition, 14,* 709-715.

Rintala, M. (1968). Political generations. In *International encyclopedia of the social sciences* (Vol. 6, pp. 92-96). New York: Macmillan/Free Press.

Schuman, H., & Scott, J. (1989). Generations and collective memory. *American Sociological Review, 54,* 359-381.

Sehulster, J. R. (1996). In my era: Evidence for the perception of a special period of the past. *Memory, 4,* 145-158.

Swidler, A. (1996). From the chair. *Newsletter of the Sociology of Culture Section of the American Sociological Association, 10*(3/4), 1-2.

Terdiman, R. (1993). *Present past: Modernity and the memory crisis.* Ithaca, NY: Cornell University Press.

Tiryakian, E. A. (1997). The wild cards of modernity. *Daedalus, 126,* 147-181.

Warner, W. L. (1959). *The living and the dead: A study of the symbolic life of Americans.* New Haven, CT: Yale University Press.

Wetzler, S. E., & Sweeney, J. A. (1986). Childhood amnesia: An empirical demonstration. In D. C. Rubin (Ed.), *Autobiographical memory* (pp. 191-201). Cambridge, UK: Cambridge University Press.

CHAPTER 15

"Performing Montana"

NORMAN K. DENZIN

In this chapter, I provide an example of a minimalist social science, a sociology that uses few concepts. This is a dramaturgical (Branaman, 1997, p. xlix; Goffman, 1959; Lemert, 1997, p. xxiv) or performative sociology (Turner, 1986) that attempts to stay close to how people experience everyday life. As the term implies, a performative sociology studies performances—how people enact cultural meanings in their daily lives.

Shaped by the sociological imagination (Mills, 1959), this version of sociology attempts to show how terms such as biography, history, gender, race, ethnicity, family, and history interact and shape one another in concrete social situations. These works are usually written in the first-person voice, from the point of view of the sociologist doing the observing and the writing.

In this chapter, I offer an example of this kind of sociology. I write about a little town in Montana, named Red Lodge, and I describe experiences my wife and I have had in this town during the past 8 years. Because we started out as tourists to this locale, this is also an essay about tourism (Allcock & Bruner, 1995) and community (Cruikshank, 1997). Because Native Americans and white Europeans are part of the local Red Lodge history, this is also an essay about race and ethnic relations in small town America (hooks, 1990).

It is more than these things, however, because a minimalist sociology is also about stories, performances, and storytelling.

AUTHOR'S NOTE: I thank Katherine E. Ryan, Laurel Richardson, Rosanna Hertz, and Barry Glassner for their comments on an earlier draft of the manuscript.

William Kittridge, a Montana author (1987, 1994, 1996) and coeditor (Kitttridge & Smith, 1988), says that the West is an enormous empty and innocent stage waiting for a performance (1996, p. 97). He continues, "We see the history of our performances everywhere . . . inscribed on the landscape (fences, roads, canals, power lines, city plans, bomb ranges)" (p. 97). Moreover, the West is contained in the stories people tell about it (p. 97).

Montana is both a performance and a place for performances. It is a place where people enact their version of the West, their version of being outdoors, of being in nature, of looking for a place where a river runs through it (Maclean, 1976). Stories grow out of these performances. Kittridge (1996, p. 164) says we need new stories about performing Montana. Here, I provide some of mine.

RED LODGE, MONTANA[1]

In 1994, my wife and I bought a small piece of land outside Red Lodge, Montana, population 1,875. We bought an acre with a cabin on the river called Rock Creek and a big bluff of a rock outcropping behind the cabin. Indian paint brush and lupine grow everywhere. In the summer, horses and deer graze in the valley above the road to our cabin. Off the big boulder under the big cottonwood tree I catch rainbow and brook trout for breakfast. I fish, and my wife quilts, hikes, and collects wild flowers. Last Christmas, we took up cross-country skiing. I prefer winter fishing on Rock Creek. In the summer, we go to auctions and yard sales, drive into town for groceries, to pick up an item at the hardware store. The town has more restaurants per capita than any other town in Montana.

This is south central Montana, 20 miles from the Wyoming border, 69 miles and 10,942 feet up and over the Beartooth Highway to Yellowstone Park, the road Charles Kuralt called "the most beautiful drive in America." Our little valley is marked by lakes, snow-capped mountain ranges, alpine meadows, and sprawling ranches with double-wide house trailers as homes. Early June brings fields of yellow sunflowers, and raging, dark, angry rivers filled with melting snow and fallen trees from the upper mountain ranges.

Red Lodge is 4 miles from our cabin. It was primarily a mining town until the 1943 mine explosion that killed 74 miners. Hit hard by the depression, even before the mines closed, looking for a way to stay alive, the town fathers pushed for a "high road" (the Hi road) that would connect Red Lodge to Cooke City and Silver Gate, the two little mining communities just outside the northeast entrance to Yellowstone Park. It took a 1931 Act of Congress and 5 years of hard work to build the road over the mountain; the Beartooth Highway officially opened in 1936. Ever since, Red Lodge has been marketed as the eastern gateway to Yellowstone. That's what got us there in 1990.[2]

After reading Kittridge, and studying Turner (1986) and Bruner (1986, 1989, 1996), I have come to see our little part of Montana as a liminal place—Turner's no-person's-land, a place for new performances, new stories, a place betwixt and between the past and the future. When you are in Montana, you occupy this liminal place, a place that is constantly changing you.

We are learning how to perform Montana. We are learning to engage in the ritual performances that people do when they are in and around Red Lodge—performances such as going to parades, shopping in the little craft and antique stores, buying things for the cabin, driving over the mountain, eating out, having an espresso on the sidewalk in front of the Coffee Factory Roasters, having a fancy dinner at the Pollard (which is on the National Registry of Hotels), picking up pictures from Flash's Image Factory, buying quilting materials at Granny Hugs, volunteering in the local library that is computerizing its entire collection, and talking to the owner of the Village Shoppe who at one time dated the niece of the former University of Illinois basketball coach.

EXPERIENCE AND PERFORMANCES

We watch other people do what we are doing, separating the experience of being in Montana from its performances and representations, constructing culture and meaning as they go along (Bruner, 1989, p. 113). Three years ago, I overheard a man talking to the owner of the tackle shop in Big Timber. His BMW was still running, the front door open. He had on an Orvis fishing vest. He had driven with his family from Connecticut. "The kids saw that movie, *A River Runs Through It.* Where do we have to go to catch fish like they did in that movie? Can somebody around here give me fly-fishing lessons?" The owner said "No" on the lessons, but told the man to "Go about 20 miles up river, past 4-mile bridge. You can't miss it" (Dawson, 1996, p. 11).

Of course, the meanings of these Montana performance experiences are constantly changing. It is not appropriate to judge them in terms of their authenticity or originality. There is no original against which any given performance can be measured. There are only performances that seem to work and those that don't. In any case, Montanans always help you muddle through.

One perfect sunny, blue-skied Montana Sunday afternoon, I was fishing with a bobber and a worm off a big rock in a large pool near the headwaters of the Clark branch of the Yellowstone just outside Cooke City. There was a large group of persons fishing the same area, and many were catching fish. I wasn't. My wife was back reading a book in the shade at a picnic table near the path to the water. When I cast, I kept catching my line in the trees behind me, or the line would dribble down in front of me, and the bopper would plop into the water. I was looking rather foolish.

The foolish feeling was compounded by the fact that I was fishing near a young man, no more than 13 or 14 years old, who was having very good luck. He had a simple casting rod and was using a small wholly fly. He'd tied a casting line, a tippet, to the end of his regular line and was getting good distance out over the water, especially in the shaded area near a big pine. He asked me if he could help me. I said sure, and within minutes he'd rigged me up with a setup like his, and I nearly caught a big trout with my next cast. This is what I mean. People in Montana help you muddle through these performances.

It is not possible to write an objective, authoritative, neutral account of performing Montana. Every account is personal and locally situated. In fact, people in Montana go to almost any length to respect personal differences. Kittridge (1996) is right. Montana as a place where "independence, minding your own business . . . and self-realization [are] regarded as prime virtues" (pp. 108-109).

The following are some of the ways Montana is performed.

CREATING LOCAL HISTORY

Every year, we try to observe part of the Festival of Nations celebration. This is a 9-day ritual performance that reenacts the town's white European ethnic history. Each day of the festival is given the name of a country, state, or nationality: Irish-English-Welsh, German, Montana, Scandinavian, Finnish, Italian, Slavic, Scottish, All Nations. At the turn of the century, men from these European countries came to Montana and became miners. Later they married, and their wives taught school, cooked, had children, helped run little shops, and carried on native crafts from the home country. Red Lodge tries to keep this history alive.

According to local history, the festival started shortly after World War II. Local community leaders decided to build a civic center. They wanted a place for community activities, for an annual summer music festival, a place for art and craft exhibits, for flags and cultural items from each of the nations represented in the town. Thus was born the Festival of Nations, and Red Lodge was soon transformed into a "tourist town, a place that offered good scenery, fine fishing, the Hi-Road, the rodeo, cool summers" (Red Lodge Festival of Nations, 1982, p. 4). They had more to offer, however: "The inhabitants themselves were a resource" (p. 4). Nine days every summer, Red Lodge puts its version of local ethnic culture on display, turning everyday people into performers of their respective ethnic heritages.

In these performances, residents only had their own history to go on, so they made it up as they went along, one day for each ethnic group, but each group would do pretty much the same thing: a parade down Broadway with national flags from the country of origin, people in native costume, an afternoon performance of some sort (singing, storytelling, or rug-making), ethnic food in the Labor Temple (every day from 3 to 5 p.m.), and an evening of music and dance in the civic center. This is improvised ethnicity connected to the performance of made-up rituals handed down from one generation to the next (Hill, 1997, p. 245).

Two years ago, the ladies who run the event wanted to shorten it from 9 to 7 days. They were mad because there was not a big turnout for All Nation's Day, so they wanted to combine it with Montana Day and put the Scots in with the Irish, English, and Welsh. The Scots wanted their own day, and the merchants got angry and said they would lose business, so the proposal was dropped.

PERFORMING ETHNIC HISTORY

I like Finn Day. The little booklet that describes the Festival of Nations says that in 1910 one fourth of the population of Red Lodge was Finnish. They even have an area still called Finn Town. On Finn Day, the all-male Finnish band plays marching songs. The women display their hooked rugs at the Festival Museum, just across the street from the Depot Gallery. Everybody who goes through the museum after the band plays gets a small paper plate filled with Finnish pastries and a cucumber sandwich on brown bread. You can go back for seconds. You are served by women dressed in native Finnish costume. Next to the food, in a corner of the museum, is a display of a Finnish kitchen, circa 1910. There is a coal-burning stove, a wood cupboard, a small kitchen table, a broom, and pots and pans hanging from a rack.

I also like Montana Day, especially the part that involves ranch women reading their stories about being Montana wives. A tent is set up over the dance pavilion in Lions Park, just next to the Depot Gallery, which is housed in a converted red train caboose. White plastic chairs are lined up in rows on the lawn. Loudspeakers are on each side of the stage. An old-fashioned Montana meal is served afterwards—barbecued beef, baked beans, cole slaw, baked potatoes, jello salad, brownies for dessert, and coffee and ice tea for beverages.

Tall and short middle-aged sun-tanned women take the stage. These are hardworking women, mothers, daughters, and grandmothers who live in the ranches in the Beartooth valley, along the East Rosebud, Rock Creek, Willow Creek, and the Stillwater River south of Columbus and Absarokee.

Some have on cowboy boots, others wear Nike sneakers. They are dressed in blue jeans and decorated red, white, and blue cowboy shirts and skirts, and have red bandannas around their necks. They have short and long hair, pony tails, and curls. They read cowboy poetry and tell short stories about hard winters and horses that freeze to death in snow banks. Some sing songs. Country music plays quietly, and people come and go, some stop and listen for awhile. As these women perform, old ranchers in wide-brimmed cowboy hats close their eyes and tap their feet to the music. Young children run around through the crowd, and husbands proudly watch their wives read their poetry.

The Old West and Reading the Montana Face

There are many Montana faces here, few that strike the kind of poses that Fiedler (1971a, 1971b, 1971c, 1988), writing as an easterner in the 1940s, said were inarticulate and full of dumb pathos and self-sufficient stupidity (1971a, p. 135). The faces I see have lived through harsh winters. Some are lined and wrinkled. The hands are strong, brown, callused, and freckled. These faces and the stories behind them hide complicated emotions, yet they give off a gentle, weathered friendliness, a worldly, unself-conscious self-sufficiency.

Montana Day is about as close as many of the people in Red Lodge get to being cowboys, or to being near cowboys and cowgirls. This is about as close as they get to the old West, to the West that exists in cowboy movies and in the national imagination. Oh, sure, you can still hear Patsy Cline, Hank Williams, and Dwight Yoakam on the juke boxes at the Snag Bar and the Snow Creek Saloon, and tourists can sign up at Paintbrush Trails, Inc., for a trail ride, or a scenic pack trip. (The ad shows a cowboy on a horse.) In the summer, before Montana Days, they do hold a Home of Champions Rodeo. It is part of the Professional Rodeo Cowboys Association of America. Cowboys wrestle steers to the ground, while Timber the rodeo clown shows off his pet chicken who walks around on a leash.

The Gathering of Mountain Men occurs every year, just before the Festival of Nations ceremonies, and just after the Annual Summer Music Festival, which features classical musicians from Europe and all over the United States. We went to the Gathering of Mountain Men last summer, it was out near the fairgrounds, up past the airport landing strip. It was like an all-male costume show, men dressed up as mountain men, men in leather, men wearing loin cloths, men as Indians, men as cavalry soldiers, as scouts, buffalo hunters, whiskey runners, muleskinners, bullwhackers, ox drovers, and horse traders.

It was Big Sky country, circa 1880, the days of Lewis and Clark, mountain men, and Indians living together in a little high plains village, big Tepees, campfires, men shooting old-fashioned guns, bartenders serving homemade sassafras and old-fashioned root beer. There was even a mountain man general store where you could buy skins, baskets, beartooth necklaces, whiskey jars, and blankets. There were men making knives, selling beads, men (and some women) selling clothes so you could look like a mountain man.

There was a man dressed as a British trader working in front of a big white Tepee. (In another life he sold real estate.) He claimed to be selling the kinds of beads Indians liked to put on their warbonnets and headbands. Just as he finished his sales pitch to us, the camp commander, a local banker, came marching by. He was accompanied by a bagpiper, Frank the butcher, who would be playing in Scottish Days at the Festival of Nations.

Dead Indians

Fiedler argues that Montana as a white territory became psychologically possible only after the Native Americans, the Nez Perce, Blackfeet, Sioux, Assinboine, Gros Ventre, Cheyenne, Chipewayan, Cree, and Crow, were killed, driven away, or placed on reservations. He claims that the struggle to rid the West of the noble savage and the "redskin" was integral to the myth of the Montana frontier as a wild wilderness (Fielder, 1988, p. 745). Fiedler said the Indian was Montana's Negro, an outcast living in an open-air ghetto (p. 752).

With the passing of the redskin came trappers, mountain men, explorers, General Custer, Chief Joseph, and then ranchers and homesteaders. Indian sites would be marked with signs such as "Dead Indian Pass." Entering Red Lodge, you drive past a Native American Indian wooden statue—a male Indian face sitting on a big stone. It was carved by a non-Native American.

The history of Montana's relations with the Native American is folded into mountain man festivals and events such as Montana Days in Red Lodge. It is a history that simultaneously honors the dead Indian while denying the violent past that was so central to white supremacy.

Two summers ago, we drove over Dead Indian Pass, taking the Chief Joseph Highway back from Yellowstone Park. Chief Joseph lead the Nez Perce over this pass just months before Custer's last stand. At the top of the mountain, there is a turn off, and you look back across the valley, 10,000 feet below. While it is called Dead Indian Pass, there is no mention of Chief Joseph in the little plaque that you walk up to. Instead, there is a story about the ranch families who settled the valley while fighting off the Indians, hence the name Dead Indian Pass. The whites, and not the Indians, are honored in popular memory.

Trout Fishing in Montana

I like to fish for trout. I grew up in a midwestern family and sometimes went fishing with my father. Unlike the Maclean family (Maclean, 1976, p. 1), in my family there was no clear line between religion and (fly) fishing. In fact, I connected fishing with harsh, dark childhood memories. My father and I would go out after work, ending up alongside some small muddy river or creek. Darkness, swarms of mosquitoes, and my father's heavy drinking went together. I'd be slapping away at mosquitoes and my father would be yelling at me to sit still. It was seldom a pleasant time, and if he caught a fish it would be a dirty catfish or an ugly carp. He didn't let me fish.

So I gave up fishing and did not take it up again until Carl and Dee Dee Couch got us to visit them in 1989 at their cabin on the Boulder River 30 miles south of Macloud, Montana. There I started to see what Maclean meant about fishing and religion. The Couch's took this stuff pretty seriously. Carl even had wooden versions of trophy fish nailed up on a post in the screened-in porch off the kitchen to their cabin, with names, lengths, and dates burned into the wood beneath each fish.

Still, it took me 3 years to learn how to catch a fish on Rock Creek. The first three summers we came out here I swore there were no fish in the river. At that time, I was fishing with a big red bobber on my line, a worm at the end. I used the bobber because it told me where my line was in the water. I used the worms because I could easily buy them at the True Value hardware store in town. I also used worms because I had no idea how to use a metal lure and, besides, I kept catching lures on nearby trees and shrubs. Fly-fishing was a mysterious art to me. It was outside the limits of the image I was building of myself as a person who fished in Montana. I was happy to be known as a rod and reel—worm fisherman who used a red bobber.

I had a pretty simple fishing strategy. I would find a wide spot near the river, sit on a rock, pour a cup of coffee, light a cigarette (I was still smoking then), and throw my red bobber into the water and wait for a fish to strike. I connected catching fish to smoking cigarettes, feeling that a fish would only bite when I had a cigarette in my mouth. I believed this because I caught a fish on the Yellowstone once when these two events happened at the same time. For three summers, I went through a lot of cigarettes, without catching any fish. So I changed the color of my bobber. Still no fish.

One afternoon I was on the Lake Fork branch of Rock Creek, about 300 yards up river from the start of the trailhead. Walking along the river, I came to a big boulder that sticks out in the river. The water runs around behind it, forming a deep pool. I climbed up on the big rock, lit a cigarette, and started to prepare my line. I found myself without my trusty bobber. So I threw my line in with just a worm. I was smoking and sitting on top of the big boulder. All of a sudden I felt a pull on my line, and I nearly fell off the big rock. I looked over the edge and fed a little more line into the water, and the line pulled taut. I jumped off the rock onto the bank. I jerked my line and a trout came out of the water. It flew over my head and landed on the bank behind me, flopping up on down on the ground, my hook still in its mouth.

In that instant, I knew what Maclean (1976) meant when he talked about "spots of time [and] fishermen who experience eternity compressed into a moment. No one can tell what a spot of time is until suddenly the whole world is a fish" (p. 44). Maclean adds "and the fish is gone." Thankfully, my fish was still there. But I had compressed my entire consciousness into this single moment, landing that fish. I was breathing pretty heavily, excited, my first trout on Rock Creek! I put out my cigarette, knocked over my coffee cup, and inspected my prize. It was about 10 inches long, a Brookie. I took out my red Swiss Army knife and cleaned it right there on a flat rock next to the river. (This was before they asked you to stop cleaning fish by the rivers because of the swirling trout disease.) I got right back at it, and in no I time had caught four more 8- to 10-inch brook trout. I cleaned them too. I put them in a sealed plastic bag.

I walked on up river and met my wife, who was returning from her hike. She took my picture near that big rock. There I am in my tan walking shorts, dark green fishing hat, blue fishing shirt, thongs on my feet, pole in one hand, holding four 10-inch trout in a plastic bag in the other, the mountains in the background, a real outdoors man. Huck Finn in Montana.

Later that same summer, we drove over the mountain and fished on the Soda Butte River, just outside the northwest entrance to Yellowstone Park. If you go down over the hill off the road and turn left, about 30 yards upstream a little sandbar extends out into the Soda Butte. Just behind the sandbar are three tall pine trees. They caste a big midday shadow across a deep pool in the river that was created when two big trees floated down river and jammed together on the sandbar.

My wife hooked a worm on her line and caste it into the water. A big cutthroat took the worm. She yelled, "Get the net! Get the net." I did, and she had a 15-inch cutthroat on her line. We landed the fish, and I ran a stringer through its mouth, and staked the cord to the bank, putting the fish back in the river. In 15 minutes, we had eight cutthroat. It was like catching fish in a barrel. And twice a big cutthroat took a worm off my wife's line and slipped away. Time stood still. We were in a zone, in a groove, our entire existence was compressed into that spot on the Soda Butte.

We came back 2 years later with our son Nate. The river had changed somewhat. Nate went to the spot where his mother had lost that big cutthroat. We drove back into town. When we returned, Nate was coming up the hill toward the road. He had that big cut on a stringer, and a smile a mile wide on his face. He'd caught his mother's fish. We were quite angry. That fish belonged to his mother, and he should not have caught it! To this day, we talk about that fish that Nate took away from his mother on the banks of the Soda Butte just outside the northeast entrance to the park.

These two experiences changed my fishing style. The red bobber disappeared. I now modeled myself after Carl, no frills fishing, caste out into the dark pools, fish along the edges of the river under the little water falls, get down into the trees and shrubs that grow next to the water, look for little eddies of water behind big rocks. Go out after supper and look for the spots where the insects swarm, and the trout feed in the cool evening waters. Keep it simple, a worm, the rod and reel, catch and release.

PERFORMING MONTANA

There are many ways to perform Montana. Montana is a place where locals and tourists constantly comingle, where Orvis-outfitted fly-fishermen from Connecticut connect with Huck Finn look-alike local kids who fish with worms and old bamboo poles. These Montana performances mix up many different things at the same time, different identities, different selves: cowboys, rodeos, classical music, antique hunters, skiers, mountain men, Finnish women who make rugs, rancher's wives who write poetry, fishing for trout. Anybody can tell a story about doing and being one of these things.

But sometimes words fail. In its naturalness Montana is a place that is stunning in its beauty, a world that defies words. How do you create an image of the thousand shades and hues of brown and gold that shimmer at midday off the rocks and stones at the bottom of Rock Creek? How do you put a word to the color of the blinding light that comes off the water in the early morning? Words cannot adequately describe the stone structures that appear in the river when the snow falls, and the rocks are turned into upside down, toad-like mushroom stems with white hats.

Being in nature is a major part of my Montana self. To perform Montana is to shed a little bit of my midwestern skin. These Montana performances teach my wife and I how to first see and then how to love the mountains, the rivers, and the valleys, how to get outside ourselves, and go back to a more basic self. We enact nature, we bring it to ourselves through the very act of bending down and smelling a wildflower, of walking along the river. This contact with the "natural world is an experience that comes to us like a gift" (Kittridge, 1996, p. 108).

So our corner of Montana is a sacred place, a hole, or house in the sky, to use phrases from Kittridge (1994) and Doig (1978)—a place where wonderful things happen, and they happen when we perform them.

These are the kinds of things a minimalist, storytelling, performative sociology makes visible. In these tellings, the world comes alive. The sociologist attempts to make these meanings available to the reader, hoping to show how this version of the sociological imagination engages some of the things that matter in everyday life.

NOTES

1. There are various stories about how the town got its name. The generally accepted theory is that the Crow Indians who inhabited the area colored their lodges with red clay (Graetz, 1997, p. 23).

2. They have a web site. Using Netscape, type Red Lodge, Montana on a web browser such as Yahoo. Within seconds, you can be looking at a map of downtown Red Lodge.

REFERENCES

Allcock, J. B., & Bruner, E. M. (Eds.). (1995). *International tourism.* London: Sage.

Branaman, A. (1997). Goffman's social theory. In C. Lemert & A. Branaman (Eds.), *The Goffman reader* (pp. xvl-lxxxii). Malden, MA: Blackwell.

Bruner, E. M. (1986). Experience and its expressions. In V. M. Turner & E. M. Bruner (Eds.), *The anthropology of experience* (pp. 3-30). Urbana: University of Illinois Press.

Bruner, E. M. (1989). Tourism, creativity, and authenticity. *Studies in Symbolic Interaction, 10,* 109-114.

Bruner, E. M. (1996). Abraham Lincoln as authentic reproduction: A critique of postmodernism. *American Anthropologist, 96*(2), 397-415.

Cruikshank, J. (1997). Negotiating with narrative: Establishing cultural identity at the Yukon International Storytelling Festival. *American Anthropologist, 99,* 56-69.

Dawson, P. (1996). Not another fish story from occupied Montana. In R. Newby & S. Hunger (Eds.), *Writing Montana: Literature under the big sky* (pp. 10-23). Helena: Montana Center for the Book.

Doig, I. (1978). *This house of sky.* New York: Harcourt Brace.

Fiedler, L. (1971a). Montana; or the end of Jean-Jacques Rousseau. In *The collected essays of Leslie Fiedler* (Vol. 1, pp. 133-141). New York: Stein & Day. (Original work published in the *Partisan Review* as "Montana," December, 1949)

Fiedler, L. (1971b). Montana: P.S. In *The collected essays of Leslie Fiedler* (Vol. 2, pp. 331-336). New York: Stein & Day.

Fiedler, L. (1971c). Montana: P.P.S. In *The collected essays of Leslie Fiedler* (Vol. 2, pp. 337-342). New York: Stein & Day.

Fiedler, L. (1988). The Montana face. In W. Kittredge & A. Smith (Eds.), *The last best place: A Montana anthology* (pp. 744-752). Seattle: University of Washington Press.

Goffman, E. (1959). *The presentation of self in everyday life.* New York: Doubleday.

Graetz, R. (1997, July/August). Sojourn to the sky: The Beartooth Highway. *Montana Magazine, 144,* 18-26.

Hill, R. T. G. (1997). Performance and the "political anatomy" of pioneer Colorado. *Text and Performance Quarterly, 17,* 236-255.

hooks, b. (1990). The Chitlin circuit: On black community. In b. hooks (Ed.), *Yearning: Race, gender, and cultural politics* (pp. 33-40). Boston: South End.

Kittridge, W. (1987). *Owning it all.* San Francisco: Murray House.

Kittridge, W. (1994). *Hole in the sky.* San Francisco: Murray House.

Kittridge, W. (1996). *Who owns the West?* San Francisco: Murray House.

Kittridge, W., & Smith, A. (Eds.). (1988). *The last best place: A Montana anthology.* Seattle: University of Washington Press.

Lemert, C. (1997). Goffman. In C. Lemert & A. Branaman (Eds.), *The Goffman reader* (pp. ix-xliii). Malden, MA: Blackwell.

Maclean, N. (1976). *A river runs through it and other stories*. Chicago: University of Chicago Press.

Mills, C. W. (1959). *The sociological imagination*. New York: Oxford University Press.

Red Lodge Festival of Nations. (1982). *Festival of Nations, Red Lodge, Montana*. Red Lodge, MT: Author.

Turner, V. (1986). *The anthropology of performance*. Performing Arts Journal Publications: New York.

CHAPTER 16

A Personal Passage
Identity Acquisition and Affinity Groups

PEPPER SCHWARTZ

The study of progress and conflict is often about the intersection of identities with social structure and transitory opportunity. People operate in a system of rewards and costs that is set up to serve (or defeat) some larger system, and personal outcomes depend on a mix of luck, hard work, and the ability to figure out how the system works and what one needs to do to please gatekeepers.

Figuring out these minimaps of social discourse is no small challenge. Social genius, however, is like any other talent: It is rewarded when done brilliantly. In retrospect, as I examine my past at midlife, it seems to me that I have always been in awe of people who could either shape their identity to the needs of the system they wanted to enter or be so charismatic that the system would reshape around them. Perhaps this is why I have always been drawn to entering new subcultures; I have looked to the system to tell me who I was by finding out, as a participant, if I "fit," if I was a leader, or if some essential part of me was unused or abused. This testing process could occur sequentially or by existing in several parallel worlds. I have never thought of multiple identities as schizo-phrenic but rather like having more than one leg on a table—therefore creating a more stable and more interesting piece of furniture. If identity is created by location—or alienation—from a community, family, or society, it seems correct that the accumulation of having been in multiple communities, societies, and families must also have an impact, though not a straightforward one. For example, if one lives a "double life"—existing in conflicting communities of interest (e.g., being a public Democrat but having all Republican friends) or hidden relationships (e.g., having a home and family but being gay in anonymous ways in public parks)—there is no question that it will affect identity formation, although it is not clear which of these statuses, if any, is the master.

Most people exist with a multiplicity of presentations of self—sometimes sequentially and sometimes contemporaneously. Most of us are one thing to our parents and another to ourselves—at least in childhood. We may also leave one identity as we seek another. Like many people, I have left some identities, formed new ones, and ultimately existed in parallel selves that cohere enough to avoid an identity crisis. The idea of consistency, I believe, has been oversold. We all have paradigms that allow people and ourselves to make sense of us—to be able to predict who we will be the next day. My conceit, however, is that really interesting people resist total incorporation. They diversify. Even someone such as the president of a corporation often has a double or triple life that gives the ego room to breath and roam. That self might be deviant (have a mistress and second or third family as did the late great financier James Goldsmith, who was politically conservative and personally flamboyant), or it might just be articulated in eccentric ways, such as when Paul Newman, successful at so many professions, became as good a race car driver as an actor. At least in American culture, we understand that being too narrow may have dignity but not flexibility. *Death of a Salesman,* the classic tragedy by playwright Arthur Miller, is the story of a man who had one identity he held very tightly, in which he was self-deceived and, ultimately, failing. His was a doomed identity, and there was little else in his life that could save him when his core vision of himself started unraveling.

The search for identity begins, for most of us, because human beings need a central theory of who they are before they can start to embroider and elaborate the self. For most of us, this begins with the basics: in our families or origin, then in our work, with our children, and in other quotidian attachments. Each year of one's life is important in the process of creating the self, and it was difficult for me to think about which snapshots of my life might serve for showing how the self (mine in this case) is built as a continuing social process. To make the point that identity is a continuing adult process, not just a childhood phenomenon, and that it is to some extent chosen as well as happenstance, I decided to discuss the following three important affinity groups in my life that were passages from one thing to another—leaving permanent identity residue in some cases but also definitely part of a shucking-off process: being in a sorority in college; being at Yale at the rebirth of the women's movement and at the height of the antiwar movement; and, in midlife, the transformation of a childhood fantasy into a parallel world: becoming a horse breeder at the same time I was a professor at the University of Washington.

When I was in undergraduate school, I was not what one would call internally secure. Therefore, I was ambitious in the way that insecure people are: Instead of being able to evaluate the system, they try just to be included. If being high up in the system is prestigious, they try and do just that; but they are not independent enough to evaluate whether what is to be won is worth winning. Yearning for some kind of ratification of "coolness"—and not being secure enough to manufacture my own standard—I wanted to be a part of the sorority system at my university. The system was small. There were no houses, only meeting rooms. It was purely a social stamp: We anoint ourselves to be cool, therefore we are cool. I wanted that social ratification, even though I could see that the system was deeply flawed. Sad to say, I was almost desperately motivated because the first time I went through rush I was not pursued by the groups I coveted, and a major reason for this was because at that time non-Jewish sororities did not pledge Jews. (This is probably still true in many places). This genteel anti-Semitism was practically my first brush with any kind of prejudice and it left me—a secular, unaffiliated Jew—furious in an inchoate way. My gentile roommates (all of whom were pledging the two sororities to which I was attracted) expected me to just "understand." I did—and it forever ended the possibility of real intimacy with those women. It was my first lesson about caste as opposed to class or status. There are some things one is born into and that is the way it is. Forever. I could of course reinvent myself, but I would have had to lie and this had no appeal. No, it was more necessary to acknowledge in a personal way that, like race, some religions leave their mark—even if one is not observant, not even a believer. Of course, I knew this from the history of the Holocaust, but this was my first personal accommodation to the idea that Jews were still considered the "other"—something I was trying hard not to be. It was also my first experience with an organized exclusion of Jews. I had grown up in an almost all-Jewish neighborhood, and the last thing I had ever had to consider was prejudice.

One would think that the discovery of organized anti-Semitism and my friends unthinking adherence to it would have been enough for me to chuck the whole sorority system in a fit of righteous insight. Nope. I wanted to be cool in the way some people want money enough to knock over a bank. I had been popular and a leader in high school, and I was so psychically propped up by my previous place in the social firmament that I could not imagine turning away from proving myself in a similar hierarchy, even with full knowledge that many of its tenants, rules, values, and activities were abhorrent to me. I had acted in a professional theater company and a student theater company during the past few years of high school, and I knew the people there found the sorority world I coveted pitiful, even laughable. I didn't disagree. I still wanted it, however.

Therefore, I observed the sorority system for 6 months, and when I went through rush again I had it more or less figured out: The system was built around good looks (basically, attracting boys was criteria 1 through 10) and, after looks, upper middle-class presentation of self and, for lack of a better word, "coolness," an almost indefinable amalgamation of characteristics including the right clothes, the right family, and the right amount of "charismatic cuteness"—all these ultimately predicted "popularity."

I did the best I could to pull these characteristics together and joined a sorority during my second semester. I was an intense pledge, and I became rush chairman and eventually president; I loved many of the rituals, the musical productions, and the company of women. I also loved being a leader: It became clear to me that if I joined anything, I would either lead it or leave it. Therefore, I stayed and became a strategist and mainstay of the group.

Of course, this eventually fell into the category of "be careful what you ask for, you might get it." It is painful to put down in print how I took my analytical skills and used them to help our sorority to become one of the most prestigious on campus. What it took was a no brainer; in fact, it relied on forgetting about brains—we pledged the prettiest girls that walked through the door and we dropped every other category, every pretension of well-roundedness, and signed up anything that looked like a beauty queen. Bingo.

This required not pledging some pretty interesting people, not being courageous, and not challenging the system. I remember when a black woman was brave enough to face the then all-white groups and signed up for rush. I remember that she was a nifty person, and during that first day when she came through the door I was wondering what we should do. I like to think we would have gone after her, but we never had the opportunity. She dropped out right away—an act of wisdom and contempt that I knew, even then, should have been my own first reaction. It was not until my senior year that I looked around at the system I had helped create and realized that although I had done some things in this group that were fun and of which I was proud, I could not be who I wanted to be if I stayed within this context. I admitted to myself that I had made the wrong choice. This was the mid-1960s, however, and I was not the only one changing. The times seeded unrest in many of my "sisters," and we performed small rebellions such as pledging a catholic girl and resisting the serious pressure we got from our national organization to cease and desist. It all came to naught, however. She eventually dropped out, and our gesture was feeble. I knew it was time to get out. It was time to get on with the part of me that was becoming more dominant: my role as a student and the emergence of my desire to write and to discover things worth reading. I left the whole student leader, sorority image behind when I went on to graduate school, and I was for many years too embarrassed to ever admit to having been in a sorority, much less having helped run one. Graduate school at Yale was about the woman's movement, the Black Panthers, sexual liberation, and the Vietnam protest—a rejection of just about everything I had been doing in sorority life. I lived in a commune, became more sexually adventurous (I have to admit, this was a continuing act of rebellion; I never understood why recreational sex was just for men), and aligned myself with intellectuals, activists, and people who I thought were more noble and more politically pure than myself. I joined women's consciousness-raising groups, began to understanding how gender had affected my life and my identity, and also started studying—and protesting against—the Vietnam War. I became engaged to a Yale law student who had claimed conscientious objector status against the war, and his fight, which went all the way to the Supreme Court of the United States (where he won on a 5 to 4 decision), made me rethink the way government related to the governed. Like many other privileged kids coming of age, I couldn't believe that I could be on the other side of the line from my government. I couldn't quite believe that I might have to leave my country. All this created daily drama, a self-important sense of one's place in the world, and a point to one's life. It so overshadowed the purely educational aspects of graduate school that by the time I followed my husband to the West Coast, I realized I was thoroughly unsocialized professionally. I was intellectually engaged, I had begun to think of myself as a writer, and I had changed from the sociology of law to the sociology of gender, sexuality, and family. I did not really think of myself as a professor, however, but that was surely the road I was on. I had the training but not the identity. When I left and took a job, it took me a few years before I became what I seemed to be. At Yale, we were trained to be intellectually adept but not to have a career. I had had good intellectual colleagueship but no one had ever taken me aside and asked me where I was going and how I was going to get there. In all fairness, I never asked. It was a time when we all thought we could just cut our own swath through the country and make it up as we went along. When I came to the University of Washington, it hit me right away that my colleagues had an occupation, and that if I wanted to stay I better figure out how to have one too. I hooked up almost immediately with a man, who would become a dear friend and coauthor, who read me the "riot act" and told me I had better get serious— and so I did. I took on a new core identity in about 2 months. My friend Philip Blumstein, however, was living a double life at the time: He was gay before it was safe to be "out" publicly. His double life gave me permission to have a few of my own; I felt comfortable with parallelism.

I won't discuss the many years I have spent as a professor—let others analyze that particular category. I will, however, discuss one other formative culture in the creation of my identity. It came from reaching back into my childhood fantasies and hobby. As I became more secure as a professor (tenure, as we all know, helps a lot) and as I added other identities that once would have threatened my legitimacy as a scholar (journalist and TV commentator), I felt strong enough to leave yuppie city life and create yet another self in the world of horses and horse people. It crept up on me. Over time, however, the horses increasingly moved to the center of my existence.

I have, from the time I was a child, been obsessed with the beauty and grace of horses; I have made a major commitment of my time, money, and lifestyle to living with them—and about 14 years ago I changed my life so that I could fully participate in the horse world—not as Dr. Pepper Schwartz but as someone who loved horses and worked in the horse business.

My dad (who grew up on a farm) put me on a horse when I was about 3 years old and, like many other little girls, it was a revelation—a life-changing event. I could write a whole paper on little girls and their horse fixations, but suffice it to say, unlike most little girls, I never grew out of mine—even with some heavy-duty competition (career, marriage, children, writing, etc.). I was so besotted with horses that I was clueless about how norm-breaking it was to have a horse in the academic world. In fact, talk about blind class privilege, I bought my own horse in undergraduate school and took it to graduate school with me. (Imagine this: Girl comes to graduate school with own horse in the time of Students for a Democratic Society and other radical movements, rides with the Chair of the department and doesn't quite get the bizarre nature of this in terms of professional socialization, political delicacy, etc. So much for my claims to an understanding of social systems. If this hadn't been Yale—home of the truly elite—I would have been ridiculed right out of graduate school.)

In any case, my horse went anywhere I went—even to my first job, at which point I realized that I had to work 20 hours a day and that this wasn't fair to the animal. I sold my horse, but once I managed to get tenure, this abstemiousness didn't last long. In fact, after I met my second husband, who also liked horses, things got more intense. The culmination of this was selling everything and moving to a ranch outside Seattle, getting more involved in the business of horses, and, in fact, becoming a serious breeder of horses from Kentucky called, variously, Rocky Mountain horses, Mountain Pleasure Horses, and Kentucky Mountain horses.

Now here is a world truly in a parallel universe. Not that class, gender, status, and power don't operate in predictable ways in this world. Indeed they do. All my other accomplishments up to this point, however, really counted for nothing in this world. The people who I wanted to affiliate with were different, and the challenges and norms and values of this world existed along new criteria.

First, I had to learn how to run a business (with my husband), hire people (and deal with a hierarchy more frank and class linked than the one between student and professor), and, most interesting, negotiate Kentucky, the place where all these horses came from. That was a mix of sociology and anthropology. In the horse world I work in, there are two Kentuckys because there are huge class divisions and mixed-up status allocations in the breed world. Western

Kentucky is made up of "flatlanders" and "hill people." The flatlanders are the people around Lexington who live middle-class lives or much better, who are educated, and who can afford to buy much of what they want. The other people, who live in the hills and hollows of Appalachia—or less posh places in the state or contiguous states—are horse traders and hobbyists who live by their wits and their knowledge of good horseflesh and gain their status by besting anybody they can in the show ring. The show ring is the great leveler—although the wealthier the person, the more he or she can network with judges, buy winning horses instead of having to raise them, and increase his or her odds of winning and dominating the show circuit. Wealthy people cannot dominate the show ring completely, however, and this is the premise of countless kid's books and movies about the little girl whose horse is rescued from the glue factory (or some such fate) who wins over the fancy breeders. It happens.

This is not the only social drama of the horse world, however. There is also the drama of trying to create beautiful creatures through a breeding program, protect them, suffer with their vulnerability, exalt when one turns out to be extraordinary, and wonder what one is doing as the bills mount up and the clients ebb and flow with the seasons and less explicable reasons. There is also the drama of discovering genetic issues, creating alliances with other horse people, and, yes, being stupidly seduced into buying the wrong animal or being betrayed by an acquaintance in the breed world. When fellow breeders support each other through hard times and risky business, strong friendships get established. These friendships, based on survival in the horse world, become as intense and as rewarding as any others one can have.

There is an unexpected discovery and pleasure in this. In my life, this world is the first in which class boundaries have really disappeared. This is the first time in my life when class boundaries have seamlessly faded away. People of diverse class backgrounds have close friendships and business relations because prestige and respect accrue because of a person's horsemanship, breeding program, or history of service to the breed. My friendships in the horse world span each class level (that is not a hyperbole), and we operate in a way that is different from that of any other world I have inhabited or do inhabit. Most, although not all, of my breed friends are women, and besides the horses, we bond in the way that women do: small and deep talk about husbands, children, lovers, or whatever is going on in our lives. Recently, in the Northwest there was a crisis regarding a genetic problem in the breed, and my close friends and I offered each other free stallion service plus the emotional support to get on the road to getting the problem solved. I tried to think of a parallel situation to this in any of the other lives I have lived, but I could not. There are individuals I have helped and who have helped me—but not as a group. It reminded me of being in a union, in which people help each other pull through a strike, or when a disaster hits and a whole community pulls together. There is something about common vulnerability that brings an honesty that makes leadership less important and unity extremely critical.

Part of this community was formed during the years when all of us attended the national show. We all stayed in a mutually affordable motel (with as many as six in a room: children, grandchildren, lovers—whoever anyone wants to bring) and spent the next 72 or more hours together. We talked horses ad nauseum. We visited with the most influential breeders, some of whom have become friends over the years and others of whom are either not interested in people outside Kentucky or who are separated from us by various national feuds having to do with everything from nasty infighting gossip to real issues over how the breed association should be run. Some of these divisions swirl around us but are not caused by us. They are the accumulation of years of horse trading and class clashes (e.g., flatland daughters running off with hill trainers) and serve to make juicy conversation. Another bond that crisscrosses class lines is that both big and small owners and breeders feel screwed at one time or another by the judges. Therefore, a great interstitial cement is the endless groaning about the bad values, sight, honesty, and so on of the judges of the moment.

All this feels very inclusive, unsullied by outside identities. It is only later, when one realizes that the man who owns the stallion of the moment holds a blue-collar job and lives out of a trailer or that the Trainer of the Year also drives a bus, that you realize you are operating in a world that has its own validity and reality and does not depend on other identities. Sure, some of the truly wealthy or professional classes have their own spiffy trainers, but their advantage, although resented, becomes insufferable only if they are insufferable—or if they have a clean sweep of the show.

I love this world so far away from my others. I like who I am in this world, and I like visiting the characters in this world, whether they live on multimillion dollar horse farms or hills where everyone has the same last name and first name (this is not an exaggeration) and where no one cares too much about what happens outside of the reality of the horse community. In my breed, there is plenty of great horseflesh at prices that more people than one would think can afford (I have seen women who are hairdressers and janitors buy the very best horse of the season). This makes for a world with an unpredictability and diversity that I love.

More to the point of this chapter, I also love who I am in this system: one of the group, struggling along with everyone else, participating in my friends lives—not as their boss, teacher, or colleague but as their fellow traveler—even though there is no other way we all would be together or would have become this close and this equal in most other settings. My friends are ranchers, secretaries, and wives of truck drivers—in other words, people who I would never have met in my circuit through Washington University, Yale, or the University of Washington. They are smart, savvy, funny people with powerful personalities. Knowing them has taught me much about my prejudices and the insularity of my previous friendship networks. It has also given me an unexpected insight into the social world most of us inhabit today: the big city. The city puts us together with like others, whereas the small town puts us together with everyone and a variety of people have dignity and value within its borders. My ranch is in a small town, and my friends in the horse world also comprise a small world. Maybe we all need a small and a big place in which to live. The size of your world affects your identity as much as what you do in it. Although I have learned some continuing parts of my identity (or identities) from the various pursuits, affinity groups, and friends I have created throughout the years, I have also learned that I am a different person when I am living in a different mode. If we don't have multiple selves, we miss a lot—both in insight and in experience. The push for the resolution of ambiguity, to be something, someone, is a process we go through and which our significant others wish us to resolve, especially among the professional classes in which the imagery is that the more single-minded the preoccupation, the more successful the result. It is also possible, however, to be many people. Obviously, I think it is not only desirable but also almost impossible to resist unless we live in total institutions or compressed communities with strong social control mechanisms. Even then, the self is a wild thing. It searches for expression, exploration, and change. It scares us: We call change in midstream a midlife crisis when it is really just an appropriate new variation—and not really a crisis at all. What is a crisis, if we have never given our identity a chance to be examined, to multiply, or to modify. The natural progress of the life cycle is to let this happen, and the process makes us all into sociologists of the self—with at least one very well-studied subject.

CHAPTER 17

Standing on the Threshold and Tripping

Awkwardness in Becoming a Field-Worker

ARLENE KAPLAN DANIELS

It is quite common nowadays to celebrate reflexivity in fieldwork, and science generally—that is, the idea that a researcher is not a remote and neutral agent in a study but rather one who is interactive with and is affected by the data collected so that what is collected inevitably bears the mark of this interaction. Proponents of this idea disagree about whether it should be encouraged or promoted rather than merely recognized. Whatever the stance, however, they all agree that it is always present and therefore has to be accounted for in analyzing the results of the study. Although the idea of reflexivity has taken on new salience, it has always been important in fieldwork. The topic of the field-workers' experiences or "war stories" has always been a popular area of discussion and publication. These stories, of course, cover both what happened to the field-worker and how his or her temperament, background, and class position affected the "natives" and what they then thought of him or her. In my case, I told stories about and from my research long before I published papers from it. The stories had at their core the unsettling experiences from the field involving what the respondents thought of me and what I thought of them. Invariably, these experiences illuminated conflicts in my own personal life.

Whether or not I realized it at the time, the stories were designed to rationalize and resolve the problems I encountered.

In this chapter, I consider what one learns about oneself in the process of interacting with respondents and learning what they think about the researcher. In my case, two important lessons concerned understanding how to manage flirtatious interactions and stay in control of the situation and how to come to grips with my own concerns about my social class position. I came to understand the significance of these difficult issues through my tendency to tell stories about fieldwork situations that had been bothering me. Also, from my experiences with the military, I told many stories about my association with a military psychiatrist captain who had been designated as an assistant to me in a survey of recruits who I had received a grant to study.

The stories became monologues that I developed to tell of my adventures—and mishaps—in the military. They were not just intended as entertainment for my friends; I discovered that they were also personally cathartic. It has been my pattern, whenever personally troubled or upset about an experience, to make the troubling experience into a tale or anecdote to tell my friends. The telling must have a funny edge to it, something amusing or exotic, so that I can interest my friends in whatever it is that is bothering me.

This pattern certainly was already well developed before I became a sociologist. I can remember my husband telling me, during our courtship, that some of his friends had warned him about dating me. Richard said his friends told him, "Don't take her out, because afterwards she will tell funny stories about it at your expense." Of course, these advisers could not realize that the funny stories were a way to encompass the pain and confusion that followed a series of unsuccessful romantic adventures. (Fortunately, Richard did not take their advice.) The pattern continued, however, and it continues to this day so that any difficult or painful experience becomes grist for anecdote to be told and retold until the embarrassment or problem has dissipated. In a sense, my habitual manner of handling problems carried over into professional life rather than sociological perspectives informing personal life.

This pattern of resolving personal problems, however, created other difficulties—problems of maintaining anonymity and respect for the informants. The confusions and pangs created by some of the encounters with respondents were issues I worked through by telling stories to make myself more comfortable about the data-collecting experience. Two studies in which I engaged that gave me the most difficulty—and engendered the most stories—were those of military psychiatrists and of upper-class women volunteers. I discuss what I learned through these uneasy and even painful interactions: how the experience of fieldwork inevitably leads to self-revelation and to a deeper understanding of one's own strengths and weaknesses.

In the first instance, the study of military psychiatry, one of my keenest realizations was that I am a control freak. I had understood that I was supposed to be in charge of a small study of recruits' attitudes toward the military experience and that the local military psychiatrists were assigned to me to help collect the data. Because I was not allowed to deal with the recruits directly, I had to depend on one particular psychiatrist assistant delegated to me. Unfortunately, this psychiatrist was not keen on taking direction from me. Therefore, a struggle emerged between this ostensible assistant and me before I realized that he would be absolutely useless as a researcher. His response to my overt and explicit desire to be in command of the research operation was, in psychiatry jargon, "passive aggressive." In this instance, passive aggressive meant that the young captain would not follow my instructions but would, instead, respond to my insistence on the agenda by becoming flirtatious and seductive. My response was to become implacable about my directives, but I was also terrified. I could not understand the reason for his behavior, and I had no idea how to respond in an appropriate manner, either as a researcher or as a young married woman. One evening, he invited me to his quarters, ostensibly to discuss the study. When we arrived, he excused himself to change clothes and returned wearing only the bottom half of what looked like some kind of playsuit. I was appalled and picked up a journal and said as firmly as I could, though I feared my voice might be trembling, "I think it is quite chilly this evening." Then I put the journal in front of my face. After awhile, I heard footsteps dragging away and, on their return, I lowered my journal to face the captain, now wearing both top and bottom parts of his outfit. I was still unnerved and entirely at a loss about how to proceed, however. When nervous, my tendency is to become compulsively talkative; thus, I started a rapid, lengthy monologue about the nature of the research experience, the importance of the project on which we had embarked, the possibilities of future research, my own previous experience with research and hopes for further research, and my hopes that we might collaborate in some of these projects. The captain had provided some cheese and crackers, which I consumed while talking. When they were completely gone—I must have made my way through an entire box of crackers and all the available cheese—I could not think what else to do, so I got up and left.

I responded to these mystifying changes in our relationship by an even greater tenacity about control. On every possible occasion, I reminded the captain that I was older than he and that he should keep that in mind. I brought up my credentials and experience in research as often as I could and tried to persuade him that there was much he could learn from me in this area that might prove useful to him in his own professional career. I even pointed out to him that the glibness of his manner betokened a cleverness in interpersonal interaction that might be put to good use in the study of relationships. He was none too pleased to be praised for his cunning, but I gave it a shot anyway. In the end, I never could persuade the captain to engage in research in a systematic and serious manner. Therefore, I turned to a study of the military psychiatrists themselves. What I learned about myself in that abortive survey was that there were unanticipated areas of interaction in which I did not know how to behave and in which I could not master the situation. As I realized how important control in such situations was to me, however, I quickly learned about the issues of coquetry and flirtation that had so terrified me previously. I learned to dress and comport myself in an appealing and even seductive manner. When it became clear that I could manage flirtatious behavior from others without becoming flustered, these behaviors disappeared. Therefore, in the end, my confrontation with the military psychiatrists was a considerable benefit to me, and, in an odd way, gave me a chance to learn how to handle myself with poise in situations I had never encountered while in graduate school or even after—until then.

In addition, I distanced myself from the seductive captain by telling stories about him: his "administrative" approach to psychiatry in the military, his disinterest in therapy or research, and his endless, manipulative efforts to keep a soft spot for himself at a desirable post. One of the stories that I told included a comparison between his own lackadaisical or indifferent approach to professional responsibility and another captain's more involved, although vengeful, attitude toward patients whom he thought were malingering or hypochondriacal. I nicknamed the two of them "The Sleeping Prince and the Beast" for the purposes of some analyses of the military psychiatric endeavor. Also, without using any names or identifying characteristics, I spoke of them with these sobriquets when giving a talk about alternative responses to the issue of offering treatment in military psychiatry. Unfortunately, another military psychiatrist recognized the protagonists behind these nicknames and angrily left. He also spoke angrily to me later about my tendency to satirize and to mock the military psychiatry mission. Here, as in my later work with women volunteers of the upper class, I was not entirely aware of how much my own self-confidence had been threatened by the people I studied nor how much I had been protecting myself by patronizing and mocking them and their ways. It was only after I had a severely angry or disapproving confrontation that I was jolted into attention. I needed to pay attention; I had to purge these feelings from my writing about military psychiatry before I could publish it.

When I began to study women volunteers, I found other, somewhat painful, opportunities to learn about myself in ways that almost threatened the success of the study. At first, I was not aware of how much these elegant and well-bred women had gotten my goat—made me feel threatened—because of my own working-class and raffish background. My upbringing had been so helter skelter that I had arrived at college without many of the middle-class skills essential to survival in college.

I began to be aware of my shortcomings in high school. My family lived in Los Angeles at that time, and I had started to study Latin in junior high. The high school in my district did not teach Latin, so I petitioned to enter Los Angeles High School because it did have a highly rated Latin program. I did not realize that this school, at that time, was also socially elite, drawing Jewish children from quite well-to-do homes. My realization was delayed by poor eyesight. My mother was a health food adherent and follower of various theosophical and metaphysical cults. She did not believe in medical interventions: As a consequence, I did not have glasses. Because I was quite nearsighted, my schoolmates were not clearly distinct to me. I was bookish and absorbed in my own interests, so their vague outlines at a distance in the hallways were not a significant issue to me; I could get along, however, because I could discern the build and shape of my acquaintances. Because I was a smart kid, I got along well with the teachers. I got good grades only when I was seated at the front of the room, however: I received poorer grades when, from the back, I couldn't see the blackboard very well—a disadvantage when exams were written on it.

During the 1940s, when I attended high school, I gradually became aware that something about me was not quite right. For example, the other girls mainly wore brightly colored peasant skirts (called broomstick skirts at the time) and white wedgie shoes (manufactured by Joyce). My clothes were acquired in a hit-or-miss fashion. Mostly I wore the bemberg sheer prints with crocheted lace collars inherited from a deceased aunt and whatever shoes that could be purchased on sales in odd shops. The dresses were too long and the hems hung unevenly; my general turnout left much to be desired. Fortunately, my sense that something was amiss was only vague and amorphous. I did notice that all the girls wore pins on their sweaters and that pins were much admired and talked about. Actually, at that time, there was discussion about the protosororities then prevalent in the high schools. In the news journals of the day, columnists would argue about whether these organizations caused pain to those excluded and placed too much emphasis on social acceptance for those too young to manage it. Most of this discussion escaped my notice, but I did focus on the pins. I realized, dimly, that it was important to have a pin. I belonged to a pre-Communist youth club called The Young Pioneers, but they did not have a pin. Therefore, I joined the Philharmonic Club at my high school. I was interested in music and they did have a pin, which I pinned on my dress and was perfectly satisfied with the effect; the larger issue of acceptance or rejection by social clubs had escaped me.

Nonetheless, I knew something was still not quite right—about where my family lived (in a ramshackle and not too well-kept home), how my parents made a living (as small shopkeepers running a health food store and restaurant), and about the eccentricity of my parents. (In my parents' health food store, there was a large sign over the counter that read "What You Eat Today Walks and

Talks Tomorrow," and my mother propounded odd theories about the body and its management to the customers along with doses of mysterious elixirs such as Hydrocon. A neighborhood pharmacist told us that Hydrocon was actually bicarbonate of soda but my mother claimed it was "dehydrated water from the High Saharas.") This background hardly made me a fit companion for the middle-class and well-to-do children of my high school. Because I was already a budding intellectual with self-conscious airs and graces by adolescence, however, their attentions were hardly missed.

I did have a few fellow aesthetes as friends. We ushered at the opera, the symphony, and the ballet. Also, we read "serious" books, turning up our noses at the big hits of the day such as *Forever Amber,* and we attended the newly available foreign films from France, England, and Italy while refusing to see such popular and much discussed American films as "The Outlaw" starring Jane Russell. These friends and interests protected me from the growing unease that my family background and idiosyncratic social experience generated whenever I had occasion to move into "polite" society. I gathered, somehow, that the parents of my friends looked at me in a somewhat askance way. I also knew, of course, that in general my high school peers and their families were bewildered and none too pleased by my manners. I did have ardent supporters among my teachers, however. I remember one, in particular: My Latin teacher, George R. Purnell, made a great effort to meet my mother and urge her to send me to college. He may have been sorry he made the attempt when she burst into tears and said, pronouncing his name wrong, "Oh Mr. Parcell, you don't know what it means to be a mother!" She was responding defensively, I suppose, to the implied criticism in his remarks about how necessary it was to make such plans for one's children. The larger issue was that my family had no funds and no real understanding of the higher-education system: My mother had no education beyond the second grade and my father was not educated beyond the primary grades. They did not stand in my way, however, and when I decided to go to Berkeley, they helped me as much as they could.

Fortunately, there was no tuition, only a moderate registration fee, when I entered the university in 1948, and one could live and work 5 hours a week at the University of California Student Coop for a very reasonable room and board. With the acquisition of a job at the library for 20 hours a week, one could just scrape by. Those first years away from home were a revelation to me. The health food business had been all-consuming for my mother and father, and my mother was never interested in domestic arts. In consequence, I reached late adolescence without much experience of regular or "ordinary" meals. In my home, the fare was catch as catch can: open cans of sardines, blocks of cheese, bread, crackers, and slices of onion and green pepper were often the kind of food one would find when dinner was arranged for guests. There were also stacks of napkins and plates and piles of flatware: One helped oneself. Ordinarily, however, everyone ate individually, either at the store or at home. With this background, the coop was a revelation to me. There were regular times for meals, and one waited until the house mother sat down before eating, although sometimes I forgot and had to be forcibly reminded. Each place was set, and food was passed in an orderly fashion. The food was plentiful and unimaginative but quite good. I had not eaten so well since we came to California from New York City in 1939 and set up in the health food business; I soon learned, however, that it was proper to grumble about the institutional fare. I also learned that I had a lot to learn about living with other people from more conventional backgrounds. My lack of "manners" was indicated by my willingness to poke fun at and ignore middle-class expectations when they were inconvenient. I would gather the unused desserts at the table, for example, and polish them off. I and a friend or two would interrupt bridge tournaments and demand a table at which to play "go fish"—the only card game that I knew how to play. I would insist on playing the Metropolitan Opera broadcast on Saturday afternoons without regard for the wishes of others using the living room. In short, I was inadequately socialized for the courtesies and regard for others that "oil" social life in the manner propounded not only by Miss Manners but also by established, middle-class custom.

During my undergraduate years, although I made friends among the other English majors and found my own crowd, I became increasingly uneasy and uncomfortable about the ways in which I was different. Once I became interested in sociology and learned about socioeconomic status, I saw that some of it had to do with my class background. The part that I was most concerned about was the disorder and casual chaos of my family home. I wanted those parts of order that I had found at the coop: regular meals served in courses with proper place settings; flowers and candles on the table; clean sheets and towels every week; hygienic housekeeping arrangements; and, most of all, the expectation that all these aspects of living could be regularly taken for granted—not just for a special occasion or time. By the time I was in graduate school, I had learned to do some of these things for myself. The finer points of social interaction still escaped me, however.

I spent some painful years in graduate school learning about how to be, as I called it, "mc." I used to tell my friends I wanted to be mc; so when my behavior was not polite or discreet enough, they would laughingly chide me by saying, "Arlene that is not mc!" In this way, I learned not to ask overly personal questions and not to intrude on the conversations of others. I also learned about table manners and some of the finer points of personal grooming. These lessons, understandably, occurred through some embarrassing moments in my social life. Although I had arrived at a reasonable mastery by the time I was interviewing women volunteers, the finer points had not made much of an impression on me because in the circles within which my own social life occurred, an emphasis on formalities and the niceties of upper-middle-class life did not arise.

My difficulties were compounded, at first, when I attempted to interview members of the Junior League for the study of what I had called "status attainment volunteering"—that is, the connection between volunteer work and establishing or maintaining one's place in "society." I had approached the local Junior League chapters in hopes that they would let me interview their members. Artlessly, I had told them that they represented such a uniquely homogenous group—so clearly a society of young women with common values, backgrounds, and aspirations—that they presented almost the characteristics of a tribe. Anthropologists were always looking for a tribe to study, but sociologists rarely had such an opportunity. I would feel fortunate, I told them, if they would be my tribe. Well, of course, I should have known better. Also, of course, the Junior League was very wary of potential researchers, having been burned by exposés and mocking, satirical put-downs in the past. The members had no desire to be studied, and the undertones of mockery in my pitch to them, although not at first consciously deliberate, were hardly likely to make them change their mind. Like the well-bred young ladies that they were, averse to open conflict—or even unpleasantness—they never said "no" but just politely postponed a decision again and again. Because my time on the grant was finite, I had to turn elsewhere for informants. I was terribly lucky to chance upon one woman, a former Junior League member and local chapter president, who thought a study of the work of serious and well-connected volunteers would be useful. She directed me to her colleagues in the earlier generation—the foremothers of the women in the group I had vainly tried to infiltrate—who had succeeded and made names for themselves in the kind of work in which the Junior League members were still apprentices. I was fortunate to have escaped the consequences of my mocking and jeering ways. Also, to my credit, I had been quite taken with and impressed by the first women I had met in the elite circle into which I had been introduced, and I showed these feelings by being both delighted with and respectful toward them. Indeed, they were impressive: in their credentials and experiences, making their way in the world of community service and creating important institutions; in their grasp of the project I was contemplating; and in their understanding of how much more it could be than a description of status attainment or maintenance. They were shrewd enough to see that I had a greater potential for telling their story than I myself had envisioned. I had a great distance to go, however, before I could fulfill their expectations. I had to learn some things about myself first.

In the early stages of the study, when I would report on my findings informally to other groups of volunteer women in other geographic areas, I would often find that the audiences would not find my anecdotes amusing. They would see the mockery and the delight I would take in reporting ladylike foibles, and they would be cold to or even angry with me. At one talk, a woman approached me afterward to reproach me for my mocking manner and, in effect, my lack of professionalism in the style of reporting. She pointed out to me that a good ethnographer would not take such delight in creating amusing tales that would throw a pejorative light on the respondents. She was, of course, quite right, and I took to heart these signs that I was not "getting it" or getting the story quite right. I thought about it a lot and discussed it with my colleagues. Eventually, I purged the deprecatory tone from my writings. I came to understand that I was not seeing beyond the ordinary stereotypes of upper- middle-class women to a clearer picture of what could be elicited from my data. I was, after all, a sociologist of work and occupations. Also, whatever their foibles, these women were engaged in serious and seriously underestimated work for their communities. As a sociologist, and certainly as a feminist, it was my duty to give serious attention to this invisible work of women. Therefore, in the end, I did do what they had hoped for—I wrote a serious monograph on the work of women volunteers who rise to leadership positions. It is interesting that my brashness and mockery endangered the possibility for study, but my curiosity about and admiration for some of the qualities of these "grandes dames" created real friendships that then offered entry into the world I wished to study and space and time to learn and rethink my earlier half-baked ideas of how to analyze the data I was collecting.

In the course of this study, I came to realize just how much ambivalence had remained with me over my own social mobility and my own achieved status as a middle-class woman with bourgeois leanings. I think I felt mingled emotions of admiration, envy, scorn, and pity (very complicated to unravel), and these feelings created a funny kind of ambivalent feeling toward these women that took me some time to understand. In the end, I believe I did sort it out—and also sorted through my relations with these women, some of whom became dear friends beyond the scope of the study. My departure from the group was marked by a party—two parties, actually. The first was a surprise party to mark my first return to the geographic area of the study. It was a proper party produced by volunteer women of the upper class; it was held in a posh home with a photographer to memorialize the event, and it was catered with decorations to note my idiosyncrasies (the table flowers were presented in upturned straw hats to note my fondness for large hats). The second party was to note the publication of my book about the volunteers and was a great luncheon at a fashionable city restaurant. After the party, the participants at the affair trouped down to the nearby bookstore to buy copies of the monograph *Invisible Careers* and to have them autographed. I had surmounted enough of my early ambivalences to be very pleased and proud to be friends with these women—and I had learned to squelch the mocking overtones of addressing them as "ladies."

In the course of the luncheon, however, I had reason to believe that some of my shortcomings as an arrival to the middle class, even if they no longer created difficulties, were still with me. The lunch was served in a Chinese restaurant with a first course of various dim sum—steamed dumplings on little plates. We had elegant carved ivory chopsticks with cloisonne handles that were easy to manage. Therefore, when I noticed that a tiny friend with a bird-like appetite and a reluctance to eat exotic food was leaving all her dim sum untouched, I reached over another woman to snaffle these untouched goodies with my flying chopsticks. The intervening friend, who knew me well, was moved to laugh and to say, "Why should this day be different from any other day?" She was referring, of course, to her habit of urging me to eat much of her meal whenever we lunched together and to my habit of accepting it without question and so eating a double lunch. Of course, she was also referring to my insouciant disregard for the ordinary niceties of the table. The point, however, is that she was referring to them indulgently and she was looking at me fondly at the time. I had managed to accept my differences from the more ladylike women, and they had come to accept me despite some of the eccentricities these differences might involve.

Doing fieldwork becomes less painful as one finds one's way and chooses one's context with more assurance. Fieldwork never loses its ability to teach and to confound one's picture of one's self as a "proper" field-worker, however. In an ethnographic study of a primary grade school in a ghetto, I spent months observing on the playground, in the lunchroom, and in classes and interviewing teachers. In the course of this study, there were several uneasy moments when I realized how ethnocentric and class biased my approach to the world could be. As a result, my intrusions into the lives of students, comments on their behavior, and interventions in their activities were not always proper for a field-worker. I have one daunting memory of standing outside the lunchroom immediately after the bell for the beginning of lunch had rung. Almost immediately, a round, good-natured Samoan first grader came out of the room. "Aren't you going to eat your lunch?" I called to her. "I just did," she called back amiably. "Good heavens," I cried, "How could you possibly eat that fast! Surely you need more time than that!" She just continued to smile and then ran on past me. I immediately kicked myself for my intrusive values, but I was clearly "going native" and taking the role of a teacher or caretaker trying to instill the "proper" values regarding eating behavior. I also had to acknowledge ruefully to myself that I had become more middle class than I had realized, and that I expected deportment rules regarding eating to be enforced in the school.

It was also difficult to remain impassive and neutral when one child would beat up on or bully another. Many times, I would find myself with my fingers around a miscreant's neck, shaking him hard and separating him from the object of his attack, rather than waiting to see if real damage might be inflicted or calling an appropriate caretaker to manage the situation. I had difficulty separating myself from my own system of values to stand back and allow the school system to operate. I was also rueful about the encouragement of gender-stereotyped behavior I would inadvertently give the young girls. One tomboy usually attended school in raggedy attire, with her hair, frizzy and unattended, sticking straight out on her head. On one occasion, she arrived with her hair in neat curls, wearing a pretty dress, white socks, and polished shoes. The teachers made a great fuss over her, and I unthinkingly reinforced their special attentions by telling her how nice she looked and, by indirection, suggesting that her ordinary appearance was a cut below acceptable. The poverty and general neglect of her home notwithstanding, this little girl was a brave and even fierce competitor with the boys in games on the playground and deserved a lot of credit for sticking up for herself. These qualities, however, were not the ones I or the teachers had singled out for attention.

On some matters, the teachers were more sophisticated and conscious of differing value systems than I. I recall asking students solicitously why they had missed school and telling them I missed them until a teacher drew me aside and said quietly,

> We try not to make an issue over absences here because so many of the students come from homes where they are kept out to care for younger siblings. We don't want to make them feel bad about that when they finally can come back.

Why hadn't I thought that out for myself? The unconscious and inappropriate assumptions of privileged people were hard to shake loose.

In thinking about fieldwork experiences during my professional lifetime, it has become clear to me that the problem of "tripping," as I have called it in the title of this chapter, is not only a problem at the beginning of a career but also an ongoing problem whenever one stands on a threshold—on the edge of a new social world or seeking entry to a group of respondents. Many professionals, including academics, as they become older and successfully settled in their careers, can, ideally, contrive to avoid nasty or uncomfortable surprises. This means that they can protect themselves from importuning or disagreeable others, and they can choose, more or less, what they want to do and where they want to go. The advantages are clear: They can "wax fat," as it were, in comfort and learn to think well of themselves when contrary evidence does not enter their daily rounds. Of course, many professionals are not in these enviable circumstances. They may have to face disagreeable and critical clients, some of whom have enough power to make their reproaches felt. Still other professionals choose to work in arenas in which conflict and controversy are always present. Journalists may face such environments when called into question about the reliability or appropriateness of their reports; public officials who find themselves in the limelight when their performance is criticized are another example. I conclude by saying that field-workers are another example. Those researchers who do not cocoon themselves in the academy or in the upper reaches of bureaucratic or administrative work are always finding opportunities for more painful acquisition of self-knowledge as they blunder into the shibboleths of those they study. Particularly in settings in which one studies one's peers—or one's superiors in worldly status—the opportunity to learn more about one's self as one learns about others is always present because they will be more than happy to point out one's shortcomings.

CHAPTER 18

My Life With Xena and Billy

JOSHUA GAMSON

I have long been a fan of lesbians, but never more so than when I discovered Xena the Warrior Princess. I was sitting with my friend Rebecca in a park overlooking San Francisco, catching up and gossiping, when it became quickly clear that Rebecca and Xena had become very close. Rebecca has been thinking about Xena day and night, talking about her nonstop with friends. She has written stories, erotic ones, starring Xena. She has videotapes of Xena demolishing whole tribes, Xena congratulating a transsexual beauty pageant winner, and Xena in a hot tub with her sidekick Gabrielle, the bard of the "Golden Era of Myth and Legend." As she began to tell the story of their relationship, she inadvertently unleashed my inner sociologist. I wanted all the details. Just who is this warrior princess, and why are so many lesbians obsessed with her? What exactly do they do with Xena, who is, after all, a fictional character on a self-consciously cheesy syndicated television program?

My interest was not academic—and besides, I was behind the curve on this one because, as Rebecca informed me, there was already an organization devoted to Xena studies. I was interested in Rebecca's life. I was also interested in the goings-on in lesbian circles. What a lot of lesbians are up to is inherently interesting to me, in large part because of my own identity: We march in the same parades, share a similar marginalized political status, and have parallel and intersecting communal histories. I found myself translating ethnographic habits and pieces of sociological knowledge to bring Xena into my everyday consciousness, to enrich my own identity-driven connection to lesbian life, and to make her—or more accurately, Rebecca's fandom of her—comprehensible to me.

This is how qualitative sociology gets imported into my life outside of academia—a process I expect is quite common and not limited to sociology: In the midst of constructing and building on various parts of my self (my identity, my self-image, my relationship to various communities with whom I identify, and so on), I stumble onto someone or something I don't quite understand or a nagging sense of disturbance. A small investigation ensues, with comparisons to things I know and questions about things I do not. I loosely apply sociological pieces and sociological skills and wind up transforming or clarifying my identity a bit. Indeed, without such a process, my personal and social identities would be much less defined. Everyone, I expect, does something like this in their everyday life; the difference for me is that my work as a sociologist has turned the process into a somewhat honed set of skills, routines, and ideas.

Therefore, I absorb Rebecca's stories, watch her videos, visit her web sites, and go with her to search for a new Xena t-shirt to give to her girlfriend. I read a story in a San Francisco magazine with my synapses snapping. At the Chat House in San Francisco, and at Meow Mix and the Boiler Room in New York, the article reports, fans "jeer, cheer, and bring the house down" while "munching sandwiches and drinking beer or espresso" during Xena showings—not unlike the *Dynasty* parties that popped up in gay bars across the country in the 1980s. Xena contingents have joined the Gay Pride Parade and the Dyke March. "One of my friends is getting the letters XWP [Xena Warrior Princess] tattooed on her chest," a San Franciscan tells the magazine (Federico, 1997, p. 24). On the internet, where computer technology has made linking up those with very specialized interests quick and simple, there are hundreds of on-line Xena sites, including a top-secret lesbian group that Rebecca tells me she shouldn't even be telling me about. There have been two official Xena conventions. "It's all these kids and all these lesbians," reports Rebecca, to my delight.

Despite the campiness of the show itself and the echoes of both old-style male homosexual star worship (Dyer, 1984, 1986) and gay-bar hooting and hollering, the affinities with gay male fandom evaporate quickly. Xena is no Judy Garland. Spun off of the action-series *Hercules,* Xena has few soft edges and little of the physical and emotional fragility found in the classic film icons worshiped by many in a previous generation of gay men. Unlike her male action-hero counterparts, she has regular moral worries, but like them she settles scores with swords and fists and well-placed kicks. She is played by Lucy Lawless, whose body itself is hardly skinny, self-conscious, supermodelesque, or drugs-and-diet-ravaged: Tall, broad Xena walks tough, like she's just gotten off a horse; talks tough (except to Gabrielle, her constant companion); and comes in a big, tough package. She is not ruled; Xena rules. I start to like her, seeing her through lesbian eyes. Through my habitual ethnography, she is becoming mine.

It's not just the sexy-tough, soft-butch, ass-kicking imagery that triggers such enthusiasm in my lesbian buddies. There is also a strong suspicion, actively fueled by the show's producers, that Xena is a woman-loving woman. Certainly, there is much in the text itself to go on, especially the flirtatious, loving relationship between Xena and Gabrielle. In addition to the I'll-scrub-your-back hot tub scene between the two, there's the moment when Xena, whose body at the time is inhabited by a male antagonist, kisses Gabrielle with great, sexy passion; many other such moments come and go. The producers, including one who is openly a lesbian, have few qualms about feeding the lesbian fire; their show, which in 1997 surpassed *Baywatch* and *Star Trek* to take the number one syndicated television spot, does not seem to be suffering. "We talk about it on the set," Lawless told *Frontiers,* "One of the best parts of the job is getting to throw in references that [gay] fans will pick up on. We are aware and we're not afraid of it. This is a love story between two people" (Federico, 1997, p. 25). I begin to share the lesbian excitement. Starved as the sexually marginalized have been for images of ourselves (Fejes & Petrich, 1993), and not entirely satisfied by the relatively tame sitcom images popping up in shows such as *Ellen,* here is a show that is aware and unafraid, in which two women love each other, bathe together, and kiss.

None of this is all that explicit, of course; it is always coded so that what lesbian and gay fans pick up, they pick up under a straight radar. Upon my return home to New York, I proudly report to Rebecca that I had caught part of a *Xena* episode involving vampire-style creatures and a guy who is only a head. "Did you see the end," Rebecca asks, immediately recognizing the episode, "where Xena says to Gabrielle, now a vampire, 'Gabrielle, do it!' and she bites Xena on the neck and then we see Xena writhing in ecstasy? That was fun." (Truth told, I got a bit bored before the writhing scene and went outside.) It is not difficult to find the lesbian subtext in such an episode, what with the classic lesbian vampire theme (Weiss, 1992) and the ecstatic reception by one woman of another's neck bite. Indeed, among the options at a lesbian Xena web site, I find the "museum of subtext," which goes through each episode, in meticulous and humorous detail, and highlights lesbian content. Like fans of many kinds (Gledhill, 1991; Lewis, 1992), my lesbian colleagues spend much of their time digging underneath the text for the stuff that meets their own identity needs and desires.

Then there's the World Wide Web, on which a simple keyword search yields multiple ongoing Xena conversations, photos, articles, and storytelling. Zoom around the web sites, and one can see that the relationship to Xena goes much further than reading: These fans are "textual poachers" (Jenkins, 1992) extraordinaire. Lesbian fan fiction abounds, including voluminous "Xenerotica" (some of it written by Rebecca), in which a love-and-sex subtext becomes an explicit, highly developed plotline. "She had fought this for so long," says one of Rebecca's (Hall, 1997) Xenerotic stories, in the tones of the romance novel, "squelching her desire and love for Gabrielle, convinced that letting it go would cause Gabrielle harm." Xena feels the tears she used to fight, lets them roll down her face. Rebecca writes,

> Before Gabrielle she couldn't remember when she had cried last—when her brother was killed she felt the tears dry up inside her. Gabrielle taught her how to cry again, how to feel again. It was scary, but it felt so good.

Later, Xena traces her fingertips over Gabrielle's breasts and abdomen, "causing muscles to twitch in their wake," and then her strokes grow longer, "now trailing down [Gabrielle's] thighs, tracing a path of fire across her skin." "Your breasts are so beautiful. I love touching them," Xena whispers in this story, "Look how hard your nipples are now." The nipples, as is often the case, are just the beginning. Until an attack on the Amazon army interrupts them and the warrior princess must go save the day, Xena and Gabrielle make hot, detailed love.

I do not do much more with all of this information than sit with it and ponder its meaning for me. I recognize in these activities, so familiar from my more academic researches, the creativity of both fan subcultures (Harrington & Bielby, 1995; Jenkins, 1992) and identity-based subcultures (Chauncey, 1994; Davis & Kennedy, 1994). It is this knowledge, along with my ethnographic habits, that facilitates my interpretations of the response to Xena: the overwhelming desire for frankly sexualized images of love between women, of women with strong bodies and wills who can kick ass; the use of these images to strengthen existing social ties within lesbian communities, and as an excuse for a party.

My use of the information is personal, however. I try to see myself in these activities—to see, in effect, how much of a lesbian a gay man can really be. Our desire for images of people of the same sex "doing it" the way it's done, passionately and unapologetically, is similar, for example. Batman and Robin notwithstanding, we have little gay superheroism to work with. Gay men have plenty of semipublic sexual institutions, however, and do plenty of sexual self-symbolizing. I am not deprived of public images of people like me as erotic beings. Therefore, I am struck by an intensity in this lesbian fandom that I do not share: the enthusiastic drive toward finding the erotic, or simply creating it, in a culture that offers the thin choice between straight-porn pseudolesbians and desexualized actual ones and in a subculture that, acutely aware of sexual violence against women, has historically been ambivalent about building institutions and imagery around sex. These are not new insights, of course, but I have never felt so strongly their emotional weight and ferocity for lesbians and their comparative lightness for me. I can walk away before Xena says "do it!" I do not need Xena like a lesbian needs Xena.

Back in New York City, I find the everyday sociologist sparked again by the flip side of this phenomenon—a man named Billy. Walking down Eighth Avenue in the nouveau gay ghetto of Chelsea, I notice him. He is a bit over a foot tall, blond, muscular, and dressed today in leather pants and a harness. One cannot help but notice a significant penis inside his leather pants. He is, his makers suggest, "anatomically correct," although a quick trip to any locker room might suggest he is anatomically exaggerated. He is the first mass-marketed gay doll, or, as an ad for a party in his honor at a popular dance club—produced by local party promoters along with the doll's manufacturers and clothing designer Raymond Dragon (who does Billy's clothes), and sponsored by Captain Morgan rum—stated, "the world's first out and proud gay doll." Given my Xena-inspired desire for a gay superhero, perhaps I should be thrilled: Here is a heroically endowed doll who dresses better than the genitalless, macho G.I. Joe and the genitalless, suburban Ken and who is a full inch taller than both. I am disturbed, however, and so must poke around Billy a bit, bring my diluted sociological business to bear on this bit of plastic, to figure out what he is doing here and why I am not so certain I like him.

Not surprisingly, it turns out I am not alone in my irritation. I start reading the letters columns after Billy's coming-out party. "Sure, he's cute, but gimme a break," writes a man named Marc. "Billy's just a clone—another reminder that the ideal gay man is buff, built, blond, and smooth. . . . We've had our fill of tired stereotypes" ("Letters to the Editor," 1997, p. 7). Billy, this time dressed in cutoff shorts and a cutoff flannel shirt over a Billy t-shirt, looks out from the page next to the letter, with the caption "Billy: Friend or Clone?" Billy's creator tells a local gay weekly (Downey, 1997), "Some [gay] journalists think he's a representation of what a gay man has to look like, but that's far from the truth. . . . Billy is an individual gay man who celebrates the concept of diversity" (p. 25). Later, perusing a Gay Billy web site, I begin to get a glimpse of this "concept of diversity": In the United States, the doll is available in San Francisco Billy (flannel shirt and gay freedom rings around his neck), Master Billy (a leather-man in a harness), Wall Street Billy (suit and tie), Sailor Billy (button-front pants and a sailor hat), and Cowboy Billy (jeans, boots, and cowboy hat). A boyfriend is rumored to be in the making.

Inside the box, a circular explains that Billy is from Amsterdam but travels a lot and is gay and proud. "I'm just your average gay guy," he is quoted as saying. Of course, all versions of Billy, as Marc the letter-writer noted, are white, blond, and pumped. In response to the charge that Billy is a "steroid freak," his creator argues that "he goes to the gym, but is how he looks so wrong?" (Downey, 1997, p. 25). He returns to Billy's extra claim to a "technical first" in the doll manufacturing business—his genitals. He says, "Really just getting the penis together was a lot of work" (p. 25). The first shipment of 5,000 Billys from the United Kingdom, I read in a Knight-Ridder report from the internet, sold in a few days at $49.95 a piece (Nevada, 1997). I cannot bring myself to set foot in the stores that sell him.

Why so hostile? Doesn't everyone need a doll of their very own? After all, isn't this good "visibility"? Doesn't this serve me, too? There is no question that the discovery of gay and lesbian markets has increased the "mainstream" visibility of lesbians and gay men: Companies such as Subaru, Miller Beer, and Ikea seek our loyalty by showing us advertising images of ourselves; their advertisements have underwritten an explosion of "community" publications during the past decade—magazines such as *Out, Curve, Genre,* and *POZ* in which clean, upbeat images of gay men and lesbians abound (Gluckman & Reed, 1997; Lukenbill, 1995; Strub, 1997). Even Disney, which owns *Ellen,* did not back down when targeted by the religious right for producing images of homosexuals as acceptable, decent people. As Mark Stern of Overlooked Opinions, a firm that calls itself the "gay market expert," told a reporter writing about the Billy doll, "Money is money" (Nevada, 1997, p. C1). Billy would seem to be a part of this commercialization-leads-to-visibility-leads-to-tolerance scenario. Unlike Xena, he is produced by and for gay men: There is no subtext to be uncovered or invented.

Confronting Billy, however, means once again revisiting my own relationship to the commercialization of gay life, and to what it means to be identified with its products. As many critics have pointed out, myself included, advertiser-sponsored visibility is very circumscribed, tending not surprisingly to produce disproportionate images of affluent, white men who conform to gender conventions and other "mainstream" norms (Gamson, 1998; Gluckman & Reed, 1997; Hennessy, 1995). Embracing Billy means embracing this model of gay "community." Whatever the protestations of his producers, it is no accident that Billy would be more comfortable on Fire Island, with its affluent, gym-bodied, predominantly white and male clientele, than in, for example, Brooklyn. In the context of all this commodified visibility and visible commodification, Billy-the-first-gay-doll cannot help but be read as collective self-representation—an imagined ideal.

Even the sexualization of this "for-adults" doll gives me pause, I find, in a way that the eroticization of Xena did not. As with Xena, the eroticized body becomes the focus—although here, through the simple manufacture of large genitals, much less creatively so. My encounter with Xena, however, reminded me of the very different paths sexuality has taken through lesbian as opposed to gay male cultures. Whereas with Xena and Gabrielle it is subversive fun to imagine an erotic life, with Billy I recognize a well-worn path: The hypermasculine body becomes a mark of gay pride—the penis a marketing tool. I have never objected to the pleasures involved in all this, but Billy pushes me away with a politic that alienates.

Therefore, my short journey into subcultural trivia, guided by sociological habits, takes me again back to myself, to the boundaries of my identity, and to my relationship to an existing community. Is this "my" doll? I am not so distant from the affluent, gym-bodied, Manhattan-and-Fire-Island man—but Billy, as I come to understand him, reminds me of my distance from an urban gay identity as it is currently being produced, often for profit. Celebrating Billy would feel like disloyalty to me because Billy helps draw the lines of community membership in ways that exclude so many people with whom I identify, and in his own small way he participates in a politics that is too far from my own, in which purchasing power is the path to liberation. Oddly, bringing a sociological perspective to my own daily life has made an identity harder to hold. The lens brings certain things into my vision that then keep me distant from my own sense of membership. My everyday ethnography leaves me standing between Xena and Billy, clearer about but more distant from my own identity: too gay to love Xena and not gay enough to love Billy.

REFERENCES

Chauncey, G. (1994). *Gay New York.* New York: Basic Books.

Davis, M., & Kennedy, E. L. (1994). *Boots of leather, slippers of gold.* New York: Penguin.

Downey, A. (1997, February 21). Guys and dolls. *HX Magazine, 25.*

Dyer, R. (Ed.). (1984). *Gays and film.* New York: Zoetrope.

Dyer, R. (1986). *Heavenly bodies: Film stars and society.* London: British Film Institute/Macmillan Education.

Federico, L. (1997). The (lesbian) adventures of Xena: Warrior Princess and her faithful sidekick, Gabrielle. *Frontiers Magazine, 16,* 24-26.

Fejes, F., & Petrich, K. (1993). Invisibility, homophobia and heterosexism: Lesbians, gays and the media. *Critical Studies in Mass Communication, 10,* 396-422.

Gamson, J. (1998). *Freaks talk back: Tabloid talk shows and sexual nonconformity.* Chicago: University of Chicago Press.

Gledhill, C. (Ed.). (1991). *Stardom: Industry of desire.* London: Routledge.

Gluckman, A., & Reed, B. (1997). The gay marketing moment. In M. Duberman (Ed.), *A queer world* (pp. 519-525). New York: New York University Press.

Hall, R. (1997). Heaven down there [On-line fan fiction]. *www.obsession14.com/XenaRotica.*

Harrington, C. L., & Bielby, D. (1995). *Soap fans: Pursuing pleasure and making meaning in everyday life.* Philadelphia: Temple University Press.

Hennessy, R. (1995, Winter). Queer visibility in commodity culture. *Cultural Critique,* 31-75.

Jenkins, H. (1992). *Textual poachers: Television fans and participatory culture.* London: Routledge.

Letters to the Editor. (1997, March 7). *HX Magazine,* 7.

Lewis, L. (Ed.). (1992). *Adoring audience: Fan culture and popular media.* London: Routledge.

Lukenbill, G. (1995). *Untold millions: The gay and lesbian market in America.* New York: HarperCollins.

Nevada, C. (1997, March 8). Gay Billy doll is "out," proud, and not for children. *Akron Beacon Journal,* pp. C1, C5.

Strub, S. (1997). The growth of the gay and lesbian market. In M. Duberman (Ed.), *A queer world* (pp. 514-518). New York: New York University Press.

Weiss, A. (1992). *Vampires and violets: Lesbians in film.* New York: Penguin.

PART **IV**

Workplaces

CHAPTER 19

Affirmative Action and Me

SHARON M. COLLINS

It is no happenstance that my work so far revolves around the perceptions and experiences of being marginal and of black people. These themes are constantly filtered through the prism of my day-to-day life; they emerge in the sociology that I do because, in part, they are my biography. There is much about me that lends itself to taking this "outsider" perspective. I am a woman in a man's world, a black person in a white world, and a black person who looks white. To a large degree, the social actors that my work attends to reflect me. They are anomalies in their environments and living lives that are shaped by organizations and cultures dominated by people significantly different than themselves. In this chapter, I continue the theme of the interplay between the academic and the personal. I discuss how individual lives inform scholarship and become transformed into sociology.

I recently published *Black Corporate Executives: The Making and Breaking of a Black Middle Class* (Collins, 1997). The idea for this project was spawned by the serendipitous intersection of several "daily life" factors. Most directly, this research was the product of my introspection on how my own life chances differed from my parents and how my career came into being. Second, it emerged from a new life adventure: I was introduced to—and intrigued by—a new black middle class of businesspeople. In this context, I became a foreigner operating in an exotic new community of black business owners and executives. As such, I was a daily witness to the lives of these black folks around me. Finally, my research interests were further influenced by my reading of newspaper coverage of a rapidly escalating debate on the relationship between public policy and black progress, a topic that at the same time was also hotly contested in scholarly circles.

I mentioned previously that my research was, in part, a product of my introspection about my own career. What sustained such an evaluation and how did I transform my experience into sociology? A survey of my resume reveals an intertwined pattern of nontraditional jobs and atypical mobility. By "atypical" I mean different relative to the average type of jobs attained by black people. Not that long ago, blacks were employed almost entirely in jobs that reflected a cultural norm in the United States of de facto and dejure segregation and of racial discrimination against black workers. Until approximately the 1960s, blacks overwhelmingly and disproportionately filled a job ghetto composed of low-paying, physically demanding, and subservient blue-collar and service work that provided manual labor for white private industry (Jaynes & Williams, 1989; Wilson, 1978). The etiquette of race relations existing at the time dictated the exclusion of black people from jobs that were the peers of, or that supervised, white people (Collins, 1989). Against this retrospective, I could clearly see that when I entered the labor force in the early 1970s with a college degree in hand, I was part of a new breed of black workers.

For example, I was hired as the first and, of the approximately 50 staff members, only black professional in a urban private mental health clinic. Approximately 13 years later, in the early 1980s, I had the rather imperious and entirely symbolic job title of "Third World Coordinator." Once again, I was the only black with a professional degree, man or woman, working on a large federally funded university health sciences project. There were certainly other black people employed in this setting, but they were concentrated overwhelmingly in clerical and low-paying service occupations. Now, as the 1990s come to a close, I can be counted among the university faculty who are tenured. The television documentary, *Shattering the Silences,* shown on the Public Broadcasting Service (*http://www.pbs.org/shattering*) and funded by the Ford Foundation, makes clear that, although I am not entirely unique, very few people of color share this status with me either at this or any other predominately white university. In summary, the intriguing issue of my work history is that it is composed of higher-paying white-collar jobs in predominately white settings in which I am the "one and only" black person or one of a very small number of black people.

How did this knowledge become sociology? There are a couple of ways we can interpret these facts of my work life. One explanation for my job opportunities and steady upward mobility is that I am simply unique among black people. That is, I am smarter, I work harder, I plan better, and I am more skilled than the one third of all black people who live in poverty, the unemployed or underemployed, and an unspecified large number of other black faculty who tried but failed to get tenure.

An alternative hypothesis is that I am a product of shifting social trends and history. I first entered the workplace in the early 1970s, about the time when employers first sought actively to employ college-educated black workers. Consequently, I was part of the first cohort of blacks who could enter and advance in higher-paying white-collar jobs, which also made me a part of a newly emerging college-educated black middle class of professional and managerial workers (Freeman, 1976). This is not to say that no black middle class existed before this period. My job and lifestyle, however, clearly were different than that experienced by college-educated black people in the generations before me (Drake & Cayton, 1962). Much of sociology is about social change, and I recognized the sociology in my own life when I realized that "something" changed and asked a question: "What was it?"

I am a product of affirmative action. I benefit from affirmative action programs that opened access to higher education in previously closed institutions that are perquisites of higher-paying white-collar jobs. Moreover, I benefit from other race-conscious programs that created funding sources to pay for this level of training and education. For example, I was in the first cohort of students that included black recruits in a master's degree programs of a prestigious, and very expensive, private school. This recruitment was an explicit goal of the school's affirmative action efforts. At the time, my parents, despite all their hopes and aspirations, could not afford the costs of the education for which I competed. Attendance would have been impossible without the government financial support package created explicitly to increase minority graduate enrollment. In short, private and government financial aid programs that were targeted to assist the upward mobility of black people during the 1960s and 1970s opened the route to my graduate degree. The same dynamics can be seen when I entered the job market. I was part of a racial vanguard in social work, which now tends to be thought of as a well-integrated profession. My recruitment into this job and my future recruitment into a variety of subsequent work settings were part of an organization's affirmative action plan to hire at least one black professional.

My book on black executives argued that race-based private and governmental programs were necessary for the upward mobility of college-educated black people. I did not automatically understand the role that affirmative action and other public policies played in shaping other black lives. I started down the road to this discovery as I became aware that some historically unique ingredients were in place that pried open new avenues to higher education and job opportunities for me.

To some readers, I suspect, the statement that I am a product of affirmative action will imply that I am an unqualified and untrained academic situated unfairly in a job that should be reserved for better qualified (probably white) people. I pause here to make the point that this view of affirmative action is a distortion of its effects. Both the course of my work life and my research on the topic indicate that affirmative action requires employers to broaden (not pollute) the pool of competition for job openings (Crosby, 1995; Reskin, 1998). Affirmative action makes the competition for jobs more, not less, fair.

In part, this is because in the world of work connections count (Granovetter, 1995). The old saying, "It's not what you know, but who you know," is partially true and especially relevant when applied to getting a job. Referrals tend to come from informal sources, and positions are filled through the networks of the existing workforce, such as friends and relatives. Not being "connected" to the workplace in this way adds more burdens to job-seeking individuals and creates disadvantage. The disadvantage borne by African Americans therefore comes not just from overt discrimination; I argue that it is a predicament created by their relative underrepresentation in higher-paying white-collar jobs that excludes them from informal job-finding resources. In 1989, for example, black and white college-educated men had sharply different occupations (Meisenheimer, 1990). Employed black men were less likely than white men to be managers (22 vs. 29%, respectively) and also less likely to work in professional specialty occupations (31 vs. 37%). Conversely, in 1989 31% of college-educated black men and just 14% of college-educated white men worked in lower-paying occupations that typically do not require a college degree. The view from the room that is my life informs me that I was part of a talent pool of people who likely would not have competed well without affirmative action. At the same time, affirmative action has never meant "any black person" will do. If that were so, black progress within the middle class would be more dramatic and, conversely, my own career would be less of an anomaly.

Affirmative action did not create me entirely, of course. I can see in my own life the relevance of sociological research on mobility that finds that family and socioeconomic background is related to future class position (Blau & Duncan, 1967; Kalmijn, 1994). I was raised by two parents whose own thwarted high aspirations fueled the hope and the expectation that their children would go to college. Luckily, by the time I was ready to enter college for an undergraduate degree, they were able to pay for my liberal arts education. Moreover, I grew up in a working-class neighborhood in east Los Angeles that had a very good high school that produced a good share of graduates who won scholarships to U.C. Berkeley and Stanford. This was prior to the passage in California of Proposition 13 and at the time it still received enough public funding to attract a committed faculty. The high school also had an abundance of extracurricular activities. Discourse on public education currently paints a dismal picture, but I, and I suspect others, can attest that the absence of educational resources now so obvious in inner-city environments was not always the case. Thus, I benefited not only from having aspiring parents but also from living in a neighborhood that afforded me a chance for a relatively good high school education. Both elements, the familial (or private) and the neighborhood (the public), created the springboard that propelled me successfully through the admissions process of a small liberal arts college situated in the outskirts of Los Angeles. This nearly all-white institution admitted me in the mid-1960s. This period was just after the Watts riots and just prior to the unprecedented onslaught of recruitment undertaken by educational and business institutions in search of black people. I did well enough there to become an attractive candidate in my future applications to graduate schools.

One can see that I am not just a product of affirmative action. There are also what social scientists might call "human capital" and class-related factors (such as access to social resources, including education) underpinning my work history. Nevertheless, from the degrees I had in hand—and with what I perceive to be the necessary additional push provided by affirmative action—flowed friendships, social environments, and a variety of other life experiences of which my parents and members of previous generations of black people could only dream.

Other aspects of my personal experiences provided ingredients for my research on black executives, when I moved to Chicago in 1980. There, I was introduced to a new sphere of middle-class black people that included a small business elite of administrators and entrepreneurs. During this time, I moved in social circles that stretched far beyond the salaried mental health professionals in social work and psychology with whom I was familiar. I met people, mostly men, who worked in business settings, including highly paid corporate executives and public officials appointed to head large government bureaucracies. They were highly successful and powerful in their various fields. I was awed by them. Growing up playing in the streets of east Los Angeles, I never imagined that I would meet entrepreneurs whose pictures appeared on the cover of business magazines because they owned the only—or the largest—black-owned company of its type in the nation. Being star struck, I noticed everything about them. In other words, my fascination with these businesspeople transformed my new Chicago environment into a field setting and me into an ethnographer.

I noticed that these men moved in a milieu that was embellished by conspicuous consumption and that rare (for blacks) privileges flowed from their social status. For example, most did not live on the south side in Chicago where, I eventually read in Drake and Cayton (1962), the old black middle class of doctors, dentists, and segregated professionals sprang up—and still congregate. Rather, they lived in the renovated brownstones and high-rise buildings in Chicago's almost entirely white "near north" side. Racial discrimination and residential segregation both historically and currently exclude blacks from such Chicago settings (Farley & Frey, 1992; Massey & Denton, 1993). From external appearances, however, race no longer seemed to play a significant role in shaping these people's lifestyles and economic opportunities. Indeed, they appeared to be solidly upper middle class, even affluent. Their children attended white private schools, they owned second and even third, homes, they dined out at upscale "in" restaurants, and they traveled extensively. I did not know the incomes of these people, but I can say that, having come from a working-class background, I had never before heard the phrase, "I make six figures," which I heard while moving in these circles. My reading informed me that since the mid-1960s, a dramatic increase occurred in the proportion of black men in business-related and managerial occupations (Freeman, 1976). In 1960, only 5% of employed black men worked in better paying white-collar occupations; by 1979, 11% did so. Between 1960 and 1979, the proportion of black men in professional, technical, and managerial fields more than doubled (United States Bureau of Census, 1979, 1980). It soon dawned on me that I had met some of the very people that I was reading about.

This was the period in which Ronald Reagan was entering office, and I was privy to many private and informal conversations among blacks that focused on the impact of the upcoming White House administration. When these black businesspeople conferred among themselves about what they perceived to be the beginning of a new era of entrenchment in race relations, it struck me that their tones of voice conveyed fear. In particular, the people I observed expressed a great deal of concern about the potential for cutbacks in social programs and affirmative action efforts under the Reagan administration. This I found perplexing. If indeed they were solidly assimilated into the social and economic mainstream of a major American city, changes in national policy that might reduce efforts to assist a more needy black population should have little, if any, effect on them. What, then, were these talented, educated, and highly privileged people afraid of?

Over time, I discovered that, like me, many of them were "firsts" in a company. They integrated major corporations during the mid-1960s and early 1970s when access to professional and managerial jobs first opened to college-educated blacks in the midst of civil rights upheaval. I also discovered that, like me, some form of affirmative action or other race-conscious consideration, along with the requisite education, played a role in their success. In other words, this was a middle class of people ushered in as the direct beneficiaries of affirmative action and other policies and programs generated by the civil right movement. For example, some were able to start businesses in nontraditional areas, such as advertising, accounting, and management consulting, because the federal government and corporations created set-aside programs. Set-aside programs helped black owners compete for sizable business outside black communities and participate in cross-racial networks that helped to increase both the size and the type of black firms. Others got their start when efforts to successfully compete for federal contracts forced companies to recruit blacks into their professional and managerial workforce for the first time in history.

Another pattern emerged as I thought about myself, these people, and the friends whom I had known in other professions. I discovered that many of us functioned in "soft" jobs that focused on addressing the problems and progress of black people. I was hired into a job title, Third World Coordinator, for a research team, for example, because the funding agency stipulated minorities must be represented on the project. A public servant who I encountered headed the disproportionately black-utilized "public welfare" function in the city that also expanded and contracted according to external political pressures. Others made a living by designing and running variations of affirmative action efforts or in public relations and advertising helping white corporations exclusively to penetrate black consumer markets. I saw that, when setting occupations and titles aside, we were a group that earned a living by filling race-related roles in white companies. With this discovery, sociology was not only "in" my work life but also began to play a much larger role in my understanding of it. So it was that I started to seriously contemplate the role of the federal government in creating the economic opportunities that opened to the new black middle class.

Much of sociology can be found in newspaper stories and other journalistic accounts of social life. Articles that appeared in the popular press about the emergence and meaning of a new black middle class also informed me. This informal literature review was performed in conjunction with my reflections on my own life and my discovery of other people like me.

While having coffee one Sunday morning in 1980, I discovered by accident an article in the *New York Times* (Gershman, 1980) that reflected the two sides of a debate on whether class or race affects blacks' economic opportunities. I did not subscribe to this paper, and the importance of this accident is symbolized by the fact that, although almost 20 years old, torn, and illegible, I still have this article. One half of the debate, that touted the importance of class, reflected emergent national attitudes that viewed race-based programs to improve the socioeconomic standing of blacks, such as affirmative action, as ineffective— even harmful—for impoverished blacks. This stance also reflected strong sentiments that typified affirmative action as unnecessary favoritism bestowed on blacks in the middle class who could well compete without this federal assistance. In this view, the race-specific agenda tied to programs such as affirmative action created job opportunities, but only for those blacks who did not need this advantage because they possessed the skills and education to compete for them.

The unconvincing other half of the debate countered that racial discrimination was still well entrenched in society and was a generalized experienced for black people, regardless of their social class and economic position. Given the nature of social change I have described and witnessed in my generation, this seemed like a recalcitrant view that was difficult to sell.

This debate in the *New York Times* neatly summarized the popular attitudes about public policy that congealed around the election of Ronald Reagan to the White House. It also summarized some of the issues underpinning scholarly concern about social policy and the deep socioeconomic cleavages that separated the "haves" from the "have nots" in the black community. Increasingly, it seemed to me, both white and black scholars were stepping up to openly challenge the efficacy of the social programs that proliferated during the 1960s' War on Poverty and the wisdom of race-conscious policies, such as affirmative action (Glazer, 1976; Loury, 1985; Sowell, 1983; Wilson, 1978). These scholars accused traditional black civil rights leadership, and the black middle class by extension, of exploiting the black poor to manipulate federal policies to gain narrow and self-serving resolutions. Although this view may have elements of truth to it, my own career and my interaction with black professionals and businesspeople around me raised suspicions that it also may be overly narrow and not tell the full story. In other words, the sociology of my daily life implied that there were more factors involved in settling the disputes surrounding this issue.

Although the people I observed were affluent, they were not as solidly assimilated into the mainstream work world as they appeared to be. They arguably were segregated in the labor market because they filled jobs implementing programs and policies designed to ameliorate the problems of black people. Moreover, the system of jobs that supported their lifestyles was a product of a particular historical period in which the federal government made efforts to improve the status of blacks. As federal policies and programs oriented toward blacks multiplied during the 1960s and 1970s, the number of professional and administrative jobs available to expand the black middle class multiplied dramatically. Many of these were "racialized" jobs, such as affirmative action and social welfare jobs, that funneled new social and economic resources generated by social policy into black communities. In 1980, however, the Reagan presidency, and its powerful challenge to antibias legislation and welfare policies of the previous 15 years, demonstrated that this period was ending. Black civil rights upheaval abated and, not coincidentally, so too did federal expenditures and supports for improving blacks' socioeconomic opportunities. In short, when the government's approach to welfare expenditures and antibias policy changed, the foundation of jobs and functions that enabled these people to rise and maintain their lifestyles was directly threatened.

Self-interest certainly played a role in the response of black leadership to shifts in public policy; the nature of their response, however, reflects the fragility of their socioeconomic position more than exploitation. As I argued in *Black Corporate Executives* (Collins, 1997), their lifestyles are supported by incomes that depend on a continued social commitment to solving the problems of black people.

You can now see how I discovered sociology in my life and also how my life became formal sociology. I did not start this research journey as some sort of conscious choice, but this journey does reflect and is a product of self-consciousness. The message here is a simple one: We live sociology. The relationship of sociology to everyday life is strong and direct, even though students may sometimes find this relationship difficult to fathom.

REFERENCES

Blau, P. M., & Duncan, O. D. (1967). *The American occupational structure.* New York: John Wiley.

Collins, S. M. (1989, October). The marginalization of black executives. *Social Problems, 36,* 317-331.

Collins, S. M. (1997). *Black corporate executives: The making and breaking of the black middle class.* Philadelphia: Temple University Press.

Crosby, F. J. (1995, September). Remarks at briefing for Congressional Staff Members and Journals, Washington, DC [Speech].

Drake, St. C., & Cayton, H. R. (1962). *Black metropolis* (Vol. 2). New York: Harper & Row.

Farley, R., & Frey, W. H. (1992, August). *The residential segregation of blacks, Latinos, and Asians: 1980 and 1990.* Paper presented at the annual meeting of the American Sociological Association, Pittsburgh, PA.

Freeman, R. (1976). *The black elite.* New York: McGraw-Hill.

Gershman, C. (1980, October 5). A matter of class. *New York Times* (Sunday Suppl.), p. 22.

Glazer, N. (1976). *Affirmative discrimination.* New York: Basic Books.

Granovetter, M. (1995). *Getting a job; A study of contacts and careers* (2nd ed.). Chicago: University of Chicago Press.

Jaynes, G. D., & Williams, R. M., Jr. (1989). *A common destiny: Blacks and American society.* Washington, DC: National Academy Press.

Kalmijn, M. (1994). Mother's occupational status and children's schooling. *American Journal of Sociology, 100,* 4222-4275.

Loury, G. C. (1985, Spring). The moral quandary of the black community. *Public Interest, 79,* 9-22.

Massey, D. S., & Denton, N. A. (1993). *American apartheid: Segregation and the making of the underclass.* Cambridge, MA: Harvard University Press.

Meisenheimer, J. R. (1990, November). Black college graduates in the labor market, 1979 and 1989. In *Monthly Labor Review* (pp. 13-21). Washington, DC: Bureau of Labor Statistics.

Reskin, B. F. (1998). *The realities of affirmative action in employment.* Washington, DC: American Sociological Association.

Sowell, T. (1983). The economics and politics of race. *The Firing Line* [Transcript]. New York: Public Broadcasting Service.

United States Bureau of Census. (1979). *Social and economic status of the black population in the United States, 1790-1978: A historical view* (Series P-23, No. 80). Washington, DC: Author.

United States Bureau of Census. (1980). *Current population reports, money and income of persons in 1979* (Series P-60, No. 129). Washington, DC: Author.

Wilson, W. J. (1981). The black community in the 1980s: Questions of race, class, and public policy. *The Annals, 454,* 26-41.

Wilson, W. J. (1978). *The declining significance of race.* Chicago: University of Chicago Press.

CHAPTER 20

Making Sense and Making a Difference[1]
Murder and College Administration

DERRAL CHEATWOOD

Career paths wander. Mine wandered into a concern with homicide, and through incremental movements into criminology and criminal justice. I expected to be a sociologist, I wasn't surprised at becoming a criminologist, but I never expected to find myself a department chair or a division director (same thing with more headaches). And yet more and more I find parallels between that odd journey and those of the homicide offenders I talked to in prison or read about in their case files—kids who use phrases like "I never intended to kill her" or "I don't know what happened." Because as I sit here in this office and look around me, I have to agree kid—I don't really know what happened either. I hope that to understand that about our own lives helps us understand theirs.

In my academic travels in the study of homicide, I used both quantitative and qualitative methods when and where they were needed, but all of it was based on a qualitative perspective. This reflects the original goal of the journal. Barry Glassner and I founded *Qualitative Sociology* to provide a venue for publication of works that were having a hard time seeing publication in other journals in sociology at the time. It was not to be a call to battle against the number counters, but was to be a chance to give some who were asking different questions, using different data, or approaching their data from a qualitative perspective a chance to be heard and counted. The journal was a forum which, at least indirectly, could answer the question of how this enterprise of qualitative sociology shapes a professional and personal orientation.

Now, 20 years later, I come back to a fundamental question leading to the establishment of *Qualitative Sociology*, but with a specific content: What difference does it make if one looks at homicide as a qualitative sociologist? Part of the answer is that it makes a little difference in terms of the methods you use. It makes a big difference in how you conceptualize the study of homicide. And it has the potential to make a significant difference in terms of what policies and programs you might suggest to help alleviate the problem. And through it all a small nagging question remains—so what has all that got to do with me?

A QUICK NOTE ON QUALITATIVE
(AND QUANTITATIVE) METHODOLOGY AND MURDER

First, how do qualitative methods help us to understand homicide?[2] Beginning with David Luckenbill's study in 1977, many of the traditional qualitative methodologies have been focused on homicide.[3] Interviews with convicted homicide offenders and other violent felons have helped significantly to understand why they think they do what they do. Those studies have helped us to see that in a violent world, one is violent and carries the tools of violence primarily in self-defense (Katz, 1988; Wright & Rossi, 1986). They have also helped us to understand the social context in which offenders create their world and act on that construction (Kathleen Heide, 1984, has an interesting discussion of this for the adolescents she calls the "players"). As always, the primary contribution of the qualitative approach has been to emphasize the reciprocal interplay that the immediate social setting has on creating a personality type and that type then has on reinforcing the culture of that setting. The player in the gender and ethnic culture of the streets (Campbell, 1986; Heide, 1984; Oliver, 1989) lives in a world where the fast action of crime is seductive (Katz, 1988) and homicide is so common that the meaning it holds for these young men does not exist in the lexicon of respectable society used by social scientists. For these young men, homicide is neither a rare event nor the product of a psychological aberration. It is a normal, everyday fact of life.

It is important to note that quantitative methods focused our initial view of homicide. When we look at those raw numbers, we see that homicide is not evenly distributed across society, but is disproportionately located in poor minority communities, particularly among young African American men in large cities. Statistics show murder to be the number one cause of death among African American men between the ages of 15 and 34, and at the present odds something between 1 out of every 10 to 15 young black men in America can expect to be involved in a homicide as either a victim or an offender during his lifetime.

Those are incredible odds. In any social group, something that common must have a whole set of roles, expectations, and meanings attached to it. Yet quantitative methods cannot provide us any entre into that culture so that we could learn those roles and meanings or make any sense out of this. In a complete inversion of the misunderstanding most of us were taught as gospel truth in graduate school, quantitative methods can only provide us with clues or hypotheses for test. Only qualitative methods enable us to actually begin to understand the way that the truly relevant pieces of any social structure fit together, and that is the only source of solid explanatory theory.

For example, one of the contributions of qualitative homicide studies has been to stress the idea of rehearsals. When you live in a world where your odds of being in a shooting are so high, you think about it and ready yourself for the day. Looking at everything around you and everything you do as a qualitative sociologist sometimes gives you insights coming from odd places. I am a member of a reenactment shooting group on the Old West. The academic veneer, anyway, is that it is a reenactment and sporting association, the reality is closer to a bunch of old geezers getting to play Cowboy again with some of the neatest toys you ever saw. But the odd part is that as we stand about with working six-shooters on our hips, and with range safety and unloaded weapons the cardinal rules, it is impossible not to realize that if these weapons were loaded and we were all twenty-something years old getting drunk in some bar in 1880s Texas, sooner or later somebody would get shot, probably a lot of people. And with that knowledge you could not help but be a little more on edge, a little more willing to shoot first. It would all depend on the wrong person saying the wrong thing at the wrong time or in the wrong place—just a chance of interactions.

In an ironic sense, homicide is one of the most social of all crimes, yet prior to the application of qualitative methods we actually knew very little about the interactions among victims, offenders, and witnesses that took place during a homicide. Qualitative methodologies have allowed us to look at the people involved in homicide at the level of scale where the homicide event occurs, in the streets and apartments where specific individuals progress through an escalating chain of interactions which results in one of those individuals being dead at the hands of the other. Qualitative methods study these settings and the roles played by those people that lead to that death. By bringing the scale down to this human level it moves toward the geographer Harold Rose's (1996) admonition to "put a human face on homicide" (a qualitative geographer, imagine that).

As such, qualitative methods have had an increasingly important impact on the empirical studies of homicide. That is, of course, a little like saying that this methodology has an influence on methodology, and it may be that superficial. Let's hope not. But if "qualitative methodology" is merely seen as a type of methodology, it really misses the point, and remains just a method of gathering or analyzing data. It is the qualitative approach to the world and the understanding that comes from that approach that more significantly affects the conceptualization of homicide.

QUALITATIVE SOCIOLOGY AND MURDER AS EVERYDAY LIFE

"Polite" society views homicide as a tragic and final ending—a distinct event set apart from all other events in a life. It certainly is easier to study it that way. Beginning at such a dramatic end and tracking backward we can always see that where everything wound up was strictly contingent on all the prior variables fitting into place. All the pieces fit together because we know the outcome, we have seen the picture on the box, and we just have to re-create it piece by piece. But life is not a linear process, not even with logarithmic transformations, and quantitative methods are most at home with linear processes. Life is a stew, with a few identifiable pieces appearing out of the gravy from time to time. The real importance of a qualitative approach is not in being a method to better distinguish the potatoes from the peas, but in making understood that the whole mess is the topic, not the potatoes and peas themselves. A qualitative approach tells us not to focus on a homicide as if it were a distinct, disconnected, abnormal event, some lumpy potato with distinct borders in an otherwise smooth social gravy. Certainly there is a need for theory and for policy to abstract out beginnings and ends, to say that some process or interaction started here and ended there, and that an interaction that ends with the death of a participant needs to be addressed by society. But when you begin to ask why a homicide occurs, what is the nature of the interactions that lead to one person killing another rather than merely why rates differ across space and time, a new perspective opens on both the act of murder and the culture in which it occurs.

For a young "gangster" in the streets the killing may merely be a first important step to a life of fame and status in his world. Qualitative study tries to understand the normal life of the subjects being studied, and in that process comes to accept those subjects' perspectives on what is—in fact—normal or unusual. Specifically, a homicide is merely one outcome of a variety of actions. Until the very moment that the victim expires there is no such thing as a homicide, much less a murder. In a culture where physical confrontations are common, weapons are prevalent, gender status is paramount, sensitivity to status slights is extreme, and a number of undereducated unemployed young men experiment with robbery, it is only normal and expected that some of these acts will, intentionally or not, result in a death. Any theoretical approach or attempt at policy intervention which is based on causal beliefs in evil people, poor values, mental aberration, or poverty must take that into account.

Similarly, in "our" world, how some of us wound up as professors or teachers or researchers or chairpersons or directors or deans is just as nonlinear and sloppy. We can look back and explain it in the vocabulary we all accept (shades of G. H. Mead), but it only makes sense if we stick to an accepted lexicon. Sometimes I think a "mental aberration" may make as much sense in explaining how one becomes a dean as it does at explaining how one becomes a murderer, but fortunately for us we get to choose the vocabulary used to do the explaining, because we made most of it up in the first place.

When murder is seen as part of the normal process of life, we are forced to allow the participants to define themselves on their own terms. For example, much of the work coming from a qualitative tradition has allowed us to see that the "present" time of a homicide stretches further into the future and the past than we had thought. What the homicide actually means to the participants, ironically often including the victim, quite often extends across a time much greater than the limited interaction in which the victim was killed. Before their own victimization, battered women often leave their settings because they come to see, often accurately, their own murder in the future (Campbell, 1992). And after the event, offenders often use the homicide to attempt to gain status or prestige (Katz, 1988). Again, only a qualitative approach suggests this to us, much less provides us with an understanding of what is going on. Even here it is not the act of the murder itself which confers status, but the manner in which the event is handled by the participants, and in which the murder and the participant's handling of it are viewed by the audience. Sometimes the attempt to handle it backfires—as one witness described a homicide offender: "He wanted to be Billy the Kid and impress his little clique [by shooting the guy]. He's stupid as shit." There is no way that quantitative methods could have given us this jewel of insight. So whether our goal is to improve our theory of what brings a homicide about, or to devise policies to reduce the probability of any given homicide occurring, a key is this knowledge brought from qualitative methods.

QUALITATIVE UNDERSTANDINGS OF HOMICIDE AND THEIR IMPACT ON POLICY

There is another significant question. What recommendations can be derived from qualitative sociological approaches that will help society reduce the level of murder? The basic goal for many of us is to understand the evolution of the homicide event sufficiently in order to intervene and prevent many of the homicides that occur. This goal is shared by the scholars employing quantitative methods as well. But quantitative studies are, by their very nature, suited for looking at large aggregate numbers. There are a multitude of studies of homicide rates at large aggregate levels, and perhaps a dozen or more relatively distinct theories attempting to explain changes across time and differences across space in homicide rates. Following Durkheim, the better researchers and theorists properly seek to explain a social fact, a homicide rate, by other social facts, including poverty rates, ethnic composition of the population, patterns of family composition, age demographics of the population, and the like. Changes in rates of any of these correlate with changes in the homicide rate, but they do not address the homicide event itself.

But knowing that poverty or the age composition of the population contributes to higher homicide rates is of little use to the police chief in Akron or the city council in San Antonio. Any attempt to enact policies which might have an impact at large levels of aggregation must confront a reality which locates much of the ability to enact change at more local political levels. Knowing that homicide rates are higher among young males and among African Americans does not lead to any ethical solution to change society's composition. Knowing that poverty is a relatively consistent factor in homicide does not provide society with the knowledge, means, or the will to eliminate poverty. And any changes are political, which means that they depend fundamentally on the culture of the time. Local agencies find themselves data rich and information poor, with dozens of studies finding the same basic factors correlating with homicide, yet saying little about what a practitioner or policymaker might actually do to have an impact on the problem. As a consequence, politicians, practitioners, and the public tend to discount many good scientific studies and rely on single-cause punishment models. Any study that supports those models then becomes the faddish answer, so we are sequentially told by econometricians that the increased use of capital punishment is decreasing the murder rate, the significant increase in prison populations is finally causing a decrease in the murder rate, or most recently that the right-to-carry concealed weapons laws are causing a decrease in the murder rate.

Yet both these scientific studies and practitioners' responses share the problem we discussed above, they move from an empirical consideration of rates to a theoretical explanation of why the homicide happens without ever considering the homicide event itself. And this is where qualitative sociology offers a unique and constructive approach not only to understanding what is happening in the day-to-day world in which homicide occurs, but to devising policies and programs at the pragmatic levels of city and county government.

Our goal is to intervene in ways to prevent as many homicides as we can. Both qualitative studies and a qualitative approach demonstrate that we might be able to intervene at very basic levels in the process of homicide. For policy as for theory, it is important to think about the setting and interactions of the homicide itself more than watching changes in the homicide rate over years. One of the things that local policymakers and practitioners can have an effect on are those settings and, hopefully, the interactions. In the policy arena, the change in scale emphasized by the qualitative approach matches a theory of interactions to the scale at which homicides are actually occurring. Scott Decker's analysis of the role of witnesses in homicides (1994) and mine of the role of multiple offenders (1996), for example, both suggest that other actors in the interaction may serve as enablers or sponsors of the final lethal actions. Programs that attempted to make adolescents understand their role as enablers or contributors, and suggested to them that they could play an important role in keeping their friends out of trouble with little effort on their part, might have an effect.

Perhaps most promising, all of the research confirms the importance of what Scott Decker calls "homicide networks" (1990). So much of our excess of homicides exists in limited social and cultural settings in which one carries a weapon in self-defense, based on personal knowledge of a friend or family member recently murdered. Yet a weapon increases the probability any encounter will result in a homicide, and to be prepared to use a weapon means that one must rehearse situations in which the weapon would be drawn and used. These rehearsals themselves come to shape encounters and increase the probability that an encounter will evolve to a murder. All of this increases the probability of another homicide occurring, and when that homicide occurs it increases the number of persons who have a personal knowledge of a friend or family having been recently murdered, and so on and so on.

Because this problem is indeed focused in neighborhoods and based in part on personal knowledge, it means that we should begin to look for ways to break this chain or disrupt this homicide network at a very local, and manageable, scale. The qualitative study of homicide, and those insights that come from constantly gazing at life through qualitative lenses, offers the promise that we can effectively intervene at very small levels to prevent the occurrence of some homicides and thus to reduce homicide rates. We do not yet have the solutions, but this approach offers a unique way of looking at the problem which, in itself, can help to suggest unique answers that we may not have tried yet.

CONCLUSION

Making a qualitative approach an integral part of the way we look at social life has an effect on our understanding of even those events most of us will, fortunately, never encounter. It moves us from our own perspectives, meanings, and assumptions into those of the populations which, in fact, are encountering those events on a day-to-day basis. Analyses of homicide based on qualitative approaches have begun to shape the way we look at homicide. We have found that within defined areas it is not a rare event, but one which is common and can be used to establish or maintain status. We have begun to understand that homicide is not a distinct aberration, but merely another potential tool in a young man's repertoire of status, one he and those around him will rehearse and be prepared to use and witness. The young kid wandering in a world where confrontations over honor occur frequently is no different than a young professor in a world where committees dealing with administration abound. It is inevitable that sooner or later you will find yourself in one of those settings, and for some individuals, either through their choice or external events that seem to carry them along, they will find themselves murdering someone, or becoming a dean.

If this is true, and acknowledging the fact that there will never be a complete absence of deans or of murderers, effective intervention can occur at any number of points and at levels of scale not apparent from more quantitative studies. People give meaning to the events around them, and some of those meanings increase the probability that the individual will be involved in a homicide—if we understand and accept that we may be able to do something to change those meanings, or at least interfere in the chain of interactions.

The tradition of qualitative study brings theory to the scale of those interactions. So much of what surrounds all of us in life is just that sort of mixture of apprehension about the future, rehearsal for those things good and bad that we expect, and encounters with luck that wind up putting us where we are. The conditions of most of our lives are very different from the conditions that kids face in high homicide areas, but the process is the same. At one time or another, we all wind up in places where we never expected to be. This suggests some promising ways to intervene at pragmatic levels for these kids. Qualitative sociology not only puts a human face on homicide, but allows us to think of ways to show that face to people who may be able to do something to reduce the problem.

NOTES

1. Reprinted with permission of Human Sciences Press, Inc. (1997).

2. In this chapter, the word *homicide* is used as a synonym for murder, but this is merely a stylistic convenience. Technically, homicide, murder, and nonnegligent manslaughter are distinguishable actions. Homicide is any killing of a human being, murder is an illegal homicide involving malice and premeditation, and nonnegligent manslaughter is an illegal homicide involving malice. For a variety of reasons, murder and nonnegligent manslaughter are treated together, and the word homicide is commonly accepted as a synonym.

3. Obviously, the grandaddy of all qualitative methods—participant observation—is the one method not used, and ethically not applicable, to the study of homicide.

REFERENCES

Campbell, A. (1986). The streets and violence. In A. Campbell & J. J. Gibbs (Eds.), *Violent transactions: The limits of personality.* New York: Basil Blackwell.

Campbell, J. C. (1992). If I can't have you, no one can: Power and control in homicide of female partners. In J. Radford & D. Russell (Eds.), *Femicide: The politics of woman killing.* Boston: Twayne.

Cheatwood, D. (1996). Interactional patterns in multiple offender homicides. *Justice Quarterly, 13,* 107-128.

Decker, S. (1990, November). *Reconstructing homicide events: The role of witnesses in fatal encounters.* Paper presented at the meetings of the American Society of Criminology, San Francisco.

Decker, S. (1994). Exploring victim-offender relationships in homicide: The role of individual and event characteristics. *Justice Quarterly, 10,* 585-612.

Heide, K. (1984, November). *A preliminary identification of types of adolescent murderers.* Paper presented at the meetings of the American Society of Criminology, Cincinnati, OH.

Katz, J. (1988). *Seductions of crime.* New York: Basic Books.

Luckenbill, D. (1977). Criminal homicide as a situated transaction. *Social Problems, 25*(2), 176-186.

Oliver, W. (1989). Sexual conquest and patterns of black on black violence: A structural cultural perspective. *Violence and Victims, 4,* 257-273.

Rose, H. (1996). *Session on: The homicide research working group: Past and present.* Meetings of the Homicide Research Working Group, RAND Corporation, Santa Monica, CA.

Wright, J. D., & Rossi, P. H. (1986). *Armed and considered dangerous: A survey of felons and their firearms.* New York: Aldine.

CHAPTER 21

Feeling at Home at Work[1]
Life in Academic Departments

BARRIE THORNE

ARLIE RUSSELL HOCHSCHILD

As long-time residents of academic departments, we're familiar with the routines of office hours, chatting in the hallway, attending committee meetings, picking up mail, and using the Xerox machine in the main office. Every department we've experienced has been laced with gossip and occasional intrigue, and sometimes disrupted by heated conflict and smoldering feuds. Why, we got to wondering one day, do tempers flare so easily in faculty meetings? Why do we "regress" just where you'd think we would be the most "grown up"—at work?

Departments are set inside the infrastructure of a bureaucracy and profession and would thus seem to invite an attitude of mild, appropriate concern. Why, then, do matters of recruitment, course scheduling, and Xerox paper sometimes evoke strong, and apparently infantile emotions?

Using an analogy (one of sociology's finest tools), we've come up with a clue to the emotional and relational mysteries of department life: *Departments are like families.*

Like families, departments are small, face-to-face groups sharing space, material resources, and everyday life. The members did not, by and large, choose one another, and (given the sorry state of the job market) they anticipate being stuck with one another for the long haul. Periods of adoption or marriage (faculty hiring) tend to be especially contentious, raising issues of collective identity and fears that the existing balance of power may become realigned.

Department members sometimes leave home, having been "courted away" as happens to eligible young people under the rule of exogeny. Indeed, departments don't like to hire from among their own graduate students because it's too "incestuous." It's often believed that the prospective hire should come from another village, and bring in "fresh blood."

Members of a department, regardless of gender, may become estranged, or "get a divorce." And then the in-laws and children are tacitly required to take sides. Students may walk into an oral exam with the hope of "bringing both parents together," just as the children of divorce may try to reunite a broken family by becoming the totem symbol of a "merry Christmas" or a birthday party which brings warring parties together.

Departments develop reputations in the eyes of both local and national outsiders. Like a specific family, a department may be known for continual infighting or for being friendly or standoffish ("closed doors"). Departments, like families, are positioned in systems of social stratification; there is even a national blue-blood registry: the ranking of "top" departments by the National Academy of Sciences. Some departments wage campaigns for upward mobility; others affirm missions which break with mainstream criteria for ranking.

Like families, departments are structured by generation and gender, and they have a long tradition of patriarchy. The vast majority have a male "head" who deploys the labor of the other members and who sits at the end of a long table as he presides over gatherings of the whole (department meetings resemble family dinners as scenes of ritual solidarity and of dramatic fights).

Department generations divide into older and younger parents (the tenured seniors and the untenured juniors), and graduate students, who, like dependent children, are expected to move on after a period of training and nurture (faculty are pleased if their children "marry well"). The junior faculty are positioned much like adolescents, since the seniors keep secrets from them and actively control their fates. At faculty meetings (as at Victorian family dinners), the junior faculty tend to be seen but not heard, fearful of publicly challenging their more powerful elders. Behind the scenes, however, junior faculty may feel pressure from seniors to take sides. The juniors maneuver for position, since resources are limited and ascent to the highest and permanent tier (a form of inheritance) is not automatic. When a junior is up for tenure and disinheritance is a possibility, conflict often erupts.

Tension also surrounds other moments of generational succession, such as the timing of retirements which will free up departmental offices and tenure lines (the equivalent of land and wealth), or struggles over who will become head or department chair. A faculty member who becomes chair may find that previously amicable colleagues turn hostile and aggressive or begin to whine for special favors. The dynamics are like those among siblings when one of their number has been singled out and put in charge.

Gender divisions are less formally marked in departments than in families, but they are present, and persistent. Men predominate in positions of authority, and there are relatively few women in the higher ranks. Feminists have challenged male dominance in departments, as in many families, with occasional moments of heightened gender warfare (as in department conflicts over charges of sexual harassment or sex discrimination). The results, in both cases, have been uneven.

Generational relations in departments, as in families, may be skewed by gender. Advising a dissertation is framed as a "professional relationship," but it involves dependence and often frustration, as the child struggles to become ratified as an independent adult. Not surprisingly, the dynamics slide into those between parents and children, or, in the majority of cases, fathers and sons or fathers and daughters. As more women become faculty members, mother-daughter and mother-son attachments, resentments, and conflicts are becoming more widespread.

In departments, as in families, the presence or absence of a particular member may become a charged issue, e.g., with widespread complaints that a certain faculty member is "never around." Just as parents often work long hours and leave their children to do their homework unattended, so graduate students fear the retreat of their "parents" to their studies, which leaves the student feeling abandoned or "home alone." As in the film by that name, a cultural scaffolding makes light of the real problem by presuming a precocious child, an affluent setting, and a sense that no real harm is done by leaving the children home alone. There is a "cool modern" "what's the problem?" gloss over the troubled waters. "What's the problem?," some faculty say, "The children are doing fine in 'self care.' "

All families manage sexuality, and healthy families manage it well, i.e., they maintain an incest taboo. While departments don't maintain an incest taboo as well as a family does, it is clear that sexual bonds between teachers and students are disturbing to the system's members, and, in a sense, signal trouble in the system. There is ambiguity about erotic connections among faculty. They may be seen as mommies and daddies who are free to mate (e.g., it is seen as fine to have married couples in the same department). Or they may be seen as children of a patriarchal head, and thus less free to mate.

Departments, like families, are sites of shared labor and of a second shift. Just as there are tensions between parents over who should do the less valued work of making a house a home, so, too, there are tensions over faculty members who refuse to "do their share." Some will do the housework (administration) but not take care of the kids (be on dissertation committees). Others do more than their share of both, and still others squirm out of doing either, creating resentment.

Like families, departments have a dominant ethos. Some value the "feminine" work of the home. Others are more masculine (publish, publish), and, although everyone in such departments does an equal amount, they do equally little (career-oriented egalitarians). Others are traditional, with women faculty devoting themselves more to teaching, and men, to publishing. The tensions—and resolutions—are similar to those in families.

Faculty allocate some of the least desired tasks, such as grading and leading discussion sections, to graduate students. Advanced graduate students are sometimes given their own undergraduate courses to teach, just as older children are sometimes made responsible for younger children. Like parents, the faculty justify these labor allocations in terms of "training" and "development," but graduate students may feel resentful and exploited.

Departments, like families, have limited material resources and there are struggles over allocation. The budget is controlled by the head, who negotiates income from outside sources, although the bookkeeping and other clerical labor is done by the department staff. The staff are positioned like paid domestic workers; they are responsible for the least valued tasks, and they have less lofty credentials than their employers. They are a part of, yet not fully in, the family, and some family members may treat them with a lesser degree of respect, as one might treat a nanny or gardener.

The chair, like a parent, has discretion in spending the department's income, and doles out salary increases (allowances) through an emotionally charged process of "merit review." Sometimes the chair has a few gifts to bestow, like new computers or extra research stipends. The faculty become like children vying for the extra goodies and sinking into states of envy toward siblings who seem to get more. Rumors circulate about parental (chair) favoritism. Sibling rivalry is a major emotional dynamic in departments, as in families.

In both departments and families, space is a scarce and valued resource. Members of equal status are supposed to have equivalent private space, and like siblings tussling over bedrooms, the faculty scan the size and location of one another's private offices, looking for signs that may indicate relative status. Sharing an office with a faculty sibling is like sharing a bedroom, a mark of lower status. The head controls the largest and often the most presentable office, which may function as a sort of parlor—a place for receiving outsiders and trying to make a good impression on behalf of the department (family) as a whole.

The next time you walk into your department office, and feel an inexplicable anxiety that you have been displaced by a new younger colleague, or ignored by a preoccupied elder colleague, smile, and understand that we all can "go home again"—at work.

NOTE

1. Reprinted with permission of Human Sciences Press, Inc. (1997).

CHAPTER 22

On the Nonnegotiable in Sociological Life[1]

ROBERT DINGWALL

Nineteen-ninety-seven is also the twentieth anniversary of the book from my PhD thesis, *The Social Organisation of Health Visitor Training* (Dingwall, 1977) and the second of the three attempts I made to understand how the process of student assessment articulated the relationship between an educational program and its environment—the first was in the thesis (Dingwall, 1974) and the third in an *Urban Life* paper (Dingwall, 1987). In the course of these efforts, I formulated a discontent with the then dominant "negotiated order" approach to organizational analysis in qualitative sociology which was eventually expressed in a paper with Philip Strong (Dingwall & Strong, 1985). This essay begins by looking back to the roots of this critique in my observations of a small academic unit feeling its way into a new era, before reflecting on the experience of British academic life in the 1990s.

WHAT IS A HEALTH VISITOR?

In the fall of 1973, I was completing fieldwork on the occupational socialization of health visitors, a British type of public health nurse. In those days, very little nurse education took place in higher education. Health visitor courses were an exception: most were offered by universities or polytechnics.[2] The course I

AUTHOR'S NOTE: I am grateful to my successor, Nick Manning, for his comments and suggestions.

studied was unusual in that it was the last to be provided by a school located within a municipal public health department and was being absorbed by the local polytechnic at the time of my fieldwork. Despite some personal contractual difficulties, the faculty welcomed this merger. Although the health department had given them strong support and built their program into a national leader, they saw the move as an essential stage in the professionalization of nursing. They were committed to its success and to seizing the opportunity to articulate their vision of an appropriate professional formation for public health nurses.

One thing I particularly noticed was their use of the assessment process to set out this vision in what I described as an "education-legal enterprise." The term paralleled Garfinkel's (1967, pp. 198-199) analysis of clinic record work as a contractual, "medico-legal enterprise." Olesen and Whitaker (1970) had contrasted approaches to socialization which saw this as passively filling empty vessels—in which case assessment would be an actuarial measure of the extent of any remaining void—and those which saw it as the active acquisition of knowledge and skills through interaction between students and faculty. I found it was necessary to extend their analysis of "studentmanship"—a term we might all prefer to avoid nowadays—and to see that the students' sense of acquisition had to be validated by the faculty. Faculty are a missing dimension in many socialization studies, although they have a critical role in deciding who is and is not going to graduate and be recognized as potentially competent. But they do not decide in a vacuum. The teachers I was watching were constantly looking beyond their program: to their national professional community and its notions of competence; to the board which accredited the program and its standards; to local employers and their feedback about graduates; to the visiting lecturers from the local university to tell them what "real" academic standards were; to the new, more bureaucratic polytechnic procedures and their concern for the formal defensibility of decisions; and so on. The assessment process was the crucible in which these layers of influence came together in a debate about who could and could not be properly certified to make home visits to the Great British Public. It formulated the contract between the program and these various environmental agents.

Of course—like most graduate students—I overstated the originality of this analysis. Although I had read a lot of Chicago-tradition ethnography, I only studied Everett Hughes's essays rather later, for example. His discussion of occupational license expresses essentially the position that I was trying to advance. Although "license" is now often interpreted rather narrowly, it is clear that Hughes intended to refer to the contract between an occupation and its social environment, the occupation's promise to deliver certain goods or services in exchange for social recognition or resources (Hughes, 1971, pp. 287-

294). Like any contract, it involves at least two parties, each of whom must be satisfied for the contract to be considered fulfilled. The power of the ecological model underlying the traditional Chicago approach lies in the ability to focus now on the niche and now on the ecosystem which defined it. An occupation might organize itself to colonize a particular space, but its continued tenancy depended on its responsiveness to the external changes which made that space available in that form.

The approach represented in the concept of "negotiated order" tends to lead to a focus on the species rather than on the environment. Both, however, need to be embraced, by sociologists as much as by actors. The health visiting faculty were asking what it was necessary to do to sustain their claim to a particular niche in the division of labor in a changing institutional context. Of course they were actors and negotiators, but many aspects of their situation had to be taken as given for all practical purposes. These included material resources, regulatory codes, and the language that could be used to legitimate their actions.

This recognition of the nonnegotiability of aspects of organizational order led me toward writers like Meyer and Rowan (1977), whose classic paper on organizational structures as myth and ceremony is also 20 years old this year, and Bittner (1965), whose more ethnomethodological approach put much greater emphasis on the discipline of organizational language. The possibilities of organizational action were limited by the cultural forms available in any historical context and by wider societal views of what constituted a legitimate way of organizing to manage some task or problem. The health visiting faculty were demonstrating their concern to legitimize their certifying activities, to be seen to be validating precisely those aspects of students' skills and knowledge in precisely those ways that were acceptable to other individuals and institutions around them.

Even if my ideas on the importance of environments for the work of occupations and organizations were not terribly original, they have been strongly reinforced by later experiences. Not all of these were intellectual. One feature of my career has been that I spent the entire period from 1974, when I finished my PhD, until 1990 in short-term (12-36 month) positions in research institutes. My first permanent job was my present appointment as a full professor, acting as department chair from 1991 until 1996. This is very different from the traditional experience of British higher education, where faculty have been employed on 12-month contracts and tended to assume that what they produced was up to them. If they chose to draw a salary, teach the minimum hours, and write something every few years or not at all, that was academic freedom. They worked under a set of structural conditions that promoted insensitivity to the environment: In contract research, if you don't produce what the environment requires, you don't eat!

THE ENVIRONMENT FOR SOCIOLOGY

What can we say about the environmental change that British sociology has experienced in the past 20 years? The sociology of sociology has tended to develop as a branch of the sociology of knowledge or the history of ideas. To the extent that material factors have been considered, it is often to dismiss them with disdain, as in Gouldner's (1971, p. 15) distinction between those who live for sociology and those who live off sociology. This is fine rhetoric but takes no account of the extent to which living for sociology requires a material base. Sociology is as much an occupation carried on in a political, cultural, and material context as it is a body of ideas. Perhaps we can be indifferent to the world if we have the wealth of an elite family or the endowment of a rich private university, where sociology might be a cultural adornment, the hobby of a leisured class with a social conscience or perhaps kept as the slave accompanying Caesar to whisper in his ear that he too is mortal. In some parts of mainland Europe, state funding for the production of an elite culture survives alongside a mass higher-education system. This is not the context in which British sociology is produced today. In the United Kingdom, the transition to the mass university has been accompanied by a demand that the system become more accountable. British governments no longer write checks to their universities with a minimal concern for the prevention of fraud and a modest amount of indicative planning. They now expect universities to deliver to centrally determined objectives. This is as true under the Labour Government elected in 1997 as of any of its Conservative predecessors since 1979. It is the logical consequence of the growth of state funding.

The justice of this demand is difficult to resist. Given what we know about the burden of taxation, most of the costs of public universities are met by people who are a good deal poorer than most of the faculty. If we are going to take money from the working class to support the middle-class lifestyles of the professoriat, then they have a right to be concerned about the efficiency and effectiveness with which these funds are used. In the United Kingdom, this has meant the introduction of national programs to assess the quality of teaching and research in every department of every university. Teaching quality is audited on an 8-year cycle and research performance every 4 years. The audits have a substantial peer-review element, although the basic criteria are defined across all disciplines. The process also incorporates "customer representatives" from outside the world of higher education and is steered by quality bureaucrats, who are an interesting new occupational group in their own right. Institutional funding is linked to departmental scores in these reviews, which also influence the decisions of many other funders. Since many universities now operate some kind of formula-based internal budgetary distribution incorporating these variables, a department's performance tends to translate directly into its own funding.

These arrangements seem to have a degree of transparency which is lacking in the more discretionary arrangements in many U.S. universities. A department which increases its share of the student numbers in the university automatically gets more funds, for example. There are some limitations in that it is contractually difficult for a department to cut staff if the budget is inadequate, thus failing fully to reproduce the market discipline of the commercial world. However, changes in departmental culture are increasingly noticeable. In particular, successful players of the system are discovering the importance of collective organization. Since much of the teaching review necessarily focuses on departmental systems of quality assurance rather than actual classroom performance, departments which cannot work as a team to produce and comply with such systems are penalized. Similarly, the research rating is of the department, rather than of individuals. A tail of underperformers hurts everybody. Neither departments nor universities can continue as aggregates of individuals: Activities need to be explicitly oriented to the environment through central and local planning and coordinating mechanisms.

Contrary to some prior expectations, sociology has done reasonably well out of these audits. Sociologists turn out to be rather good teachers, or at least rather good at producing appropriate documentary evidence to back up their claims to being good teachers. I suspect that all those studies of the social construction of data have given us an edge in the generation of paper to fit performance indicators. Overall, sociology seems to be around the middle of the research rankings, which is about what would be expected from a discipline that is heavily represented in "1992 universities" with a limited research tradition.

These changes in the organizational conditions of sociological production cannot be seen in isolation from wider political projects. The growth of a quality bureaucracy is not a pathology but a new building block of legitimacy. The restructuring of higher education and the academic profession has nothing that distinguishes it from the remodeling of other professions and their work environments. All UK professions have seen direct challenges to producer-controlled monopolies through marketization, deregulation, bureaucratized quality assurance, and purchaser/provider separation. These structural reforms are intended to promote organizational and professional cultures which are more responsive to customers' concerns. Many sociologists would, under another administration and perhaps by other means, warmly endorse such a project. It is not, of course, entirely straightforward since the customer for a public service is often rather ambiguous. Is it the recipient of the service? Is it the government which is creating the conditions for the supply of the service, whether as a direct provider or as a contractor for the provision? Is it the taxpayer in terms of his or her willingness to fund the supply, which may, of course, result in a lower level of quality and extent than the same individual would demand as a recipient? Who are the customers for a university? Students? Purchasers of research? Prospective employers of graduates? The government as an orchestrator of labor market planning and industrial strategy?

In practice, the government tends to be the most immediately powerful, partly because of its direct control of resources and its dominant role as a purchaser of research and graduate production and partly because of its sensitivity to its own prospects for re-election. Students enter as customers only when their purchasing decisions reflect the intentions of the government, for example. When they do not, market incentives are adjusted to try to persuade them to produce the "correct" decisions. So if, for example, students do not choose to study engineering, a bounty may be paid to those who do and places for humanities may be reduced to restrict "incorrect" choices.

The structural reforms, then, are the means of achieving a cultural project. The social sciences are at the center of this. As Philip Strong frequently used to observe, the perceived attack on social science by Conservative administrations since 1979 was an index of its importance rather than of its marginality. Sociology was seen to be exactly the kind of producer-controlled monopoly that it had criticized in writing about other professions and which needed to be restructured in the same way and for much the same reasons. Sir Keith Joseph, the first Secretary of State for Education and Science under Margaret Thatcher, was particularly identified with this, especially in his insistence on renaming the Social Science Research Council, which was the main channel for disbursing basic research funding. He felt that the title downplayed the key role of economics and implied a scientific status for social sciences that they could not sustain. We now have an Economic and Social Research Council instead! But these were not the views of an ignorant or illiterate man: They came out of a deep study of conservative traditions in social thought represented by the work of people like Hayek, Popper, and Oakeshott, who were skeptical about the application of technocratic positivist models to understanding or managing societies. Indeed, there was a certain irony in the speed with which many sociologists found themselves defending a claim to scientific status that they had increasingly questioned in the 1960s and 1970s. We might not deal quite so generously with Margaret Thatcher's celebrated later dismissal, that there was no such thing as society, only individuals and their families. Again, though, this is the worldview of a chemist and a lawyer, used to thinking in reductionist terms, but echoing a similar skepticism within the social sciences. Has anybody since Durkheim seriously thought that there was a "thing called society"—and even he does not seem to have been too sure about this?

The main target, in fact, was the alliance between sociology and the postwar social democratic project, whose crisis was revealed by the Conservative election victory of 1979. The diagnoses of this crisis have varied considerably and we do not need to look at them in detail here. However, what is striking is that none of the establishment figures of British sociology saw it coming. While they were focusing on the failures of Labour administrations to redistribute wealth or redress other social inequalities rather than, say, celebrating their successes in education, health, social security, or industrial policy, a massive groundswell of demands for different sorts of change was gathering particularly among skilled male manual workers. The Conservatives capitalized on this and constructed a series of election victories and an intellectual hegemony which seems likely to endure much longer than their period in government. The social sciences were seen as possible partners in constructing this hegemony. They were challenged to live up to their claims about freedom of debate and inquiry and to give serious attention to an alternative canon of noncollectivist thinkers.

In effect, the options have widened for British sociology. At one end of the range is that suggested by Barry Glassner's observation, when we discussed this paper, that many of his colleagues saw U.S. sociology as the "keeper of the nation's conscience." It might be described as the "rainbow model," where sociologists align with underdog groups, celebrating their cultures and documenting their exclusion from the societal mainstream. The postmodern turn in social theory may be an expression of this. At the other is a response to the changes in the environment: Sociologists can only be the keepers of a nation's conscience, where that conscience is on the political agenda. When morality must be accommodated to efficiency and effectiveness, would-be moralizers tread on thin ice. In effect, sociologists have been offered a chance to become allies of liberal capitalism. As both the UK government and the European Union have formulated industrial and scientific strategies for the next 20 years or so, corporate interests have told them that the keys to success lie as much in questions for social science as for the natural sciences. Generally, British science has been more successful than that of most countries at discovery: Our weakness has been in industrial product development and marketing, so we end up buying goods from Japan that result from our innovations! A sociological understanding of the structure and culture of economic activity in the United Kingdom could make a vital contribution to national competitiveness. In many science-based industries, for example, a great challenge is to reduce the costs of innovation by a better understanding of the process of discovery and the organizational conditions which facilitate this. There is a growing field of study in the transfer of technology from the laboratory to manufacturers and end-users. One of the biggest injections of private funding into British sociology at the present time is for ethnomethodological studies of the organizational use of new information technologies. There is a real commercial value in reducing the expensive record of failure among systems rationally designed by computer scientists which then fail to support the work of the intended users. Ethnomethodology's eye for detail may hold vital clues for system design.

THE CHAIR'S DILEMMA

This is, inevitably, a sketchy account of the environment for British sociology in the 1990s. However, I hope that it conveys some sense of a turbulence that I suspect others may soon begin to encounter, if the number of international delegations that have observed the restructuring of our higher education is any indication. But I also want to bring a sense of return to my observations of a small program in an uncertain time 25 years ago. The health visitor faculty did not know quite where their program was going and what would happen to it as a result of the environmental changes that it was experiencing. Their survival as a program depended on getting it right. That could only be done by careful listening to what was going on around them and by an active discussion of what kind of graduate they needed to produce and how the curriculum, the pedagogy, and the assessment could be made to interlock in order to achieve this. It also needed attention to the core values and skills of the occupation and to their reinterpretation for a new historical moment.

It is the chair's job to provoke such debate, to ensure that a department is alive to what is going on around it. Like all modern managers, department chairs are managers of culture. The structural conditions are largely given. Chairs may have a small input to the particular local versions devised by their university administration but this is relatively marginal in the context of state policy or even the mission formulated by the governing body of the university. But the chair must do this without any of the tools of his or her counterpart in industry. Individuals have a high level of contractual security. Market exit—bankruptcy—is not seen as a realistic threat. In a relatively immobile labor market, career aspirations are of limited concern for most faculty. An inflexible reward system and shortage of funding means that the differentials between the industrious and the idle are relatively small. The university is classically a nonnegotiated order, where there is an almost obsessive pretense of negotiation.

If change is not achieved, then sociology, like any other discipline, is vulnerable to decline because its material foundations are not secure. Faculty will not be replaced, students will not get jobs because their skills are not seen to have market currency, scholars will end up writing for each others' amusement rather than because anyone else is interested in what they have to say.

The rainbow model of sociology can, I suspect, survive in two kinds of institution. In institutions like many of our "1992 universities" it will prosper because it is cheap to research and teach, locks into their high level of recruitment from nontraditional student groups, and can be tolerated as a filler in a mass system where many degrees from lower-status colleges will have relatively little market value. If the United Kingdom had great private universities, I suppose that it might also survive as the plaything of the sons and daughters of wealthy families whose accumulated material and cultural capital guarantees their status. Ivy League law schools can be hotbeds of Critical Legal Studies precisely because they are Ivy League law schools. This is not a viable option in the research-oriented parts of a public university system. If students are to commit themselves to the increasing economic costs of studying in these colleges, they need to be sure of acquiring skills that will confer a market advantage on graduation. If the sociology department is to be supported within the university by the big hitters in science, medicine and engineering, then it needs strategic alliances to unlock the funding lines for social science within national and EU science and technology research programs. Sociologists in these universities cannot afford to be regarded as the jesters of the academic world: To survive, they need to join the suits at the top table.

This need not, though, betray our corporate values. It demands, rather, an understanding of what it takes to speak out for them in the contemporary world. Qualitative sociologists have become strangely detached from their own macro-canon. Qualitative sociology, indeed, has become so firmly defined as a micro-sociology that its historic roots in attempts to understand the organization of whole societies have been deeply buried. It is not, for example, widely known that the first social scientist to write of the "looking-glass self" was Adam Smith as part of his project to build an understanding of social organization, in *Wealth of Nations,* on the workings of face to face interaction, in *The Theory of Moral Sentiments.* Similarly, few of those who draw on Schutz for inspiration have traced the links to the macrotheories of spontaneous order in the writings of Hayek and other Austrians. Qualitative sociology is deeply if unconsciously embedded in the liberal tradition of social theory (Dingwall, 1997).

Albion Small once observed that his aspiration for sociology in Chicago was to produce business and civic leaders who, when confronted with a social problem, would not just wring their hands and declare that nothing could be done because of some immutable law of the market or of social evolution or whatever. The production of such an elite is still a valid mission. It may well be more persuasive to argue that a concern for the quality of public schools is a concern for national efficiency and economic competitiveness rather than a moral obligation to the poor; to argue that spending on welfare can contribute toward the promotion of risk-taking and innovation by assuring entrepreneurs of an adequate safety net if the risk goes wrong; to argue that the creation of the American Gulag is a remarkably inefficient and wasteful means of dealing with criminality. Business may prosper far more in a high-trust society. A buoyant economy and full employment may deliver a much higher level of welfare and social justice than the most elaborate social security system. A tight labor market may be a stronger pressure to deliver equality of opportunity than elaborate legal provisions. An active and integrated regional or world economy may be a better guarantor of peace than international disarmament talks. As the great, and much-maligned, English sociologist, Herbert Spencer, once observed, nations bound together by mutual trade rapidly find that they have too much at stake to fight wars with each other. We need to become as good at helping our countries to make money as we are at proposing ways to spend it. In the process, we may well find we have achieved more real progress on the values of humanity and civility that have always been at the core of our discipline and that we have delivered more benefits to those whose interests we have assumed some right to articulate and represent.

For a discipline so identified with collectivism, sociologists are remarkable individualists who remain reluctant to learn from their own discipline's work. We know the importance of teamwork in successful organizations and we reject the lessons for our own. We know that organizations need to be in constant interaction with their environment and we hide behind our campus fences. We know that legitimacy is problematic and we resist the measures necessary to manage and sustain it by maintaining the pretext that our own organizations are uniquely negotiable.

The chair's fate is often that of Cassandra, to stand at the intersection between the department and its environment and to pass messages in both directions which neither side will quite believe or act on. We are usually better rewarded than was Cassandra, but the pay does not compensate for the frustration. In the long term, the only consolation may be the bitter one of the Presbyterian minister in the Scottish story. The minister preached sermons every Sunday warning his congregation about the evils of drunkenness, fornication, and other debauchery and the eternal damnation that awaited them. During the rest of the week, the sermons were, of course, ignored. However, one day the nuclear power station down the road blew up and the minister and his congregation all passed over to the other side. The congregation were cast into the pit of fire and as they were led away to their fate, they looked up at their minister leaning out from heaven to watch. "Minister," they said, "all those sermons of yours, all those warnings, we didna' ken." To which he replied, in the best Presbyterian tradition, "Weel, ye ken noo!"

NOTES

1. Reprinted with permission of Human Sciences Press, Inc. (1997).

2. Readers unfamiliar with the status system of UK higher education should note that the difference between a university and a polytechnic is roughly that between the University of California and the State University of California, with the polytechnics being primarily involved in undergraduate, vocationally oriented programs with a

limited amount of research and graduate work. Since 1992, the UK government has decreed that all these institutions should have the title of "university" although in the argot of our profession, a distinction is still often made between "traditional" and "1992" universities.

REFERENCES

Bittner, E. (1965). The concept of organization. *Social Research, 32,* 239-255.
Dingwall, R. (1974). *The social organisation of health visitor training.* PhD thesis, University of Aberdeen, Aberdeen, UK.
Dingwall, R. (1977). *The social organisation of health visitor training.* London: Croom Helm.
Dingwall, R. (1987). The certification of competence: Assessment in occupational socialization. *Urban Life, 15,* 367-393.
Dingwall, R. (1997). The moral discourse of interactionism. In G. Miller & R. Dingwall (Eds.), *Context and method in qualitative research.* London: Sage.
Dingwall, R., & Strong, P. M. (1985). The interactional study of organizations: A critique and reformulation. *Urban Life, 14,* 205-232.
Garfinkel, H. (1967). *Studies in ethnomethodology.* Englewood Cliffs, NJ: Prentice Hall.
Gouldner, A. W. (1971). *The coming crisis of Western sociology.* London: Heinemann.
Hughes, E. C. (1971). *The sociological eye.* Chicago: Aldine/Atherton.
Meyer, J. W., & Rowan, B. (1977). Institutionalized organizations: Formal structure as myth and ceremony. *American Journal of Sociology, 83,* 40-63.
Olesen, V. L., & Whitaker, E. W. (1970). Critical notes on sociological studies of professional socialization. In J. A. Jackson (Ed.), *Professions and professionalization.* Cambridge, UK: Cambridge University Press.

CHAPTER 23

Is There a Philosopher in the House?[1]

JONATHAN D. MORENO

HERR/FRAU PROFESSOR DR.

As a philosopher who teaches in a medical school, I have long wondered about the business of using academic titles as part of one's name. Is the use of "Dr." a mark of arrogance, or is its omission self-denial and nondisclosure? The most prestigious college I was associated with before I turned away from traditional philosophy teaching identified all its instructors as "Mr." or "Ms." in the course list. But I also recall my senior colleague in another philosophy department who invariably introduced himself, with a broad smile and hearty handshake, as "Professor" so-and-so. I remember thinking that he said it as though that was his first name.

I started out in bioethics by team-teaching in medical school courses, offered in the medical school building. I noticed that my medical colleagues would usually introduce me as "Dr." to the students. It was apparent that everyone was comfortable with this mode of address, or at least not uncomfortable, including the philosophy majors taking the course for philosophy credit who knew me as "professor" elsewhere on the campus. The physical location of the course supported the "Dr." emphasis, including the meeting room itself which was a lab suitably arrayed with cabinets, beakers, bunsen burners, and emergency showerheads.

Under these circumstances, it would have been pointless to note that the title indicating degree is less prestigious than that indicating rank. First, my rank wasn't really professor at that time (where's the prestige in being an assistant professor?), and, second, the marks of status in the German academic tradition don't apply in the New World, where even generic "doctors" have at least as much clout as generic "professors." My dissertation director once recalled his work for a think tank on contract with the Navy. When operational issues came up the brass said, "Let's call the doctors." "Let's call the professors" wouldn't have been believable enough on its face to be a cute inside joke. A medical school administrator with a doctorate in another humanities field told me that he permits himself to be called "Dr." within the institution because otherwise he would not be taken seriously by the medical and science faculty, though he would loathe to be so addressed in any other context.

When still shuttling between liberal arts college and medical school, I was also able to adapt any doubts I had about the propriety of being titled one way or another to the context. This adjustment worked well until my first summer on rounds in an oncology unit. Joining the team for its tours of the bedside was an opportunity to learn more about the physicians' work style. With this experience I could formulate more relevant suggestions when we gathered around the conference table to discuss their more difficult cases.

Upon entering a patient's room, I would be introduced by the attending physician as one of the many doctors on the team. Indeed, on morning work rounds there were ordinarily 8 or 10 of us huddled around a bed, several of whom were no more medical doctors—and indeed less "doctors"—than me, but medical students or pharmacists. The attending oncologist was invariably polite to the patient, but rather than running through the whole list of people assembled would often simply say something like, "These are some of the doctors who are on the team caring for you."

Because truth-telling was supposed to be a matter for my watch, the experience was unsettling, though my colleague, the attending physician, assured me that I had every right to be part of the team and to be introduced in a like fashion. In one sense, I could hardly argue, as the psychologists were also undifferentiated as "doctors" and had the appropriate degree. My stumbling block was the knowledge that none of these people would have expected a philosopher to be among those privileged to witness their vulnerability, so how could I presume their acquiescence?

Though not the primary reason I was drawn to spend more clinical time in the neonatal intensive care unit, the title issue is less of a problem with those tiny patients. In the NICU, it is easy for the attending neonatologist to introduce me as "Dr. Moreno, our medical ethicist" to the staff without raising eyebrows. Sapient patients, on the other hand, might well wonder why such a presence is needed.

TEACHING ETHICS, DOING SOCIOLOGY

Whatever sensitivity I brought to these matters can be attributed partly to my close association with Barry Glassner and his other colleagues who founded *Qualitative Sociology* 20 years ago. At that time, fresh out of graduate school, I could not have anticipated my bioethical turn. I enjoyed reading the manuscripts submitted to *QS* and attending sociology conferences (the issues were delightfully different from those that drove my philosophical colleagues), but I had no idea that this way of thinking would ever have direct relevance to my working life.

About 10 years after my initial experience with qualitative sociology, I conducted a weekly ethics seminar with pediatric nurses. They were a marvelous group, smart and dedicated. The first several sessions were on various standard issues in medical ethics, and we then focused on the peculiar stresses inherent in the nurse's role. One of these is the need to deal with various attending physicians who have different practice styles and make very different demands on the staff. An important part of learning how to nurse in a particular unit is learning how to deal with the attendings. Some annoyance was expressed, but mostly resignation.

Then I suggested that the young residents, who are after all on wards a lot more than the attendings, must present another sort of challenge. I mentioned my impression that nurses don't deal with all these physicians-in-training in the same ways. This general remark immediately elicited smiles of recognition, some more bashful than others, and a few amused glances at one another. Emboldened, I then allowed that I have sometimes observed nurses "game" or manipulate the house staff to get what they want. Confirming anecdotes then poured forth freely, most on the order of knowing which resident to approach to deal with a problem, and how to do so. An especially memorable conversation followed about nurses' relationships with female residents. For at least some of these nurses those dealings were freighted with a great deal of complexity.

In retrospect, what I found especially fascinating about this discussion in the nursing ethics seminar was not the content of their stories about gaming the residents with whom they worked, but the zeal and amused delight with which some of them talked about it. The affect in the room differed considerably from our previous discussion of their relations with the attendings, for in that dynamic they were subordinate. When it came to the house staff they were in a position of power by virtue of knowing more about the way the unit and the institution worked, and often by virtue of knowing more about medicine than the newer residents. Of course, the young doctors had to learn, said one, but it was hard to watch them learn on the patients that they were also charged with caring for, especially when the nurses had to clean up after their mistakes. On the whole, while they were not unsympathetic to the new doctors' plight, it was pleasurable for these experienced women who perceived themselves as often undervalued by the institution to exercise a little dominance over some of the supposedly best and brightest.

I was delighted with this session and how much it had revealed about the interstices of the hospital regime. The nurses themselves also expressed their enjoyment at having a phenomenon framed for them, for though they were roughly aware of it they had not fully articulated it before or talked about it with one another. In fact, the last minutes of that class were devoted to a heartfelt discussion about interpersonal honesty and authenticity, and how hard it is to achieve in the highly scrutinized, hierarchical, and closely regulated modern hospital.

Talking openly about power and dominance is an agenda I have tried to pursue with residents themselves; even though this is arguably not "medical ethics" in a strict academic sense, the constraints on health care workers' efforts to take good care of their patients obviously has moral overtones. I meet regularly with groups of residents in conferences in which ethical issues are given the stage. If these sessions are defined as "core curriculum" rather than "patient management," they enjoy the great advantage of having no attending physicians in the room, but only the house officers themselves. After a few meetings, I am usually able to engender a level of trust that enables topics to be opened in the ethics conference that are not spoken of in any other formal setting. The most powerful such session I conducted had to do with the way that mistakes are dealt with in the department, a topic I was able to introduce by describing Charles Bosk's classic observations about a surgical residency program in *Forgive and Remember* (1979).

ALIENATED ALIENS

In the hospitals where I work in Brooklyn most of the residents in primary care departments are graduates of medical schools in other countries, usually foreign nationals on special visas. One might have thought that they would be less inclined to criticize systems of authority, especially as tenuous accredited guests, than those who are citizens and who were socialized and educated in American institutions. But in fact I have found them remarkably willing to question their situation and, because of their cultural perspective, far sharper in their critiques of our system. On rare occasions they are deeply embittered. A Russian surgeon attempting to gain credentials to practice here denounced the American colleagues he had observed as motivated entirely by greed; at least in the old Soviet system, for all its faults, there was room for compassion, he concluded, and the treatment was actually better than what he had seen here. The others in his cohort, some also Russian and some from other parts of the world, were obviously taken aback by his caustic outburst, and quickly asserted that his observations applied only to a minority of American physicians they had met.

Coming from such countries as the Philippines, Pakistan, and Argentina, these exceptionally capable people often have practiced medicine at home, have not set foot in the United States before, and within days of their arrival are at work in some of our busiest inner-city hospitals. They tend to be among the best products of their country's system of medical education, but are viewed as second class in the United States, and they know it. Current federal policy changes call for a vast reduction in the number of positions available for "international medical graduates," who give most of the inpatient care in places like Brooklyn.

For some who have difficulty obtaining a visa in time to begin their residency, the indignities begin even before they arrive. For others the shock comes later: One young man arrived in this country in mid-June, days before his orientation, settled his family in a tough neighborhood near the hospital, and had his car stolen before he even began to work. He immediately moved his wife and children to suburban New Jersey and took the long commute several times a week.

The first time I met with a group of new arrivals I realized that because they had no understanding of the American legal system and little familiarity with many of our cultural assumptions, they could hardly make sense of discussions of patient autonomy or informed consent. Sometimes their reactions to our system achieved comical proportions. One melodramatic chief resident told me facetiously that in his country "when one of my patients died the government sends me a letter—thanking me! Because there are too many people! Here, if one of my patients dies I get a letter from a lawyer!"

More usually what I have found in these sessions, which I think of as anthropologic focus groups, is amazement at our cultural contradictions. For example, one Latin American who had been a professor of histology in a medical school back home was nonplussed at Dr. Kevorkian's ability to "get away with murder" in public. In his country, he said, that would be impossible. When he was questioned, he admitted that assisted suicide probably does happen, but if a doctor did that in a publicized manner he would certainly be imprisoned. The example enabled me to explain that our Constitution gives the states authority to create their own laws on matters such as the regulation of health care professionals, and that at the time Kevorkian started, Michigan had no law on physician-assisted suicide. Although the group was frankly puzzled by the moral inconsistencies of a society that rhetorically insists on the sanctity of human life, those from Catholic countries had to admit that the same was true of their homelands, where abortion is illegal but common. In the end, these young physicians are candid that they are not here for philosophical consistency but for professional training and economic opportunity. They are willing to accept American social conflicts as minefields they must be willing to navigate in order to reap personal rewards.

TAKE TWO LOGICAL CONNECTIVES
AND CALL ME IN THE MORNING

Many of the venues in which I work are more or less academic rather than mainly clinical. They include conferences with residents in which issues in medical ethics are discussed, as well as grand rounds about topics like euthanasia. These events are in many ways extensions of graduate and continuing education on philosophical and policy problems. When these academic exercises shade into finding solutions to clinical issues with ongoing cases, a new and different role for the philosopher, the most fascinating experiences I have had in the sociology of the professions are engendered. Requests for concrete advice about managing what the physicians involved perceive to be ethical problems are, of course, common and expected for one touted as the "ethicist." More often than not the problem with a current case has to do with a concern or disagreement with a patient's family about the most appropriate course of treatment. Under these circumstances, negotiating skills are as important as philosophical insight.

Sometimes, however, requests for advice go beyond what can be viewed as ethical issues and into technical medical questions, such as what order and technique for the withdrawal of life-sustaining treatment should be adopted. Now sometimes these questions do have ethical implications, since deciding to stop antibiotics for a dying patient is distinct from turning off a ventilator, though the end result is the same. On the other hand, I have also been asked how much sedation should be given when the respirator is being withdrawn (to prevent a feeling of suffocation), or at what rate the supply of oxygen should be reduced. These questions have been asked by physicians who are quite aware that I am not a medical doctor, but they ascribe to me a level of experience with technical matters by virtue of the clinical issues that animate my intellectual work.

Another reason for this exaggerated notion of the philosopher ethicist's knowledge base is that some (but by no means all) ethicists have medical titles. At my previous medical school my rank and tenure were in pediatrics, and I held a "courtesy" appointment in medicine as well. I am sure that my opinions would be taken far less seriously if my professorship was in philosophy, as it was at another institution, rather than in central clinical departments. The assumption is that I have somehow "earned my stripes" to have these appointments; while I would like to think that is true, contingent factors are also at work in the way that ethicists are assigned their academic titles.

These generalizations are, of course, severely limited, and in particular cases attitudes toward the nonphysician presuming to speak to clinical issues vary wildly. At one extreme, even close colleagues have sometimes trumped my arguments about physician paternalism by appealing to ad hominem tactics that I heard more 10 years ago than I do now: "Well, it may look that way to a philosopher, but it's different for the physician who is actually giving the treatment." At another extreme, I have been appointed to ad hoc committees on sensitive administrative problems (such as what to do about a resident who was HIV positive but wanted to stay in the program), even though ethical expertise was not much needed. In such cases, I have come to see myself as cast into the role of a "secular priest": Even in a pluralistic and multiethnic society someone must sanctify such delicate proceedings. If responsible authorities can announce that the ethicist was part of the committee, then they are generally perceived to have taken into account something important, though it is not easy to say exactly what that is.

IS THERE A DOCTOR ON BOARD?

In spite of my frequent public professions that my goal is not to be a physician *manque* but a philosopher of medicine, immersion in a medical environment and collaboration with medical professionals has deeply affected my self-identification. I was not aware of how much I have come to identify with the physician role until a long airplane flight several years ago. I was seated in a wide-body aircraft in a row on the side of the plane in front of an emergency exit and near the galley, the kind of seat in which there is an open space that permits even the economy traveler to stretch out. With no seats in front of me and the seat next to me unoccupied, I congratulated myself that on this flight I had first-class space for a lot less.

Several hours after dinner, night descended, and I managed to drift off. Not long after that I felt something landing on top of my feet. It was a female passenger whom the flight attendants were attempting to place in a position that would encourage the flow of oxygen. The cabin was darkened and the voices muffled by engine noise, but I gathered that the passenger had collapsed after leaving the toilet. The flight attendants hoped it was only airsickness, but they feared a heart attack. Quickly the call went out for a physician on board, and first class seemed to empty as an international group of medical personnel huddled over a shrouded figure below me.

All this happened in a few moments, of course, while I was semiconscious, but I remember being struck by an urgent desire to answer the flight attendants' call for assistance, and then to join my "colleagues" at the "bedside." That I could contribute little or nothing to the ministrations being provided (which consisted mainly of a brief medical history, a self-report of symptoms, and the provision of some oxygen) had nothing to do with my reflex sense that I had a place with the "team." Since then I have had another such experience, and again I wanted to announce myself to the flight crew: "I'm not a medical doctor but I am an ethicist. Can I be of assistance?" Fortunately for all concerned, I have resisted such urges and concentrated instead on the introspection for which my training more properly qualifies me.

On the other hand, maybe someday I will answer that call.

NOTE

1. Reprinted with permission of Human Sciences Press, Inc. (1997).

REFERENCE

Bosk, C. (1979). *Forgive and remember.* Chicago: University of Chicago Press.

CHAPTER 24

The Two Faces of
Professional Discretion
A Vision From the Client's Bed

ALLAN SCHNAIBERG

RULES AND JUDGMENTS:
INSIGHTS ABOUT SOCIOLOGICAL PRACTICES

Over many years of teaching, I gradually realized that what sociologists actually did in their research practice was quite different from what they wrote in their professional articles (Goldenberg, 1992). During many years of my own research into environmental conflicts, I discovered that natural scientists and engineers also practiced their own research in ways quite different from their standard methodological and ethical prescriptions. I later discovered that the constructivist sociologists of science had been analyzing some of these practices for some time. In this chapter, I extend some of my insights to the medical profession, with which I have recently had extensive interaction (and coaction). I also try to synthesize these observations of professional life by reflecting on my own practices as a sociological researcher and my recent experience as a client of medical practitioners.

The benefit of my having stumbled about these issues was that I was independently working inductively toward a new approach to understanding the research process of scientists. I began to understand how and why the ways in which scientists practiced their research, and the ways in which they wrote it up, had to do with two factors. First, they were responding to the career structures in their professional subfields and departments. Second, each scientific practitioner was also responding according to his or her own personality (and with gender and racial components of their worldviews).

In the past few years, in directing senior theses, I observed how seniors' personalities influence their choices. First, they assessed the opportunity structures in my courses (e.g., What would I tolerate? What would I be enthusiastic about? and What kind of recommendation letter would I write them?). Second, they decided how much risk they wanted to take in structuring their topic and methods.

More revealing perhaps has been my experience in supervising doctoral theses. Two categories of students emerged in my reflection: Those could write everything but the conclusions chapter and those who rushed through all the preliminary chapters to focus most heavily on the conclusions chapter. The common denominator of both sets of researchers was that their behaviors were conditioned both by their opportunity structure and by their own personality styles (e.g., risk taking vs. risk averse).

I now realize, however, that I was observing in my students just a particular instance of the broader category of professional practice. Sociological analysis of professionalism typically emphasizes that professionals have the right to use discretion in their role performance (Larson, 1977). Central in the study of medical professions especially was the inference that these rights were a form of doctors' power over their clients (Bosk, 1979; Freidson, 1970, 1986; Millman, 1977). My recent encounters as a client of the medical profession led me to a different conception of medical practice.

PROFESSIONAL RISKS AND AVERSIONS

Some of my insights into this social structural and social psychological process of professional practice stem from being married to a therapist, who works on individual development. I suspect, however, I have been interested in this as a missing piece in much of modern sociological practice for a long time. As a graduate student, for example, I noted the strong differences between my classmates in population studies and those in social organization. The former were much more risk averse than the latter—and as one who straddled the two fields, I felt the tensions internally. Although I wanted the approval of mentors who stressed the "scientific" discipline of research, I often found the work they promoted to be limited and boring. At the same time, however, I found that some of the qualitative classmates were, in the modern parlance, "flakes." I also discovered that faculty responses in qualitative courses seemed much more arbitrary and uncertain than those in narrowly quantitative courses.

Years later, I discovered from a psychological researcher that there were systematic personality differences in teaching and learning styles. The modal natural scientist and engineer emphasizes "learning facts"; in contrast, social scientists stress "creative thinking." As someone with a previous career in chemistry, I found my own orientation mixed both approaches. Was this "fit" between personality and discipline one of social selection or of socialization? I now think both operate to some extent. There are modal role performances of natural and social scientists that are quite different. There is some important variation within each category, however, suggesting there is imperfect selection or imperfect socialization or both in these professions.

Here, I establish the linkage between professional sociologists and medical professionals. Training my sociological students by having them learn rules for research practices was not only incomplete in capturing how "real research" operated but also often quite misleading. Their training, I believed, needed to be expanded by also exposing them to accounts of how sociological researchers actually made decisions in the field. Ironically, there is a multitude of books for imparting "methodological rules" but few on how sociologists in practice make "methodological judgments." There is some recognition of this gulf: There have been repeated attempts by research training institutions to engage students in some form of apprenticeship. As early as 1964 (when I wrote my first graduate paper), however, Albert Reiss made me aware that much of the structure of apprenticeship programs served the (exploitative) needs of the masters and not those of the apprentices (a point my later colleague Howie Becker stressed in his studies of schooling and work).

I also noted, however, that some students much preferred to learn the formal rules, whereas others wanted to know about all the messiness of actual practices. Likewise, some colleagues preferred to teach rules, whereas others emphasized and illustrated the multitude of judgments required to do "good research."

Some of these tensions are evident among undergraduates being socialized to "do research." When I ask these students to actually pick a design, they become immobilized. They realize that they have to discard some options, and this makes them feel vulnerable, given the uncertainties of future research paths. Their tension is further heightened when they are either risk averse by person-ality or are more anxious to "get an A" in their thesis research or both. These younger students are preprofessionals still trying to decide whether they want to be selected into sociology training; in contrast, graduate students are being socialized into professional sociology, and therefore their anxieties are more grounded in occupational reality.

I have been struck by my recent intensive and extensive experience with medical practices, with similar tensions between their application of rules and their use of judgments (which is the core of medical discretion). To some extent, I argue that although studies of the medical profession highlight doctors' freedom to use discretion in medical practice, they often understate the con-straints imposed on medical practitioners against using such discretion. Issues such as medical malpractice risks have been much discussed in recent decades. We largely ignore, however, the more diffused and enduring microstructural and mesostructural (Mills, 1959) aspects of medical practitioners' choices to use discretion, relying on their personal judgments as much as on the rules in their medical books.

MEDICAL RULES AND JUDGMENTS IN DIAGNOSIS: INSIGHTS FROM THE CLIENT'S SIDE

Struggling Toward Defining the Problem

Recently, I have had many occasions to reflect on medical professionalism. I began to experience some shortness of breath, especially when I swam (which I did regularly). Sometimes, I also had similar experiences when walking. For several months, I chalked it up to anxiety—although always with some nagging doubts. The alternative explanation, that I was having some coronary problems, lurked in my background consciousness. Because I had experienced no chest pain (angina pectoris), however, I considered the likelihood of coronary artery blockage to be low. After all, even though I have been overweight (and diabetic in recent years), I did exercise regularly and had been on a low-fat diet for approximately 10 years. Of course, I often excised from my own judgmental processes the fact that my cholesterol ratios were very unfavorable, and that my total cholesterol was higher than what is now considered healthy. In the shadows of my optimistic judgments, however, lurked these counterjudgmental facts, accounting for my persistent anxieties about possible cardiac problems.

I finally visited my primary care provider (Dr. J) in my health maintenance organization (HMO) when it was time for my annual checkup. I mentioned the breathing problem (probably in a casual way) and then winced when he suggested it was time for a cardiac stress test (my last one was more than 20 years ago). My adverse reaction was due to my substantial faith in this physician. Although he has operated through a succession of HMO ownership, each of which has become more restrictive in approving referrals, I have been his patient for approximately 20 years. He has always been a professional who exercises good judgment: He is sensitive, attentive, reflective, and a concerned physician. Paradoxically, I often have to wait up to 2 hours to see him because he takes his own time in discussing issues with patients, regardless of the HMO pressures for increased productivity.

Although he has some rules that he follows (in my case, advising me to lose weight) and some routine tests that the HMO and he provide, he has been open to discussion about alternative interpretations of symptoms, test results, and treatment options during the past 20 years. I tend to deal with my health anxieties in part by reading about issues a great deal, and I have increasingly used the internet to follow through on more acute problems. In the standard social psychological literature, I tend to have an "internal locus of control" (Peterson, Maier, & Seligman, 1993; Weary, Gleicher, & Marsh, 1993). I react strongly against physicians and medical personnel of all types who simply "follow the rules" in dealing with me. Often, I force them to explain approaches—and if they refuse, I either switch providers or find another route to get my questions answered. This has been my style regarding my own health conditions and those of other members of my family (including several instances of surgery).

Thus, when my HMO physician advised me to do a cardiac stress test, I reluctantly agreed and scheduled it approximately a week later—with great fear and anxiety (partly because of the physical stress of the test itself and partly because of what it might reveal). I performed the test and thought I had "passed" with flying colors. Unlike my earlier experience, I did not feel dizzy when I was finished. Moreover, whenever the attending cardiologist asked me whether I was feeling any chest pains, I could answer (truthfully) that I had none. I left feeling rather pleased with this testing, and I scheduled a follow-up with my primary physician a week or two later, feeling little anxiety.

When I saw Dr. J. for the follow-up, I was surprised and distressed when he announced that I had "failed" the stress test. As I questioned him, he said there had been some "irregularities" on the test readout but did not give me any details (which was unusual and worried me further). I argued with him that I had experienced no chest pain in the test. He then dropped the other shoe: Because I was a diabetic, sometimes the nerve damage from diabetes made the coronary nerves insensitive to pain from oxygen restriction (of course, I also retained a notion that sometimes they did not, and that the test results were really a false positive). He said I should see one of the HMO's consulting cardiologists. At this point, I asked for their names because I had some bad experiences with an HMO cardiologist several years earlier. I asked for a referral to another cardiologist on their list, but I also said I needed to check his name "downstairs." I quickly went down to the cardiology test lab in the HMO and checked with the lab technician, whom I have come to know through repeated tests (for a mild congenital heart defect). She and I had previously talked about "good" and "bad" cardiologists—by which she implied those with openness to patients and the good use of judgment as opposed to those who were mechanical and rule bound. I asked her again for the names of the good ones and verified that the name I had remembered in dealing with Dr. J. was indeed one of this small set.

It took almost 4 weeks for the HMO to send me a referral approval notice for seeing this consultant. Although I was frustrated, on the one hand, I was also relieved, on the other hand. Because I trusted Dr. J's judgment, I knew that if he had believed my condition required urgent consultations, he would have arranged for a rapid approval. Hence, the bureaucratic delay I also converted into another reassurance that "nothing much was wrong." Ironically, one of the problems with judgments is that there are few rules to tell you when you are way off base—after all, judgments can be bad as well as good. Because of my own judgment, I did not rush to make the appointment, but called within a week. I then discovered, however, that the cardiologist, Dr. A., was away on vacation for 3 weeks and had no openings for a month. Having little other choice (but secretly also relieved), I made an appointment for approximately a month later.

Moving From Medical Uncertainty
to Diagnostic Precision

Dr. A. was clearly a high-performance and stressed specialist. When he interrupted our meeting to take a phone call, however, I was impressed with how much he used complex judgments in dealing with the case rather than simply applying treatment rules. Rejoining me, he answered all my questions, including a detailed evaluation of the stress test results, showing (perhaps) some "ischemia"—an electrical signal indicating that there was some possible limitation of oxygen supply from at least one major coronary artery. He also talked about nerve atrophy from my diabetes and how this might have prevented me from experiencing angina pains during the stress test and the months in which I had experienced shortness of breath. We talked about repeating the stress test, adding a dye indicator (thallium), but he indicated that this test might not have much more discriminatory power than the previous one. He then reviewed my cholesterol profile and suggested that perhaps a more definitive—more invasive— test might be better "in the long run." This was an angiogram, which requires an insertion of a catheter in the femoral artery (in the groin area). The catheter is then slowly moved into the heart area, and a dye is injected. Through X-ray technique, the major arteries become outlined by the path of the dye, which traces their openness or constriction by plaque. I scheduled the test for approximately 2 weeks later because I needed time for other medical testing before the angiogram. I also had an National Science Foundation review committee trip I believed I "needed" to complete (perhaps in preference to doing the angiogram!).

Because I was awake but partly sedated during the angiogram, I could follow the conversation of the surgeon, Dr. X, doing the angiogram. It became clear that he was having problems finding access to some of my arteries because he kept changing the size of the catheters during the procedure (so much for the rule-like implementation of this "straightforward" test). When it was over, Dr. Y, who had assisted in the testing, showed me a summary X ray. He pointed out major constrictions in at least two of my arteries. I was highly distressed, to say the least (but of course, this had been one of the possible outcomes of this test).

A few minutes later, Dr. X told me in greater detail the results: "85% obstruction in at least three of the arteries" with "ossified deposits." I understood the first of these, but did not ask about the second because Dr. X said, "This requires bypass surgery and is not treatable by angioplasty." When I asked if I could finish teaching the remaining 2 weeks, he said "I wouldn't delay if I were you: Your heart is good now, and you don't want to take chances." This effectively rendered me questionless and hence speechless.

From Diagnostic Precision to Medical and Social Judgments About Treatment

When I returned to my outpatient room later, with my wife and my research collaborator (an advanced graduate student) present, we began to discuss the findings. My collaborator assured me that he and his wife could finish the lectures, and that I should not worry about the course. When my cardiologist, Dr. A, arrived later, he indicated that "this seemed to be an open-and-shut case, with no ambiguity." I "needed bypass surgery." This would involve cutting open my chest, stopping my heart, and replacing blocked arteries with redirected and grafted pectoral arteries and veins removed from my leg. In response to my questions, he explained where the blockages were and what "ossification" meant. These were thick, hardened plaques, which could not be removed by angioplasty. Angioplasty is a less invasive treatment that involves inserting a catheter with a balloon at the end, much like the diagnostic angiogram, sometimes with "shunts" inserted to hold the artery open after the plaque has been flattened or blown out. Using angioplasty on ossified blockages might break through the artery walls, however, causing unstoppable hemorrhaging.

I then retreated to asking whether the bypass could be performed with a newer "port" surgery, in which the chest is not cut open. Instead, a small incision is made between the ribs—allowing for less trauma and far more rapid recovery. He said, in another rule-like fashion, that the placement of the blockages made this impossible—only some of the arteries could be grafted this way. Furthermore, because I needed the chest cut to do some arterial grafts, it made more sense to do all the grafts that way.

I was at a loss to challenge this, so I retreated to a final defensive question. Could I wait 2 weeks until the end of the academic quarter to have the surgery? At this point, the differences between Dr. A and the angiogram physician became clear. Dr. A said, "Well, you have been walking around with this problem for at least 6 months, so I don't see why a few more weeks should be a problem." He also set another limit, however: "But I wouldn't wait too long, because your heart is in good shape, and you don't want to risk damaging it." He implied that if I waited "too long," the risk of a heart attack would increase, and permanent heart muscle damage would impair full recovery from bypass surgery. Although this generally concurred with the logic of Dr. X, I noted how different the process of reasoning through this was with Dr. A. He contextualized my case and was willing to negotiate the timing of the surgery. When I asked what was too long of a delay, he said "probably not over a month." After discussion with my wife and my young research collaborator, I agreed to try to schedule the surgery in approximately 2 weeks. This allowed me to finish lecturing but left the final exam in my collaborator's charge.

I then asked Dr. A about which surgeons were available under my HMO coverage. He indicated that there was a group of cardiac surgeons, of whom one (Dr. Z) was the "star." He was the most senior, had done more bypasses, and was internationally known. He continued, however: "If you want someone who will talk with you, Dr. R is better at that." This was affirming of me in two ways. First, it meant Dr. A really understood how important it was for me to retain at least some illusion of control over my medical experience by talking with practitioners. Second, it indicated that he had considered this important enough to make a non-rule-bound suggestion of a surgeon other than the star of the team. When my wife and I agreed to follow this suggestion, he said he would try to see if Dr. R was still in the hospital and have him come talk with us.

Indeed, Dr. R arrived about an hour later and proceeded to sketch out where the blockages were and what he believed needed to be done. My wife had one major question: How many such surgeries had he done? He answered, about 150 during this year. Then my wife probed more deeply: "Of these, how many had survived?" He responded thoughtfully but with little hesitation: "All of those with your husband's profile survived." It was then that we agreed to have him do the surgery!

KIND AND UNKIND CUTS: SURGICAL RULES VERSUS PERSONAL AND CLINICAL JUDGMENTS

Rule-Following in Initial Recovery

In keeping with the standard sociology of medicine literature, I was generally a good (compliant) patient following surgery. Unanticipated back pain was caused by peeling back my split chest to expose the heart because my beer belly made it necessary to push the chest farther apart than would be the case for a slender patient. My major element of judgment was to contract with one of my students and coteachers to practice his form of alternative medicine. This reduced my pain and allowed me to sit and sleep more comfortably.

Apart from this, I was the "model" surgical patient. The surgeon said to walk, and I walked. Nurses said to walk more, and so I added more laps traversing the hospital floor. When I also passed the required mictatory exam and had no fever, they released me from the hospital. Before I was released, however, I was first lectured by the senior cardiac surgeon to "lose 50 pounds" (a level of loss that I had never achieved in 57 years of living). Then I was lectured by an even more rule-following dietitian, who then proceeded to "teach her grandmother to suck eggs" by telling me to follow a low-fat and low-calorie diet. She left me pamphlets in case I had not yet understood the rules she was prescribing for me (this was as close as I came to rising from bed and stabbing a staff person with my pencil!). Unfortunately, because my family members were present during these sessions, they also felt legitimated in underscoring this future dietary caution.

Mercifully, for the first 5 or 6 days at home, I could diet easily because I was nauseous much of the time. Therefore, although I was feeling crummy, I actually looked good to most of my visitors! This posed some judgmental challenges for me and for my attentive wife, however. Although I appreciated the weight loss, I hated being nauseous so often. Also, I feared vomiting my medications each time I took the array of pills. I knew some initial nausea was common (due to anesthetics and the trauma of surgery), but by the third or fourth day I became concerned. I had cut back on some new medications, trying to use the rule of concomitant variation I had learned in sociological methods courses more than 25 years ago (i.e., it must be the new medications that are causing the new nausea). Also, I ate increasingly less. Still the nausea returned.

Then my wife's judgment kicked in one morning. She remembered that during her pregnancy, she always kept some crackers by the bedstead to counter morning sickness as soon as she awoke. She suspected that my reducing my food intake only exacerbated the nausea. Alas, crackers were high in salt, which retains water in the body: I was on a diuretic to remove fluid, which accumulates in the body after surgery. Therefore, late one night my wife went out in search of low-sodium crackers, and on her return I skeptically swallowed the crackers. I happily spent my first night free of nausea, however. When I was visited by the home nurse several days later (home nursing is now relied on by HMOs to reduce hospital stays and cut insurance payments), we recounted this innovation to her. "Oh yes," she said, "We know all about that." Nothing about this approach to nausea was in the detailed literature I had been given on discharge, however.

Now I was walking every day and eating and sleeping. With a complex mixture of rule-following and judgment making, I was beginning to feel I would actually recover from this major biological and emotional trauma of cardiac surgery. There was some light at the end of this dark tunnel.

Denial and Neglect:
The Darker Side of Judgments in Recovery

This section was the most difficult to write. Indeed, my initial plan was to end the chapter at the end of the previous section. That would lead the reader to a sociological axiom that rule-following is always inferior to judgment making, however. As we all know, every sociological axiom has its counteraxiom.

Almost 1 week after my release from the surgical ward, I began to encounter some body changes. Although I had walked 3 miles (ahead of the recommended walking schedule!) the day before, I had trouble after walking a block with my wife, and we turned back home. I believed that I had a flu-like condition and retreated to bed to rest. Later that day, I had several bouts of diarrhea, which I interpreted as confirming my lay diagnosis of "the flu." At one point, before I flushed the toilet, I saw that the fluid was reddish and called my wife in for another lay consultation. We concocted a diagnosis that the color was due to my consumption of an exotic fruit the previous evening—and we concurred that this was not blood we were seeing. It was certainly not deep red enough to be blood, and so on. Denial is, after all, more than a river in Egypt.

Late that evening, I went to the bathroom, and "fell asleep" on the toilet, waking up to find myself on the floor and feeling nauseous and chilled. Although I felt terrible, my wife and I concluded once more that I had even more of the flu than we had judged earlier. The next day, I was still tired enough that I asked a visitor to walk to the corner and return my video because I was too "flu-ey" to do it. That night, I "fell asleep" again, and woke up on the bathroom floor again. "Too much flu," so I laid low and rested the following day.

The day after was my first postoperative visit to the surgeon. Two friends came over for lunch, and one then drove me to the surgeon's office. Although I felt a little dizzy, I assumed it was anxiety and (guess what) the residue of the flu. When I met with the surgeon (Dr. R), he checked my blood pressure, examined my chest incision, and listened to my heart. He asked how I had been feeling, and I reported that "until I got the flu" I had been well, but that I had "occasional" dizziness and "frequent" fatigue that left me unable to walk more than a block. When asked about bleeding, I obliquely reported my "diagnosis" of the fruit-caused coloring of my stool. Then he casually probed further about "blackened stools"; I said that I had noticed my stools tended to be darker than usual, but I assumed this was due to some medication. He then asked me to take a blood test and said he would read it "that evening." Otherwise, he said I was healing well and could now start to drive again.

I went home and reacted like a 16-year-old: I took the car "for a spin" and even took it to the car wash because this was such a liberation from being dependent on "the kindness of strangers" (and very good friends and relatives!). The next morning, my wife and I celebrated by driving to a nearby mall and having lunch. Then I napped until it was time for me to go to the department for a reception for "my" graduating seniors and their parents. I was tired and sat on a couch for the hour or so during the reception, but I was buoyed by seeing the students and meeting their parents. Also, I promised to give them their degrees at graduation ceremonies the next morning, for which I had made special provision for sitting down rather than standing and waiting for the procession to move. I thought I was doing well, but one of my colleagues later noted that I "looked pale" (we are trained observers, right?)

I was very tired and listless that evening, eating little. The next morning, I woke up barely able to crawl out of bed. I still hoped to go to convocation, but even the Nile has an ending in its delta. Therefore, I called a colleague and asked him to fill in for me. Reluctantly, I called the visiting nurse, but she believed she was unable to help and suggested I call my HMO primary care physician. Even more reluctantly, I did this; because it was my doctor's day off, I talked with his nurse instead. After an extended conversation, she said the physician (Dr. G) covering that morning wanted to see me and not deal with this over the phone. I still resisted, relying on the flu as a ongoing explanation.

My wife insisted on driving to the HMO (which I thought was being overprotective). By the time we parked in the garage of the HMO, however, I needed to lean on her to walk. We waited only a short time (a miracle in my HMO) before the physician saw us. He was very concerned at my appearance and unsteadiness and asked if I had recently had a blood test. I dutifully reported that the cardiac surgeon had taken one. Because he never called me back, however, I assumed it was normal. Dr. G then asked when and where the test had been taken and called it up on a computer screen. It was 6.5 as opposed to a "normal" level of 13 or 14 (13.5 had been my level when I had been discharged from the surgical ward 10 days earlier). This was a fairly unambiguous test: The results indicated that I had lost a substantial amount of blood.

He then said, "You're going to the hospital by ambulance," and he immediately asked the nurse to summon the municipal paramedics. When he wanted to weigh me, I collapsed on my way to the scale. For the first time, I accepted that something was very wrong with me. When I asked how long I would be in the hospital and he said "maybe a week," I started to remonstrate with him (before my wife shut me up). When the paramedics arrived, I was still enough in control (and denial) that I chatted with them in the ambulance. In retrospect, I think that my behavior in this period attests to my powerful need to maintain an internal locus of control rather than to abdicate to the external control of doctors, paramedics, or anyone else!

Denial Versus Diagnosis:
Reframing My Condition

When I arrived at the hospital emergency room, my wife was already there along with a good friend. Also, my HMO primary care physician arrived minutes later. This was both reassuring (I was in good hands) and terrifying (everyone was concerned that I was very sick). A quick blood test revealed my hemoglobin had now dropped to 4.3, which indicated that the emergency physicians rapidly needed to do two things. First, they had to induce where the bleeding was coming from; second, they had to start a transfusion. I understood the utility of the first rule but questioned the second, asking about HIV risks from transfusions. They brushed my resistance aside, essentially communicating that I really didn't have much choice. I think this was the first time in the recovery period that I fully abandoned my internal locus of control, realizing that I simply had no competence to assess or control my body by this point. I continued to monitor all discussions and evaluations, however, and to ask questions as often as ever.

The diagnostic procedure for testing where the bleeding had originated was devilishly simple: They first put a tube down my throat. When they discovered "coffee grounds" (dried blood) in my stomach, they said that this was firm evidence that the bleeding was "upper GI": It had originated in the upper part of the gastrointestinal tract (esophagus, stomach, and large intestine). This was good news, they said, because this was easier to access and cauterize by a less invasive procedure. They would only have to put me on a liquid diet for a day or so and give me transfusions. Then "it would be cleared up" the following day by the cauterization. Great, I thought: These rules sounded reasonable, although I was concerned that they admitted me to intensive care rather than a regular hospital room (just a precaution, they said). Eventually, Dr. R, the cardiac surgeon, arrived to say he was sorry that his lab had "misplaced" the blood test, but he also remonstrated with me that I had not fully indicated my problems to him 2 days earlier. I was angry because this was at the very least an overstatement, and perhaps even his attempt to obscure his bad judgment at that earlier visit.

In intensive care, the nursing staff was phenomenal (they are usually the elite members of the nursing staff in most hospitals). I was confined to bed and not allowed up for the bathroom, but the staff were attentive, cheerful, and supportive. The night before the cauterization procedure, I asked to go to the bathroom. Eventually, they compromised by bringing a chair commode to the room (because I found it hard to defecate in bed). When I started to get up from the commode, I "fell asleep" again—this time, overturning the commode (and myself). Upon getting up, I discovered a room full of nurses and doctors and fecal material and blood strewn all over the floor and my hospital gown. My first reaction was embarrassment—I had "made a mess." When the young doctor shined a flashlight in my eyes and asked if I could hear and see her, however, I realized I had actually blacked out and was once more terrified. This was a major loss of any internal control I had remaining.

Cauterization and Cutting:
Promises and Pitfalls in Treatment

Once more receiving blood, but no liquids, I was eventually ushered into the "factory" of the gastrointestinal laboratory the following morning. The specialist explained that he was going to pass a tube down my throat but would spray my throat first to minimize my discomfort. After some indeterminate time, he pronounced me hale and hearty. For the first time, he told me that I had a duodenal ulcer (i.e., in my large intestine), which had caused all the bleeding, but now I was OK.

I returned to my room and my wife with much relief. I still resisted the idea that they were going to keep me in the hospital "a few days more": Denial was once more resuming its place in my framing of events. I also felt emotionally and physically exhausted from the ordeal, however. An hour or two later, I asked for a bedpan and proceeded to use it—and use it again, and again, and again. Previously, I had been informed that blood is a laxative, that my diarrhea from the previous week was caused by loss of blood, and that the reddish color in the toilet bowl was indeed blood and not the juice of the exotic fruit. Therefore, I knew pretty quickly that I was in trouble again. The room was soon filled with nurses and physicians, and they proceeded to call off my blood pressure (I believe the last reading I remember was 70/30). They were pumping transfusions into me as rapidly as possible (I eventually had 15 of them before I left the hospital), but it was clear to everyone that I was again bleeding internally.

The tension in the room rose exponentially, and as I looked at my wife, I knew that we both wondered whether I was going to survive this round of bleeding. Soon, one of the nurses asked, "Do you have a surgeon?" I was a bit miffed—although I have come to collect a primary care physician and assorted specialists in my aging process, I didn't think it necessary to have a surgeon within my retinue. My wife and I simultaneously named a surgeon that had recently operated on her, however, because he was someone we both trusted. In her case, he had explained his judgments and where he deviated from rules— and he had allowed our judgments to enter his decision making. When I heard that he was on the floor and hence available, I surrendered the last of my internal locus of control and left my fate in his hands. I had terror in my heart, however, and experienced the pain of watching the anguish on my wife's face as they wheeled me down the hall into surgery.

Tautologically, the reader must know by now that I did indeed survive (or had a good ghostwriter). Abdominal surgery is not fun to recover from, and 4 months later I am still healing from this and the previous surgery. Also, I am trying to gauge how to protect myself from both my internal and external loci of control.

REFLECTING ON RULES AND
JUDGMENTS IN PROFESSIONAL PRACTICE

In addition to the medical messiness of the previous account, there is also an analytic messiness. It should be apparent to you that my own psychological and social preference is for an internal locus of control—marching to my own drummer as much as possible. I have also learned that there are limits to this approach, however, but there are no clear guideposts as to when and where these limits will pop up in my life.

In terms of the medical practitioners I encountered in this odyssey, the rule-followers were less sensitive and effective in treating me than were the judgment makers. An honest reflection indicates, however, that there are dialectical tensions that operate in this system, just as there are in other professional discretionary systems. Judgments may be good for the client, but sometimes they are better for the professional than the client. Also, rules may be onerous to impose on the client, but they may call attention to problems that the sensitive, judgmental, but often overstressed professional might ignore.

This dialectical tension is constructed from two psychological and social systems. First, every professional and every client has his or her own personality. For professionals, it may tilt them to risk aversion through rule-following (even to the point of compulsion) or toward risk taking through judgments (even to the point of imperiling their clients). Likewise, clients may be more oriented toward an internal locus of control—but not recognize where their own judgments are flawed or limited—or they may be more oriented to following the rules of physicians (and other professionals), even when these rules may not be appropriate to their own case.

Second, both clients and professionals are embedded in organizational and institutional systems. These may reward innovation or punish it; these may reward conformity or inhibit it. Once more I call on the Mertonian treatment of options in response to conditions of anomie (Merton, 1949): conformity, ritualism, innovation, retreatism, or rebellion. How I responded as a patient, and how the variety of my medical advisers reacted as physicians, was a complex mixture of responses to personal preferences and social structures. I have emerged from this experience alive but with considerably more uncertainty about how to ensure the practice of "good medicine" and the appropriate role of being a "good patient." At least I have some sociological models to help me understand why this uncertainty exists, and why the "perfect" medical (or sociological) practice is chimerical, in the real social and psychological worlds in which we are embedded (now made even more complex by rising cost-containment pressures).

REFERENCES

Bosk, C. L. (1979). *Forgive and remember: Managing medical failure.* Chicago: University of Chicago Press.

Freidson, E. (1970). *Professional dominance: The social structure of medical care.* New York: Atherton.

Freidson, E. (1986). *Professional powers: A study of the institutionalization of formal knowledge.* Chicago: University of Chicago Press.

Goldenberg, S. (1992). *Thinking methodologically.* New York: HarperCollins.

Larson, M. S. (1977). *The rise of professionalism: A sociological analysis.* Berkeley: University of California Press.

Merton, R. K. (1949). *Social theory and social structure; Toward the codification of theory and research.* Glencoe, IL: Free Press.

Millman, M. (1977). *The unkindest cut: Life in the backrooms of medicine.* New York: Morrow/Quill.

Mills, C. W. (1959). *The sociological imagination.* New York: Oxford University Press.

Peterson, C., Maier, S. F., & Seligman, M. E. P. (1993). *Learned helplessness: A theory for the age of personal control.* New York: Oxford University Press.

Weary, G., Gleicher, F., & Marsh, K. L. (Eds.). (1993). *Control, motivation and social cognition.* New York: Springer-Verlag.

CHAPTER 25

Qualitative Sociology and Good Journalism as Demystifiers

PAUL M. HIRSCH

"But isn't all this simply good journalism?" Sociologists mistakenly cringe when this question is thrown at them. Similarly, journalists fear being told their work is "too sociological." What each of these ad homonym attacks has in common is the effect of making it more difficult for the members of each group to do their job well. As Pulitzer prize winner Isabel Wilkerson noted (in a recent lecture at Northwestern University), first-rate ethnographies and quality journalism have a great deal in common. Writers of both, for example, experience attacks from their respective colleagues for producing works that involve "too much in-depth research," "take too long to deliver," and "read too much like" a _____'s (substitute journalist or sociologist name here). Many good ethnographies have their origin in newspaper or magazine stories. As professionals, we are not blank slates; our ideas for what to study—even about what is going on—come from many sources. Two of the most common (and least discussed or credited) are personal experience and learning about topics or issues for research projects from their coverage and discussion in nonacademic venues such as the *New York Times, Nation, Village Voice,* or National Public Radio.

Knowing what our discipline could find interesting in the subject enables the ethnographer to dive into what he or she is also curious about, and—by explaining it to colleagues in terms of the concepts and frameworks that make up the field—to learn, analyze, and write up something in which he or she is personally interested as well. An example I have experienced is my study of how the normative framing of corporate "hostile takeovers" changed—from a moral lapse, by unwelcome outsiders, to a morally neutral contest between professional insiders (the study also provides a detailed glossary of terms [Hirsch, 1986]). The idea for this project came from two sources: qualitative interviews with corporate directors, and reading of the *Wall Street Journal* and other articles and reports in the business press. I have long read the latter for fun and out of curiosity as well as to gain some professional insights. We usually deny or "excuse" this subjective side to choosing topics and "research sites" for study, having been trained to fear the impact of its discovery on the perceived accuracy and legitimacy of our analysis.

The presumption here is that we cannot be as objective or detached about something we learned of or encountered in other parts of our lives. As a result, the field often rejects their study or overemphasizes professionalism as the only reason for attending to these idea-producing but nonacademic activities and media reports.

Reading about which companies in the news are suing, fighting, taking over, or being acquired by other giants is very analogous to and can be just as engaging as following professional sports (or, more historically, probably a Roman circus!). Questions such as Which corporate gladiators will demolish their competitors? Which team will put together the winning plays? Whose contract will not be renewed? Who will be the new coach? and, Will the owners move the team to a competing city? are all equally familiar to fans of professional contests in both business and sports. Such prior familiarity and personal "knowledge of the game" increases the likelihood that our ethnographic analyses and reporting will be more accurate, insightful, and informed. Indeed, especially when we take care (as professionals) to not let it distort our interpretations, becoming submerged in this type of personal, tacit knowledge is exactly what we advise novice ethnographers to do in advance of going into the field.

After coding the changing terminology quoted by business writers and used in mass media sources to describe "takeover" contests, I ordered it into categories and time periods, began making presentations to colleagues, and published two scholarly articles on the topic. Within a year, I received a call from a *Wall Street Journal* reporter who wanted me to be an expert "source" for a story he was writing about a takeover. The newspaper that had provided the idea and raw material for my study would now report as "news" my interpretations and conclusions based on materials gleaned from its own earlier news stories. (It is usually more difficult for the "sources" whom we observe and report on to so easily comprehend our conclusions about them.) The resultant feature about the changing language and framing of business contests was aptly titled "If a Sleeping Beauty Takes Cyanide, Look for Hired Guns."[1]

Here, the idea for my project, and much of the qualitative data for the analysis, came from publications by journalists. Their reporting is useful to ethnographers for both generating ideas and gathering information. More generally, qualitative sociology and good journalism (supermarket tabloids excluded) share the common goals of finding interesting stories and puzzles to develop or address and providing sense-making frames, accurate reporting, and good analyses. Although their proportions of reporting and analyzing or theorizing do vary (the respective audiences and crafts differ, and sociologists have more time to produce their analyses), the professional interests and common grounds we share should not be minimized or denied.

Sociology as a discipline, however, continues to overly devalue journalism. After acknowledging that we must beware of journalistic excess or sensationalism, the questions remain as to why our professional dislike runs so high, how we might better understand what lies behind it, and how this developed. Part of the reason is that our field is very defensive. "That's obvious!" is a fearsome statement about sociological findings that we hear more often than we would like. Although we follow a norm of repressing this idea when it comes to assessing the work of fellow sociologists, the risk of hearing it, ironically, is also highest when the writing is most clear and understandable to anyone. Indeed, when this occurs, sociological work runs the greatest risk of being compared to, and sometimes dismissed as, "too journalistic."[2]

A commonsense solution is mystification—to write up our product more obscurely so only colleagues steeped in the discipline can decode it. Professionally, it is less harmful to be told that one's writing is unclear or filled with jargon than that it is accessible and (too) clear. This solution becomes an especially professional, institutionalized, and "taken-for-granted" assumption (Zucker, 1977) as we forget the field's more defensive basis for rewarding the more obscure style of presenting results. This process is further complicated as the jargon we develop to communicate with colleagues becomes more widely known and popularized. Ironically, it is achieving this larger following that increases the risk of seeming or being called "obvious" as the field's new language is, once again, adopted by writers for wider audiences.[3] Recall how many now "pop" ideas, such as "lifestyle," "subculture," "public opinion," and "world system," used to appear only in sociological journals but now appear frequently in everyday usage.

I can see this more clearly as a result of having studied organizations in general and the mass media in particular. Newspapers and magazines now popularize and appropriate sociological concepts at a faster rate than ever before. Our utilization of their reporting for information gathering and idea generation is clearly reciprocated; whereas our craft is to make the obvious seem more obscure, the journalist's task is to simplify it for the more general audience. If taken too far, however, the former becomes impenetrable rather than sophisticated, whereas the latter can oversimplify and miss the larger story.

Why the acceleration in the rate of sociological concepts being so popularized? The following is the simplest answer: Because of television's provision of instantaneous and continuous headlines and pictures, the print media were required to expand their offerings to continue to attract and inform readers. Newspapers were transformed from presenting "just the facts" stories and headlines, without much background, to publishing more lifestyle features, nonnews columns, and entire sections with good writers providing explanations and "in-depth" interpretations of everyday experience.

As a result, reading newspaper features focused on gender, race, work, and lifestyles has become more like taking or teaching an introductory sociology class. A professional reaction we should better understand is our field's focus and reliance on more complex, quantitative concepts and methodologies to differentiate the discipline from such mass accessibility. Understanding this connection and sequence of events dilutes the visceral response often encountered when journalism is discussed by sociologists. There must be room for both. Where there are shared goals, we are better off acknowledging them more clearly and cooperating.

I am optimistic that pursuing qualitative sociology's missions and methods will both contribute to the discipline and continue to help differentiate it from much of journalism (which, as we have seen, counsels its professionals away from being too sociological). Retaining these, and becoming less defensive when the two worlds overlap, is the direction in which I think we should be headed. When they do intersect, we can be flattered by the imitation. For example, if a newspaper feature about travel agents or bank tellers independently derives the same insights and interpretation that I attribute (in the following section) to knowing qualitative sociology, I would be delighted and welcome the overlap. The dialogue that such features provide between my own research and personal experiences is both fun and productive. Good journalism and qualitative sociology are both strong contributors to a better understanding of everyday life.

SOCIOLOGICAL KNOWLEDGE AS DEMYSTIFYING

The professional roles of teacher and researcher, of largely qualitative organizational sociology, have contributed greatly to enabling me to interpret and understand a wealth of everyday encounters. When something that might otherwise produce personal irritation and annoyance occurs, it is much more interesting and enjoyable to conceive and demystify it in a research mode, undertaking to inquire or explain why it is happening. Everyday encounters with bureaucratic routines are an example. Have you ever wondered why travel agents have trouble talking about multiple segments of your trip while also lining up the airline tickets? They are not reliving the joke about ex-President Ford's trouble with walking and chewing gum at the same time. (I used to wonder if travel agents were living proof of this.)

The reason for travel agents' apparently single-minded, one-thing-at-a-time pace of booking airline travel is that the interactive computer software programs through which they must book tickets require this linear limitation on more wide-ranging conversation. Further, even the "prices" they agree to "hold" for 24 hours are beyond their control, as airlines provide no advance notice, to even their own staff, about changes in ticket prices for flights going from one city to another. Upon arrival for the flights he or she has booked, it also helps to be able to decode an announcement that "boarding will be delayed due to an equipment problem" by knowing this is often synonymous with "we haven't a plane available for you to board."

These sense-making instances of professionally knowing details of how jobs and routines are limited, and meanings behind the language ("argot") used to communicate with "outsiders" (customers in this example), are highly beneficial in the personal lives of qualitative researchers. For example, as a result of reading Hochschild's (1983) account of flight attendants' everyday experiences on the job, who cannot better understand what they are doing. By better knowing how the bureaucratic routines of travel agents work against a more enjoyable conversation, or what the language used in the airport actually means, I benefit personally from understanding the organizational constraints that structure the interaction. It helps mitigate frustration better than presuming the voices on the other end of these lines are personally indifferent, unfriendly, or hostile.

These examples reaffirm that bureaucracy is depersonalizing to both sides of the interactions involved. I well recall a classroom discussion about this, after which one student exclaimed, "What I'm learning is it isn't the supervisors I thought were harming me at work. It's the system we're all working in, for its rules are driving what they do too!" Connecting this sociological insight to personal experience helped clarify and make better sense of everyday life on the job for this student. As "people" become "personnel" at all levels of organization, both sides of the interaction lose a more personal dimension. This loss becomes less hurtful and confusing once terms such as "job" and "for now" are understood to dilute the intensity of what would otherwise be seen as more "personal" relationships (Rousseau, 1995).

Another everyday puzzle that sociological knowledge helps clarify is the general perception that visiting the local bank today provides encounters far less personal than those experienced just a few years earlier. Because a customer can no longer select which line in which to wait, the bank tellers and officers he or she now sees are randomly assigned, each time, depending on which one frees up when it becomes the customer's "turn." When the form of the waiting line(s) is intentionally altered (from one per employee to one for all), both the customer and the teller or officer are less likely to be familiar with each other. The "client" is likely to (accurately) perceive whomever he or she is assigned to as more impersonal and "less friendly."

This does not mean, of course, that these tellers' and officers' personalities have become less attentive to or caring about customers. By the organization's design, they simply are less likely to be able to recognize the customers. Banks' elimination of customer choice in selecting whose line in which to wait is designed precisely to speed up the pace of transactions by reducing the degree of familiarity between customer and employee. Regular customers are more likely to be treated as strangers—for example, to be asked to show picture IDs. In time, some of them will feel more comfortable with the same bank's ATM machines (which charge a usage fee but make less pretense about human interaction) or decide to do all of their banking from home via telephone and computer setups.

Once the clients realize that the apparent decrease in personal attention from the bank's tellers and officers is not deliberate on their part but rather was designed into their jobs' new routines and descriptions, my personal experience is that the clients' level of discomfort in having to deal with it decreases. Like knowing that the McDonald's staffers are required to tell everyone to "have a nice day," this is another example of how sociological awareness and insight contribute to making better sense of one's everyday life interactions.

APPLYING SOCIOLOGICAL KNOWLEDGE IN MORE HIGH-STAKES EVERYDAY LIFE SITUATIONS

The following are personal instances in which I benefited from knowledge gained through sociological observation of organizations at work:

1. I understood that many "health maintenance" providers withhold useful medical information if one's insurance policy limits (or excludes) coverage for the procedure. Hence, when I know friends, relatives, or colleagues will need medical treatment, I benefit from being able to advise them to know and specify what their policies will cover to minimize the likelihood of its avoidance or denial.

2. I realized how, in some bureaucratic settings, only "squeaky wheels" applying pressure get needed or scarce resources. Rather than accepting routine, albeit polite, denials when a family member was refused admission to the local public, magnet school, I was primed to virtually camp out in front of the decision maker's office, call on whatever politically connected allies I could muster, and threaten a lawsuit if the application was again denied. Because I am not typically so cantankerous, it was the sociological insight that only this type of pressure produced the desired

result (notwithstanding all the polite refusals) that inspired this series of actions. The outcome was successful because the earlier denials ("It would be impossible") were reversed.

3. I participated in a freelance artist's personal injury lawsuit by helping to estimate the lost income of a person not employed on a regular (full-time or per-hour) basis. Sociological observation of how organizations (and courts) conceive value generated the solution of documenting "lost income" by estimating the price that would or might have eventually been realized for the art that was not (and could not be) produced while the artist was disabled. Addressing how there is no tangible compensation ("remedy") if salaries are not disrupted (e.g., annual contracts or sick leave still pay out), or if one is not regularly employed, yielded important information and insights about "labor markets" and sociological definitions of work that will also be valuable for my future work.

CONCLUSION

Because our profession is to figure out how social life is patterned and organized, it is difficult to imagine mental lightbulbs not going off as we encounter examples of these sociological categories in our own daily lives. We develop professional ideas from experience and—as this chapter indicates more clearly—also better interpret our personal experiences through the ideas gained by being sociologists. In this, as with good journalists, an important reward of demystifying the social world around us for others is the attractive benefit of better explaining it to ourselves as well.

NOTES

1. A "sleeping beauty" is the company targeted by the acquirer to be taken over. "Cyanide" is a nickname for the draconian changes adopted by the target company's management to make its shareholders less likely to sell the company to the potential acquirer. "Hired guns" are the lawyers and investment advisers hired by both sides in the takeover contest.

2. A similar professional dilemma sometimes arises when a professor's teaching ratings are very high. The following may be one reaction: "He [or she] must be diluting the more serious theories and issues, for otherwise his [or her] ratings would not be above the average [for the rest of us]."

3. This is analogous to an urban neighborhood being discovered by artists and bohemians at a time when no one else finds it attractive. After they fix up and creatively reconstruct it, a broader group of stores opens and residents ("yuppies") follow, changing the meaning, culture, and character of the area. Another analog, from popular culture, is the concern of a performer's (e.g., Bob Dylan's) early followers when he or she crosses over into greater popularity with a wider audience. The sense of invasion

exhibited by sociologists when our terminology is more widely diffused and adopted by more general writers and reading audiences is very close to the "There goes the neighborhood" concerns of the early innovators in the world of real estate once the area they set up or renovated catches on and becomes more popular.

REFERENCES

Hirsch, P. M. (1986). From ambushes to golden parachutes: Corporate takeovers as an instance of cultural framing and institutional integration. *American Journal of Sociology, 91,* 800-837.

Hochschild, A. (1983). *The managed heart: Commercialization of human feeling.* Berkeley: University of California Press.

Rousseau, D. (1995). *Psychological contracts in organizations: Understanding written and unwritten agreements.* Thousand Oaks, CA: Sage.

Zucker, L. G. (1977). The role of institutionalization in cultural persistence. *American Sociological Review, 42,* 726-743.

CHAPTER 26

Talks Between Teachers[1]

SHIRAH W. HECHT

HOWARD S. BECKER

In the summer of 1995, and continuing through the end of the fall term, Shirah Hecht and Howard Becker corresponded by e-mail about teaching fieldwork. Shirah initiated the exchange because she was teaching the class for the first time and had some questions about how to do it. She had taken Howie's class some years earlier at Northwestern and had memories of those events but wanted more details. The following excerpted version of the resulting dialogue preserves the significant teaching-related issues. So she wrote:

From Shirah Hecht: 2-AUG-1995 Subj: Still out there?
Hi, Howie. Are you still out there in cyberspace? I think of you often these days for the following reason: I am scheduled to teach the research methods course required for graduate students in sociology this fall . . .
I am trying to figure out if I am smart enough (and brave enough) to give the students as much free rein as you gave us in the field methods class, and still give them the feeling that they are getting something for their money. I guess I will have to structure it more than that, since it's not just field methods, but still would like to lean in that direction, for all kinds of reasons.
Any hints?

From Howard Becker: 5-AUG-1995 Subj: RE: Still out there?
Dear Shirah:
I don't know about the amount of freedom. I'll think about that and be back to you.

For the next month, Howie and Shirah exchanged several e-mails, which might be considered of a philosophical or theoretical nature, about good texts to use, what is the nature of research, etc. Then classes started.

From: From Shirah Hecht: 8-SEP-1995 Subj: OY VEY!
   Howie,
   OY VEY! Having sort of recovered from my first day of class two days ago, I can't help but wonder how does *anyone* teach grad students—or teach anyone for that matter—for a living. I know I'm much too sensitive . . . but OY VEY! That's really the only word for it. They're virtually just a smaller version of my seventy-five undergrads from last year's teaching experience. I guess I shouldn't expect any different: None of us really ever "grows up," whatever that is.
   How do teachers do it all the time . . . ?
   Was I like that as a grad student? I guess I now know why, after I took my last class in grad school, I swore I would never choose to sit on that side of the teacher's desk again.
   Let me know if you're too busy to read all this. This course just brings you to mind a lot, since your fieldwork course was significant for me.

From Howard Becker: 9-SEP-1995 Subj: RE: OY VEY!
   Dear Shirah:
   Teaching is a little disheartening the first day, for sure. It almost always happens that things get better. Don't expect (here's Foxy Grandpa, with his wise remarks) all of the students to do interesting stuff. They won't. But they will get better and know more when the class is over than they did before it started, which isn't bad. The thing to work for is developing a kind of group spirit in the class, so that they help each other and teach each other. You mainly do that just by expecting them to and by not doing too much of the work yourself.
   You will remember me often just sitting there until someone said something, and letting people solve their own problems instead of telling them "the answer," which I usually couldn't do because there wasn't any one answer. When they start talking to each other, then you're in business, and you can join in just like one of them. This also means that you have less work to do, always a desirable thing.
   Don't hesitate to send more Oy Veys, if it would be helpful.

From Shirah Hecht: 12-SEP-1995 Subj: Letting off steam
   THANKS for the great advice. We'll see how it goes. In the meantime, this came to me this morning, after a couple of nearly sleepless nights:

The Case of the Missing Item: Installment One
This was no common missing item.
   As he loaded the double-barreled question, and aimed it at the respondent, his hand shook. The respondent never flinched. She knew her job. She reached for the number two pencil on the table between them, pointed it at him and said

quietly, "Put the questionnaire down. Now." The researcher considered his next move. How crazy was she? Was this going to be a No Response situation? Or was he looking at the business end of a Don't Know? He knew he had asked the wrong question. Realizing he had to move fast, he turned quickly and it was then that he saw the participant observer, reflected in the mirror. This was no time to be taking notes, he thought.

Then he saw what was happening. The room he'd followed her into was close-ended, and there was no way out. He'd have to interview her, or he was a dead man.

From Shirah Hecht: 13-SEP-1995 Subj: I did it
Howie,
I did it. I filled 2-1/2 hours of time with the grad students, between them talking and me responding and asking what they thought and me responding . . . I don't know if I did it "right," but it seemed to have worked. I estimate I got to about 66%: either 2/3 of the class felt okay or 2/3 of their thoughts and feelings were that this was okay or we accomplished 2/3 of what could be accomplished in the time. Something like that.
You might not like the adulation, but you saved my butt on this one.

From Howard Becker: 13-SEP-1995 Subj: RE: I did it
Dear Shirah:
All adulation gratefully accepted. Pay no attention to any complaints I may make.
The thing to remember is that whatever you do in class is a form of training the students in what you *want* them to do in class, so be sure you teach them to do the right things.

From Shirah Hecht: 14-SEP-1995 Subj: Question
Howie,
Do students ever question your course assignments? While most of the folks are not doing this, I've gotten a serious question on just about everything I've asked them to do. Partly I know it's innocuous; I just have to clarify what I mean. But sometimes it is phrased as a questioning of how I have set things up. And some of it is wanting me to tailor the course to them individually in this respect. I just wondered if this happens to you or not.

From Howard Becker: 14-SEP-1995 Subj: RE: Question
Dear Shirah:
Gee, I don't know if it happens or not. I think maybe that's because I don't quite "give assignments." That is, I never say "You have to do this," let alone "You have to do this or else." I usually phrase things more like, "If you want to learn fieldwork a good thing to do would be to do x or y or z." I also say things like that I already have a PhD and know how to do this stuff and if they don't want to learn it it's OK

with me, everyone doesn't need to know it, but then why are they taking the class. Of course, sometimes what you've suggested they do won't work in a particular situation or locale and you have to make allowances for that.

But I think maybe the main thing to consider is that before a student can question an assignment, an assignment has to have been given. If you only give suggestions and not assignments, there's nothing to question. And I'm sincere about all that, I really don't care if they do it or not, it's up to them. Like when they ask how much fieldwork they have to do, I say, "Look. I said I would read all the field notes you wrote. So the more you write, obviously, the more work I have to do. So it's in my interest for you to do as little as possible. On the other hand, if you do that you for sure won't learn anything. It's up to you." I also confess, before they have a chance to accuse me of it, that this is highly manipulative.

Tailoring it to individuals isn't so terrible. I usually do that with the reading, not giving much or any general "required" reading for the whole class, just suggesting things that might be helpful. Maybe I should add that my whole philosophy is to get them out and doing stuff, which will surely get them into some kind of trouble, give them some problem they don't know how to solve, and then they really want to learn and will do practically anything you tell them, out of fear and desperation, which are very good motives for learning.

I don't know, is that any help?

From Shirah Hecht: 14-SEP-1995 Subj: RE: Question
Howie,

Yes, that's helpful. I realize now that I knew deep down this is the answer you would give me. While I've sort of moved in that direction, compared to what they are used to, I haven't taken it to the logical conclusion. But it's a good standard to keep in mind and shoot for (while trying not to be contradictory about it).

It's *hard* (sort of, not so much hard as contrary to knee-jerk reactions) to give up all those things we are trained to think we should do in front of people: control them and express ourselves in the usual ways, is the way I see it. It's ego. I remember you telling me in my fieldwork, when I ran into trouble getting access to the group I wanted to study: Drop your pride. It lessens your workload considerably, but isn't the way we are all raised, I don't think. I as much as told them, I don't quite have the courage to tell them what you told us on day one: You'll all be getting A's.

From Howard Becker: 14-SEP-1995 Subj: RE: Question
Dear Shirah:

People who ask me questions of the kind you've been asking usually *do* know what I am going to say. It's as though phrasing the question is enough to know the answer (as if there were an answer, rather than just answers).

It is hard to do these things, and I think some of the difficulty comes from an intellectual source, not just habits we were raised with: We find it hard to give a defensible rationale for acting in this libertarian who-gives-a-shit style. There is a perfectly defensible rationale I can trot out if I have to. Some of it you can see in the piece I did (Becker, 1972) called "A School Is a Lousy Place to Learn Anything In": People do what they have to do to get what they want, and you are in charge of what they have to do so, if you make them do X, they will. The things we don't like about student behavior are thus usually generated by the requirements we lay on them. Not laying requirements on them, making it all voluntary, gets rid at a stroke of all sorts of student *mishigas*.

From Shirah Hecht: 14-SEP-1995 Subj: Another approach
 Howie,
 So is this how it goes?

Student-Teacher:
"You're making me do this stuff and I don't want to do it."
"I'm not making you do this stuff."
"Oh."
"You didn't make me do any stuff so I didn't and I didn't learn anything."
"So that's my fault, that you didn't do anything or learn anything?"

I'm getting nervous about my course again (as Wednesday approaches). But I've finally formulated my question.
 What if you have stuff you think is neat to say? I'm thinking that if I get up and say that stuff, it will discourage discussion, because it will make them passive again. The other disadvantage is that I can't fill 2.5 hours with neat stuff to say, and now I have to, because I've squelched their need to speak for themselves. So, I am trying to have faith that in the course of conversation, I'll get to say my neat stuff, things I think they would be wise to think about. And that it's worth sitting on my hands, waiting for my opportunity. And that they *will* get something out of this course, if I do this. Is this the answer? One thing I would like to model for them is excitement about cool applications of research methods.
 And another thing! In tomorrow's session, a student is supposed to present on your article, "Whose Side Are We On?" (Becker, 1967). I suspect she'll be critical. I'm not worried about that. I'm more worried about how to do this thing, let her speak, give her the room she needs, and hope she fills it. Well, I guess there's a first time for everything, I'll just have to see how it goes, fix it later if I have to.
 This is a growth experience, I can tell. :-|

From Howard Becker: 19-SEP-1995 Subj: RE: Another approach
 Dear Shirah:
 I don't know why it is so interesting to live through this experience with you, but it is.
 Anyway, yes, that is the answer. I always have a lot of neat things to say, and I just wait and find something that the students say to hook what I have to say to. There always is something like that. As far as the student who is going to denounce my article. I often assign things of mine and practically insist that they find something to criticize. But also that they find something useful in it.

The general point is to let them find their way around and try to find answers for themselves, giving such advice as you can along the way. That's where you get to do your neat stuff.

Good luck tomorrow.

From Shirah Hecht: 2-OCT-1995 Subj: Trying to report in

Howie,

I lost almost all control over my life and time in the last two weeks, which is why you haven't heard more from me. And also, maybe being in the middle of teaching, I don't have as much perspective for reflection as I did heading into it.

I can give you the response your article received in class. One student commented: He used all those theories, from all those different sources! That gave me a chance to give them your line about theories as tools, to use so as not to reinvent the wheel if someone else has already thought about this part of the thing. I have added another perspective, too, on theory. I decided this semester that what theory does is give us a way to try to connect facts or ideas so that we are more likely to remember them, for later use. It's consciousness-raising in that way; and just a handy format, since we don't know what we'll need to remember at a later time.

On your article, another student also responded interestingly: "I would have liked to hear his tone of voice," as she read the article, as it seemed you might have been speaking tongue-in-cheek. The best perhaps was another one, who said that your conclusion seemed to be saying, and she was too delicate to say this aloud, but suggested it, "Then, fuck it."

So that's the feedback on that.

I feel like a parent sometimes to the students, but I don't seem to want to be. I am probably too supportive . . . and sometimes worry way too much that they will get into some trouble and that I will be responsible. I added a corollary to your comment that they will do whatever I do in class: They'll be doubly sure to do the stupid things I do.

So, that's the extent of my insight these days. They seem alternately panicky that I am asking them to do terrible things at which they will fail, and trying to get out of the work or get me to do something else around it because "they've already done this and want to learn more." Seems bogus to me sometimes, but other times it doesn't.

From Howard Becker: 4-OCT-1995 Subj: RE: Trying to report in

Dear Shirah:

Sounds like your class is going just fine. As long as people will argue with me, I'm happy. It's the sitting silent that gets to me.

I've started teaching: field methods. Looks like a reasonable class, but you can never tell. I leaned on them yesterday about getting started right away and we'll see what happens.

From Shirah Hecht: 5-OCT-1995 Subj: Quick question
Howie,
I have a relatively quick question. One of the students asked if I had any suggested readings to assign on doing fieldwork, something I had not previously provided. I have the long bibliography you handed out to us but hesitated to provide it. If I weren't in touch with you, I would probably just put it on reserve for them, and tell them its source. Since you are around on e-mail, I just thought I'd run it by you first. Of course, I've taken wholesale all of the insights you shared in the class I took with you, so this probably isn't much different, but I just thought I'd check. The written word, and all that. Welcome back. And may all of your fieldwork students do interesting work . . .

From Howard Becker: 5-OCT-1995 Subj: RE: Quick question
Dear Shirah:
You're welcome to give that bibliography to anyone you want. The problem with it, of course, is that it is way out of date. At one time I had this vision of keeping an up-to-date list of all good things about fieldwork and all good fieldwork studies; but I got lazy. What can you do? It's OK up to about fifteen or twenty years ago. The good side of that is that it includes a lot of stuff that people are pretty much unaware of these days. A colleague here says he is constantly shocked, because he's a generation after me, at all the good work that he really never heard of, let alone read.

My fieldwork class looks like it might be interesting. But, as I explained to them, it isn't the topic you choose, it's how you do it and that's still an unknown.

From Shirah Hecht: 5-OCT-1995 Subj: New question
Howie,
When you have the chance, maybe you'll reveal one more secret to me. Do you like teaching? I mean, are you one of those who does enjoy it?

There's something so odd, still, about the interaction. It takes a lot to bend it to one's will. So then I wonder if it's worth it. Yet, here I am, owing so much of where I've been to the fact that a bunch of people out there considered it worth their time to be what we call teachers. (Sounds like a variation on Tennessee Williams, "I've always relied on the kindness of strangers" . . . of teachers . . .).

From Howard Becker: 6-OCT-1995 Subj: RE: New question
Dear Shirah:
Do I like teaching? To tell the truth, yes, I do. I pretty much hate most of what goes with it: departments and administrations and voting and meetings and requirements and all that. But I like sitting around with people bullshitting about interesting things, which I guess is my idea of what teaching really is, if it goes the way it should. In the last few years, I've often found teaching undergraduates more interesting than dealing with graduate students. I think that's because the graduate students are now

so "professionalized," so intent on learning the right way to do things so that they can get a good job, and so nervous about "the requirements," and all that. I can't blame them, but they aren't so much fun.

Undergraduates, on the other hand—well, I often have students who don't know how to read very well, so that's what the teaching turns into: how to read a scientific article. And that is actually interesting. I like leading them through a table and getting them to see what it means. I don't know how long I'll continue to find that interesting but right now I do.

One secret about liking it, I think, is that I don't try to bend anything to my will. I guess this is kind of a Zen thing. I'd use another metaphor. I try to find out where things are going and help them get there. I never try to impose my will because, fundamentally, I guess I believe that people know what they want to do and it's not up to me to tell them they're wrong, just to help them do it. If I think it's a dumb thing to do I'll show them why I think that, why it won't get them where they want to go, or tell them to go somewhere else where they could find what they're looking for. So I never have the sense of things not going the way I want them to in class, except when I forget all this sage talk and try to get them to do something they don't want to do or, more likely, can't do without more help than I've given them.

From Shirah Hecht: 6-OCT-1995 Subj: Zen
    Howie,
    "Zen," yes, that's what I planned on writing you after session 3 (before I went into session 4 pretty unprepared). That I felt like some sort of Zen Buddhist. And, yes, these grad students are, in a subtle way, much focused on getting to some end-point, a professional end-point, and have lost some openness as a result. I think my class (when I was a student) was pretty much like that, too, which took much of the fun out of it.

From Shirah Hecht: 13-OCT-1995 Subj: Another hurdle
    Howie,
    I have another hurdle I'd like to get over and thought I'd run it by you, if I'm not overdrawing on my account here. I'd like to do something like a "mock interview" in class, but am not sure how. I remember two things you did. One was a short demo, where you asked one of the students "Where are you from" and it showed, at least on that occasion, that there can be more than one answer and more to the answer than expected, even for such a simple question. (Ha! Like how could you be sure this guy wasn't just going to say, "Toledo. Never moved." Actually, the question here lies more in your attitude as the interviewer, which I guess is the answer. To be open to the variations possible in the response, to encourage them. So, I guess that's a roundabout way to demonstrate interviewing technique.) I also remember us interviewing you, on your interest in computers. If I do that, do I have one person ask the questions? Or did the whole class get into it? Yeesh, I've never been interviewed myself before! I guess being the interviewee, I can at least control how much time we spend at it, and what direction it takes. Any suggestions?

It's sort of "cute," seeing the difficulties some of the folks have with this whole qualitative data collection process: the concern about losing control over your research, about getting the "wrong" answer. I hope I'm teaching them something. . . . I still will not grant that I "like" this thing, but I'll reserve final judgment for the end of the course.

From Howard Becker: 19-OCT-1995 Subj: RE: Another hurdle
Dear Shirah:
No, your account isn't overdrawn yet, although I'll probably have a little less time now that my own fieldwork class has begun.

What I used to do with the interviewing thing was take on some character—I used to do a Chicago bus driver, but got too far away from what I originally knew about it, and now in Seattle it's meaningless to people—and let them interview me about my work or whatever. What I'd do is have one student start, give the student a reasonably hard time at first (not be too forthcoming, answer every question that could be answered briefly briefly, etc.) and then open up at some point and give them clues to follow, things they should pick up on. I'd let the first student work at it for two or three minutes, then say someone else take a turn, etc. I wouldn't put anyone on the spot. Periodically I'd step "out of character" and ask why they had asked something, what they had in mind, or make a suggestion about something they had done that could be done differently, etc. It was always a lot of fun.

Zen, yes. It's the main thing, just go with it, find a handhold somewhere, something you can work with, and see what you can get them to do for themselves. It's the doing it themselves that's crucial, I think; they can listen to you all they want (and all you want) and write it all down in their book, but they won't know anything until they use it themselves. That's the only way the class works.

From Shirah Hecht: 23-OCT-1995 Subj: RE: Another hurdle
Hi, Howie.
Thanks for the response. You have way more chutzpah than I do, if you don't mind the phrase. I was surprised by how you told me you did the mock interview, but it made sense. It avoids a lot of the trouble I foresaw in doing this. Maybe on my second time teaching this course . . . But, hell, if I run out of things to do Wednesday, we just might do it.

Things are going pretty well, I think. That is, we've filled the 2.5 hours each time. The funny thing is that I'm getting an enormous amount out of this course (excluding the preclass funk I go into each Monday). Maybe it's because I've "done the thing." That is, I wouldn't have gotten as much out of these readings before doing the research I've done myself. In some ways, I'm a slow learner. But that idea also fits with the general tack of getting them to do things, so that your questions and the answers you might come to make sense. But it's also probably a function of the anxiety level at which one reads these things when one is responsible for teaching it.

I hope your class is going well.

From Shirah Hecht: 10-NOV-1995 Subj: Quick note
Howie,

Well, it's almost a wrap. Three or four more class sessions to go. I just wanted to share one more thing with you. (You may ask yourself: What did I do in some other life to deserve this fate?) The last two class sessions, I've been going through some physically trying stuff myself, having nothing to do with the class. As a result, I felt I had to be much more calm, not push too hard. And, I don't know if it's because of this or just because it's half-way through the semester, but those seemed to be the best sessions we've had. I felt I was more direct with them . . . and with less "noise" of "what should I say or do now" going on. After the first of these two sessions, I left the class thinking, "I'm going to miss these guys. . . ."

So, now I have a lot more grading and reading to do, but I see the light at the end of the tunnel.

From Howard Becker: 11-NOV-1995 Subj: RE: Quick note
Dear Shirah:

Probably the reason the class is going so well is a combination of everything you mentioned. One thing about a class like this is that you get a buildup of esprit and morale, as they realize they have actually done it and are doing it and can do it; it thrills them and that's thrilling for the teacher. Then, too, if you lay back, for whatever reason, they respond to that and fill the gap and that makes everything more lively. And, as you said, having done it they can now talk in a knowledgeable way about the choices and problems.

My class is going well too. I don't know why. I am really in a groove and do improvisations that seem wonderful to me on whatever they bring up and, on good days, get them to collaborate in the improv. For instance, the other day one of them, who is studying a bunch of refugee punks from Eastern Europe, gave me some notes in which she described two of the people as the "kingpins" of the group. So I said I knew what she meant vaguely, but how did she know they were kingpins, what had she seen to allow that conclusion? She was embarrassed at having used a "vague expression," but I said no, that was good, but now we should use it to move on. There was about a half hour of the two of us working out what she had actually seen that justified the expression, and then there was the question of how much of that was actually in her field notes, and why not? And I could say, repeatedly, that the point of such Monday quarterbacking was that now, when she was with these people, she would not be able to help seeing all these things we had just discussed and noting them down. Etc. It was really fun.

From Shirah Hecht: 20-NOV-1995 Subj: Misc.
Howie,

I'm rereading notes you sent me on the class, getting reeducated by them again. I fear I didn't always "get there." (And, hey, I'm not done yet.) But, maybe in response to that fear, I wanted to report to you some of what I told my students.

I remember you once saying, there's always one student in class who asks the question you need to have asked, but I didn't think it would come in this form, or hadn't had the experience I thought you meant when you said that. . . .

So, one asked, he's an avowed Marxist who wants to study on-campus black student activism, seemingly frustrated with what we were discussing about doing surveys: "What is the one thing that's most important here, about doing surveys?" The timing couldn't have been better; he must have been reading my mind. I said, and I hadn't ever thought this or read it put this way before: that it was to avoid "playing" to the easy audience, the people you know will agree with you and whose opinions you think you "like." I left out what would have summarized it well: Because the researcher lives and dies by "variation" and if you get rid of that, you're dead in the water. His response was great: He dropped his head, as if in shame or deep realization.

And then, on the same topic but maybe a later class session, a student asked me about my own dissertation survey, ". . . what would you have done differently?" In the context of our discussion, I listed a couple of things. But I also said that I can see that I would do them differently, because I have some distance on it now, and can see it differently. Implying that that will always be the case, time giving you a different perspective on the work.

It may be paranoia, but it seems to me I'll always have one student in class who has particular problems with me. It feels like passive-aggressively (or aggressive-passively) playing out larger problems with teachers or authority or other people in general in this setting. That's one out of fifteen. So, the question is: Is that the proportion (a) in the general population (b) in graduate schools (c) in sociology grad schools or (d) is my sample skewed? :-)

From Howard Becker: 21-NOV-1995 Subj: RE: Misc.

Dear Shirah:

Last thing first, while I remember it: I don't know what the proportion of these passive-aggressive types is, but my experience is that whatever the size of the class there is almost always one, usually not more. It's like it's a slot that has to be filled. I once had a student who left the class after I just didn't respond to all her attempts to get me to do what she wanted, which was to spend the class discussing what various authors had to say about fieldwork. When I said I thought it was more important to do some so that you would know what anyone was talking about in such discussions, this student said she didn't really feel comfortable doing field-work. I said I didn't either but I did it anyhow. After a while I stopped trying to persuade her and told her if she didn't want to do it I really could understand and that I certainly didn't think that everyone had to do it or know how to do it, but that this class was about doing it and not about talking about it. So she stopped showing up for class, which was OK with me, I gave her an OK grade.

The rest of what you said sounds fine to me. As you know, I talk all the time about my own experiences, it's the one thing we can talk about with assurance, and my only rule about that is one that it sounds like you followed, which is to tell the exact truth as far as you can remember it. Students, I think, appreciate being told the truth, whatever it is; I have often told students that I had a cold or whatever and felt lousy and if I was a little snotty in my remarks on their notes that was why; or that some times I did things in the field for no good reason; etc.

From Shirah Hecht: 29-NOV-1995 Subj: Need mantra
Howie,
Now that I'm well into this zen-teaching business (and happily so, I'm not complaining), I need a mantra. What to say to myself when I worry that I haven't made all of these students happy. Or when I find out I haven't made any of them happy (evaluations are next week). Something like, "I can't make you all into researchers, much less happy. OMMM" or "It's not my fault you didn't learn anything and sociology is hard to learn. OMMM." I have the feeling those aren't the zen way. I really am looking for suggestions, though the answer is probably buried somewhere in your previous advice to me.

I really appreciate that you do this teaching thing for a living, even if I am not so enthralled with it myself. And I'm not just kissing up now, since I have no real motivation to do so.

Your comment on the slot being held for the one passive-aggressive type was great. I even know who the second person is in the class who would have taken the slot on a given day if it had not already been filled.

Two more sessions to go. . . .

From Howard Becker: 30-NOV-1995 Subj: RE: Need mantra
Dear Shirah:
Bernie Beck [who teaches sociology at Northwestern] had a nice solution to your dilemma. He said that worrying about whether you were satisfying all the students or teaching them all something useful or doing a good job for all of them or any version of that was a version of the "White Man's Burden," which is to say it puts all the responsibility on your shoulders. But it doesn't belong there. I always figure that I'll do my best, not try to persuade people who don't want to learn, for whatever reason, what I could possibly teach them, help the ones who want to learn something in whatever way I can, and be glad if anything comes of it at all. If you're dissatisfied, it means you expected more than the situation could produce for you, and the easy solution is to revamp your expectations, while thinking about what could be changed to make it work better.

Does that help?

From Shirah Hecht: 13-DEC-1995 Subj: Now this is fun
Howie,
Now this is fun. I'm hiding out in my "academic office space," having told my "real job" that I needed time off to grade papers. Of course, eventually, I really do

have to grade those papers. . . . But first to let off some steam. I just held the last session of class and this is my "reflection" paper on doing this class, to the one person who most helped me get through it.

It was a tough road. I'm not convinced I did as good a job as I would have liked. I know I made it harder on myself than it had to be. The biggest problem is that I lack confidence, which makes it harder to lead well, no matter whether in a Buddhist or more structured style. It makes it hard on me and hard on them, and I don't know if I can do anything about that. You would think I would outgrow this, but I'm now well into my thirties (and I won't tell you how many therapy sessions. . . .) and I see no sign of it abating. Not only is it not going away, I seem to find more situations in which to let it show.

It's hard to feel I've read enough.

It's hard to feel I can let people go, do research, and think I can make a class based on that.

You, Howie, are very hard to emulate. The most useful thing (well, one of the most useful things) you ever said to me had something to do with: Well, of course you haven't read as much as I have; I'm a lot older than you are. No one told me that before. But, wanting to be as good as I maybe can be with a lot more work, I am not aware of what I have accomplished, if it's short of my ideal goal.

I have a specific question. Do your students sometimes take your comments on their work as criticism they don't want to hear and try to argue you out of it?

From Howard Becker: 13-DEC-1995 Subj: RE: Now this is fun

Dear Shirah:

What a sweet, thoughtful letter. I really appreciate it. Don't forget that I got something out of our exchanges too. It's why I like teaching too, you know; I learn so much from students.

The thing about self-confidence is that the one thing you can't ignore is that you actually did it this time and the floor didn't fall in, you didn't disgrace yourself, most of the students got along OK, alright a few kvetches kvetched, but that's their nature, etc. In other words, you did it and it worked. This proves (in math they call this an existence proof) that it can happen, since it already did.

I don't remember students ever complaining about my criticism. But that's probably because I almost never criticize. What I do instead, and it does work much better, is tell them what others will say if they do this or that, and ask them what they think they should do about that. And I am, of course, willing to listen to the argument that they don't have to listen to those people (because, after all, there are people I don't listen to or to whose criticisms I pay no attention).

I don't ever try to get things to be as good as possible, especially not in class, because there is too much that isn't under my control. I do my best, but I set some kind of limit beyond which that's it, enough already.

It actually sounds, for all your complaints, like the class went reasonably well.

NOTE

1. Reprinted with permission of Human Sciences Press, Inc. (1997).

REFERENCES

Becker, H. S. (1967). Whose side are we on? *Social Problems, 14,* 239-247.
Becker, H. S. (1972). A school is a lousy place to learn anything in. *American Behavioral Scientist, 16,* 85-105.

About the Contributors

Howard S. Becker is Professor of Sociology and Music at the University of Washington. He is author of *Outsiders, Art Worlds,* and *Writing for Social Scientists.* His most recent book is *Tricks of the Trade: How to Think About Your Research While You're Doing It.*

Susan E. Bell is Professor of Sociology at Bowdoin College. She received her PhD from Brandeis University. She is senior author of "Birth Control" in *The New Our Bodies, Ourselves* (1984, 1992, 1998). Recent publications include "Translating Science to the People: Updating *The New Our Bodies, Ourselves*" (*Women's Studies International Forum,* 1994), "Looking at Bodies: Insights and Inquiries About DES-Related Cancer" with Roberta J. Apfel (*Qualitative Sociology,* 1995), and "Gendered Medical Science: Producing a Drug for Women" (*Feminist Studies,* 1995). She is currently writing a book about the experiences of DES daughters.

Derral Cheatwood is Professor of Criminal Justice and Sociology and Director of the Division of Social and Policy Sciences at the University of Texas at San Antonio. He received his PhD from Ohio State University. He is a former Fulbright Scholar at the Max Planck Institute for Foreign and International Criminal Law in Freiburg, Germany, and continues to analyze homicide data from Germany and Austria. He is author (with Keith Harries) of *The Geography of Execution: The Capital Punishment Quagmire in America,* and his recent articles on homicide have appeared in *Criminology, Justice Quarterly, Journal of Quantitative Criminology, European Journal of Crime, Criminal Law and Criminal Justice,* and the *Criminal Justice Review.* Currently, he is involved in gang research and in analysis of homicide data in San Antonio.

Sharon M. Collins is Associate Professor at the University of Illinois, Chicago. She received her PhD from Northwestern University. In Chicago, she spent more than a decade researching the experiences of the "black business elite," the first wave of African Americans to enter professional and managerial jobs in the 1960s and 1970s. She published her findings in *Black Corporate Executives: The Making and Breaking of a Black Middle Class* (1997). Currently, she is engaged in a study of diversity in a large midwestern manufacturing organization.

Peter Conrad is Harry Coplan Professor of Social Sciences and Chair of the Department of Sociology at Brandeis University. He received his PhD from Boston University and has published six books, including the award-winning *Deviance and Medicalization: From Badness to Sickness* (with Joseph W. Schneider), and dozens of journal articles and chapters. He has served as chair of the Medical Sociology Section of the American Sociological Association and as president of the Society for the Study of Social Problems. He is currently studying how genetics has been reported in the news media during the past 30 years.

Arlene Kaplan Daniels is a visiting professor in sociology at the University of California, Berkeley. She received her PhD from the University of California. She began her studies of the military—particularly military psychiatrists—in nonprofit research institutes. She is author of *Invisible Careers: Women Civic Leaders From the Volunteer World.* She has served as editor of the *Journal of Social Problems* and president of the Society for the Study of Social Problems and of Sociologists for Women in Society. She also served on the council and as secretary of the American Sociological Association.

Lynn Davidman is Associate Professor of Sociology, Judaic Studies, and Women's Studies at Brown University. She was a Fellow at the Bunting Institute at Radcliffe College. She is author of *Tradition in a Rootless World: Women Turn to Orthodox Judaism* (1991), which won a 1992 National Jewish Book Award. She is coeditor (with Shelly Tenenbaum) of an original book of essays titled *Feminist Perspectives on Jewish Studies* (1994).

Norman K. Denzin is Research Professor of Communications at the University of Illinois, Urbana-Champaign. He is author of *On Understanding Emotion* (1984). He is editor of *Sociological Quarterly* and coauthor of *The Handbook of Qualitative Research* (1994). His most recent book is *Interpretive Ethnography: Ethnographic Practices for the 21st Century* (1997).

Marjorie L. DeVault is Associate Professor of Sociology and a member of the Women's Studies Program at Syracuse University. She specializes in women's work, family studies, and qualitative research methods. She has written on the organization and significance of housework (in *Feeding the Family: The Social Organization of Caring as Gendered Work*) and on professional work in the historically female profession of dietetics and community nutrition. Her articles and essays on feminist research methods are concerned with strategies for producing more broadly inclusive knowledge of the social world. Her current work is concerned with developing critical, constructionist approaches to family studies.

Robert Dingwall is Professor of Sociology in the School of Sociology and Social Policy at the University of Nottingham. His career has spanned both medical sociology, which was the field of his PhD from the University of Aberdeen, and law and society studies, through his work at Oxford University. These are united by a general interest in professions, work, organizations, and interaction. He is currently working with a consortium evaluating the introduction of publicly funded divorce mediation in England. His most recent book is *Context and Method in Qualitative Research* (coedited with Gale Miller; 1997).

Joshua Gamson is Associate Professor of Sociology at Yale University. He is author of *Freaks Talk Back: Tabloid Television and Sexual Nonconformity* (1998), *Claims to Fame: Celebrity in Contemporary America* (1994), and a participating author of *Ethnography Unbound: Power and Resistance in the Modern Metropolis* (1991). His research and teaching focus on the sociology of culture, with an emphasis on contemporary Western commercial culture and mass media; social movements, especially on cultural aspects of contemporary movements; participant-observation methodology and techniques, particularly as applied in urban settings; and the history, theory, and sociology of sexuality. Recent articles include studies of the political pitfalls in the pursuit of media visibility (*Sexualities*), exclusion processes in sex and gender movements (*Gender & Society*), organizational aspects of collective identity construction (*Sociological Forum*), and dilemmas in identity-based movements (*Social Problems*).

Naomi Gerstel is Professor and Director of Graduate Studies in the Department of Sociology at the University of Massachusetts, Amherst. Her books include *Commuter Marriage* (with Harriet Gross) and *Families and Work* (coedited with Harriet Gross). She has written many articles that focus on divorce, caregiving, homeless families, and The Family and Medical Leave Act.

Barry Glassner is Professor of Sociology at the University of Southern California. He is author of *Career Crash, Bodies, A Rationalist Methodology for*

Social Sciences (with David Sylvan), and *Drugs in Adolescent Worlds* (with Julia Loughlin). His articles have appeared in the *American Sociological Review, Social Problems,* and other journals. He is currently completing a book on how scares are promoted in American society by politicians and the media.

Shirah W. Hecht works as a consultant on the administrative side of Boston College, teaching on an occasional and part-time basis. She received her PhD from the University of Chicago and a 1989 fellowship from the Congregational History Project to support her dissertation study of recent changes in Jewish congregation. In an additional current role as Research Associate and Project Director at the Susan and David Wilstein Institute of Jewish Policy Studies, she is preparing an inter-religious conference on women's roles in contemporary American religion.

Rosanna Hertz is Professor of Sociology and Women's Studies at Wellesley College. She received her PhD from Northwestern University. Her research focuses on the relationship between family, work, and gender to understand the interaction and reciprocities of these areas of inquiry. She is author of *More Equal Than Others: Women and Men in Dual-Career Marriages,* coeditor of *Studying Elites Using Qualitative Methods,* and editor of *Reflexivity and Voice.* She is editor of *Qualitative Sociology.* She has a long-standing interest in social science methodology and has written about in-depth interviewing of couples separate but simultaneously.

Paul M. Hirsch is the James Allen Professor of Strategy and Organization at Northwestern University's Kellogg Graduate School of Management. Hirsch was selected the 1998 "Distinguished Scholar" for contributions to organization theory by the Organization and Management Theory Division of the American Academy of Management. His primary areas of research are culture, organizations, and institutions, and recently he addressed the sociology of euphemism, the social construction of markets, and organizational "downsizings," which he also addressed in his book *Pack Your Own Parachute* (1987). He is author of "Dirty Hands vs. Clean Models," a critique of efforts within the discipline to increase formal modeling at the expense of field research. He is executive editor of the *Journal of Management Inquiry* and has also served as Book Review Editor of *American Journal of Sociology.*

Arlie Russell Hochschild teaches sociology at the University of California, Berkeley. She is author of *The Managed Heart* (which concerns the emotional labor of service workers), *The Unexpected Community* (which concerns the social life of low-income elderly people), and *The Second Shift: Working Parents and the Revolution at Home* and *The Time Bind: When Work Becomes*

Home and Home Becomes Work (which focus on tension points for working parents—at home and on the job). She recently returned from a Fulbright in India exploring issues of work and family in Kerala. She heads a Center for Working Families at the University of California, Berkeley.

Sherryl Kleinman is Professor of Sociology at the University of North Carolina, Chapel Hill. She received a PhD from the University of Minnesota. She has studied graduate students, detectives, seminary students, medical students, and a holistic health center. She is author of *Equals Before God: Seminarians as Humanistic Professionals, Emotions and Fieldwork* (with Martha Copp) and *Opposing Ambitions: Gender and Identity in an Alternative Organization.* Her work has become increasingly feminist and critical, and she is interested in bridges between feminist theory and symbolic interaction. She is currently writing sociologically informed personal essays for a wide readership.

Peter K. Manning is Professor of Sociology and Criminal Justice at Michigan State University. He received his PhD from Duke University. He was a Fellow of Wolfson and Balliol Colleges, Oxford, and the Oxford Center for Sociolegal Studies. He is author of 12 books and many articles and chapters. He most recent book is *Police Work* (2nd. ed., 1997). His book, *A Communicational Theory of Policing,* is forthcoming. He is named in *Who's Who* and was given the Bruce Smith Sr. Award by the Academy of Criminal Justice Sciences in 1993 and the O. W. Wilson Award in 1997. His current research includes an analysis of private policing, fieldwork on community policing in several sites in Michigan, and the rationalization of policing, with emphasis on the role of information technology in the United States and the United Kingdom.

Jonathan D. Moreno is Emily Davie and Joseph S. Kornfeld Professor of Biomedical Ethics at the University of Virginia, where he directs the Center for Biomedical Ethics. He is also Senior Research Scholar at the Kennedy Institute of Ethics at Georgetown University, a Fellow of the New York Academy of Medicine, and an Adjunct Associate of the Hastings Center. He is author of *Deciding Together: Bioethics and Moral Consensus* (1995), *Ethics in Clinical Practice* (1994; 1998), and *Arguing Euthanasia* (1995; Japanese edition, 1997). He has published more than 100 papers and book chapters and is a member of the editorial boards of *Bioethics, The Journal of Clinical Ethics,* and the Health Care Ethics Committee Forum. He is currently writing a book on bioethics and national security.

Shulamit Reinharz is Professor of Sociology and Director of the Women's Studies Program at Brandeis University. She is author of numerous articles and books, including *On Becoming a Social Scientist, Qualitative Gerontology,*

Feminist Methods in Social Research, and *Psychology and Community Change.* She served as coeditor with Peter Conrad of *Qualitative Sociology.* She recently created the International Research Institute on Jewish Women, sponsored by Hadassah and located at Brandeis University. This interdisciplinary institute is the only one in the world devoted to research on this topic. She was also the 1997-1998 Robin Williams Lecturer of the Eastern Sociological Society.

Lillian B. Rubin is Senior Research Fellow at the Institute for the Study of Social Change, University of California, Berkeley, and a practicing psychotherapist in San Francisco. She is author of *Busing & Backlash: White Against White in an Urban School District* (1972), *Worlds of Pain: Life in the Working-Class* (1976), *Women of a Certain Age: The Midlife Search for Self* (1979), *Intimate Strangers: Men & Women Together* (1983), *Just Friends: The Role of Friendship in Our Lives* (1985), *Quiet Rage: Bernie Goetz in a Time of Madness* (1986), *Erotic Wars: What Happened to the Sexual Revolution?* (1990), *Families on the Fault Line: America's Working Class Speaks About the Family, the Economy, Race, and Ethnicity* (1994), and *The Transcendent Child: Tales of Triumph Over the Past* (1996).

Clinton R. Sanders is Professor of Sociology at the University of Connecticut. He is author of *Customizing the Body: The Art and Culture of Tattooing* (1989), editor of *Marginal Conventions: Popular Culture, Mass Media, and Social Deviance* (1990), and coeditor (with Jeff Ferrell) of *Cultural Criminology* (1995). His book, *Regarding Animals* (with Arnold Arluke, 1996), received the 1997 Charles Horton Cooley Award from the Society for the Study of Symbolic Interaction. His current research is focused on human relationships with companion animals.

Allan Schnaiberg is Professor of Sociology and Faculty Associate at the Institute for Policy Research at Northwestern University. He is coauthor of *Environment & Society: The Enduring Conflict* (with Ken Gould, 1994) and of *Local Environmental Struggles: Citizen Activism in the Treadmill of Production* (with Ken Gould and Adam Weinberg, 1996). His recent work has involved a lengthy study of the contemporary recycling movement and industry, with the collaboration of Adam Weinberg and David Pellow. He is currently focused on the flaws in current models of sustainable development. His goals are to build an accurate model of how centralization and globalization threaten workers, family life, and the natural environments and to disseminate this to both scholarly and other audiences.

Barry Schwartz is Professor of Sociology in the Department of Sociology, University of Georgia. He is author of "Memory as a Cultural System: Abraham

Lincoln in World War II" (*American Sociological Review,* 1996), "History and Collective Memory: How Abraham Lincoln Became a Symbol of Racial Equality" (*Sociological Quarterly,* 1997), and "Postmodernity and the Erosion of Grand Narrative: Abraham Lincoln in the Late Twentieth-Century" (*Social Forces,* forthcoming). He is currently completing a book-length project on Abraham Lincoln in American memory and conducting research on the Korean War Veterans Memorial and on "memory wars" in Germany and the United States.

Pepper Schwartz is Professor of Sociology at the University of Washington. She is past president of the Society for the Scientific Study of Sex and a fellow of that organization as well as a member of the International Academy of Sex Research. She is author of 11 books, including *American Couples* (with Philip Blumstein), *Love Between Equals: How Peer Marriage Really Works,* and *The Gender of Sexuality* (with Virginia Rutter). She also writes extensively for the popular press, she was the sex and health columnist for *Glamour* magazine (with Janet Lever, with whom she wrote *Women at Yale* and *The Great Sex Weekend*), and she writes the sex and relationships column for *American Baby* and the sex column for OneClickAway on the Microsoft Network. She and her family raise Rocky Mountain horses and llamas and are thought to be quite eccentric by post-yuppie friends.

David Silverman is Professor of Sociology at Goldsmiths' College, London University. His research interests are qualitative methods, conversation analysis, and professional-client communication in medical settings. He is author of approximately 60 journal articles and book chapters and 14 books. He is author of *Communication and Medical Practice* (1997), *Interpreting Qualitative Data* (1993), *Discourses of Counselling: HIV Counselling as Social Interaction* (1997), *Harvey Sacks* (1998), and *Doing Qualitative Research* (forthcoming). He is editor of *Qualitative Research: Theory, Method, and Practice* (1997) and of a new Sage series, *Introducing Qualitative Methods,* which will offer a "hands-on" introduction to qualitative methods. He is committed to a dialogue between social scientists and the rest of the community, and he is an active member of the Forum on Medical Communication, Royal Society of Medicine, London. He has held workshops on his research for parents, doctors, and counselors in the United Kingdom, the United States, Australia, Trinidad and Tobago, and many Scandinavian countries.

Barrie Thorne teaches sociology and women's studies at the University of California, Berkeley. She is a former vice president of the American Sociological Association (ASA) and a former chair of the ASA Section on Sex and Gender. She is author of *Gender Play: Girls and Boys in School* (1993) and

280 QUALITATIVE SOCIOLOGY AS EVERYDAY LIFE

coeditor of *Feminist Sociology: Life Histories of a Movement* (1997), *Rethinking the Family: Some Feminist Questions* (1992), and *Language, Gender and Society* (1983). She is currently engaged in a collaborative and comparative ethnographic study of childhoods in three California communities that vary in social class and ethnic composition and in processes of immigration and racialization.

Candace West is Professor of Sociology at the University of California, Santa Cruz. She is author of "Doing Difference" (with Sarah Fenstermaker; *Gender & Society,* 1995), "Women's Competence in Conversation" (*Discourse & Society,* 1995), "Goffman in Feminist Perspective" (*Sociological Perspectives,* 1996), and "Ethnography and Orthography: A (Modest) Methodological Proposal" (*Journal of Contemporary Ethnography,* 1996).

Christine L. Williams is a faculty member at the University of Texas, Austin. She received a PhD from the University of California, Berkeley. She conducts research on gender discrimination and sexual harassment in employment. Her book, *Still a Man's World* (1995), is a study of men who work in traditionally female occupations. She has written several papers on sexuality and sexual harassment in the workplace. Her current work addresses the topic of consensual sexuality in work organizations.

Robert Zussman is Professor of Sociology at the University of Massachusetts-Amherst. He is author of *Mechanics of the Middle Class: Work and Politics Among American Technical Workers* and *Intensive Care: Medical Ethics and the Medical Profession.* He is currently working on a study of autobiographical occasions.